This Is About Vision

This Is About Vision

Interviews with Southwestern Writers

Edited by
William Balassi,
John F. Crawford,
and Annie O. Eysturoy

New America Studies
in the American West

University of New Mexico Press
Albuquerque

Library of Congress Cataloging-in-Publication Data

This is about vision: interviews with Southwestern writers
/ edited by William Balassi, John F. Crawford,
and Annie O. Eysturoy.—1st ed.
p. cm.—(New America studies in the American West)
Includes bibliographical references.
ISBN 0-8263-1186-5.—ISBN 0-8263-1187-3 (pbk.)
1. American literature—Southwestern States—History and criticism.
2. Authors, American—Southwestern States—Interviews.
3. Authors, American—20th century—Interviews.
4. Southwestern States—Intellectual life.
5. Southwestern States in literature.
I. Balassi, William Victor.
II. Crawford, John F., 1940–
III. Eysturoy, Annie O., 1955–
IV. Series.
PS277.T47 1990
810.9′979—dc20   89-70428

© 1990 by the University of New Mexico Press
All rights reserved.
First Edition

Contents

Introduction   1

1. Frank Waters   15
2. Frances Gillmor   27
3. Tony Hillerman   41
4. Edward Abbey   53
5. N. Scott Momaday   59
6. Margaret Randall   71
7. Rudolfo Anaya   83
8. Paula Gunn Allen   95
9. Mark Medoff   109
10. John Nichols   119
11. Pat Mora   129
12. Linda Hogan   141
13. Denise Chávez   157
14. Joy Harjo   171
15. Jimmy Santiago Baca   181
16. Luci Tapahonso   195

Contributors   203

Introduction
John F. Crawford

When we in the New America Project started to work on a collection of interviews with Southwestern writers a few years ago, it never occurred to us that we would be charting a changed course for the writing enterprise in our region. But that may turn out to be what we have done.

In the time it took to complete the project, the three editors, William Balassi, Annie Eysturoy, and I, reformulated it, taking into account the responses we received from the writers themselves. Even our choice of writers to interview was influenced by the discoveries we were making in the course of interviewing them. While we regret the absence of many writers who for one reason or another were unavailable to us—Leslie Silko, Simon Ortiz, Ed Dorn, Robert Creeley, and William Eastlake among others—the interviews we did complete, chronologically arranged by date of birth, show a remarkable development of ideas and themes, and it is this unfolding set of discoveries that I am to map out in the rest of my introduction.

In the beginning, we were looking for evidences of the "Spirit of Place" (*spiritus loci*), broadly speaking the effect landscape has upon art and the artist. Though this idea is a very old one, it has been especially prominent in American regional writing since the 1960s. But as we conducted our interviews, we found that our writers expressed another sense of "place" altogether, and with it another sense of "spirit" as the source of their creative instincts. Rather than conceive of "place" as something "out there" and spirit as something "in here," the old mind-body duality of Western thought, our writers appeared to feel that "place" was internalized *in each of them,* and that this sense of inner grounding was what they called "vision" or "spirit."

Younger writers from each of the several cultures expressed this attitude. For this reason, we believe in the correctness of the statement by Paula Gunn Allen that gives our collection its title: "This isn't about race, this is about vision." Still, there are interesting intersections of the themes of generation, "race," "place," and "spirit" to consider when we look at the interviews in chronological order. This is why I want to begin here with a sort of "map," refining it as I go.

Frank Waters and Frances Gillmor are our starting point in the collection. They belong to the pioneer generation of Southwestern Anglo writers born around 1900. Tony Hillerman and Edward Abbey formed their attitudes as children of the depression and were young adults by the end of World War Two; they "arrived" just in time to see the change in the region from underdevelopment to postwar boom. Scott Momaday, Margaret Randall, Rudolfo Anaya,

Paula Gunn Allen, Mark Medoff, and John Nichols, born before the outbreak of the war, were formed intellectually by the expansion of the later forties and fifties, but they also confronted, in varying forms, the repression of the spirit that went along with that period of terribly uneven development. Two of the Anglo writers among them, Randall and Nichols, became radicals; the Indian artist and writer Momaday and the Hispanic writer Anaya managed against odds to break into the highly restrictive cultural establishment of that time. The last six writers in the collection—Pat Mora, Linda Hogan, Denise Chávez, Joy Harjo, Jimmy Santiago Baca, and Luci Tapahonso—all born after the outbreak of World War Two and all of Hispanic or Native American background—represent a new generation of multicultural artists, freed of the shackles of the past to express a new faith in the triad of land, culture, and society as they have experienced it in their lifetimes.

So (my crude map suggests) the torch has passed down from old to new, from the Anglo to the writer of color, and from the old European "civilization" to the new, still uncharted multicultural future.

But this is not the whole story by any means. For one thing, the Anglo writers, even in the narrow sample we have here, do not "represent" a degenerating society to begin with, nor do they themselves degenerate as we go along. While it is true that the ones we interviewed have gone through marked changes, including disenchantment and radicalization, the continuity of a strong literary tradition can be traced as far back as Frank Waters, that miraculous survivor whose work has influenced so many writers of all backgrounds to follow him. For instance, his apocalyptic, transcendent, mystical side is echoed in the vision expressed by Laguna/Sioux writer Paula Gunn Allen, though she differs with him in other matters. Again, Anglo writer Tony Hillerman expresses a new sensitivity to Navajo culture, though it is not without some peril, as Navajo Luci Tapahonso points out. Edward Abbey, now sadly gone from us, was unique, a slickrock Voltaire, standing watch through the night in order to save us from the future that others might force upon us. The radicalism of Margaret Randall and John Nichols is both a part of American tradition and localized in its insistence that we look at the dangers we face as residents of the Southwest. Mark Medoff, stinging in his satire, has also found his home here, both as a dramatic producer and a playwright. While the writings of these Anglos has shown a new path of development, scarcely to be contemplated by an earlier age, clearly it has retained both its vigor and vision.

Nor (to return to my map) has the development of writing in the other cultures gone in a straight, predictable line. Creek poet Joy Harjo and Chicano Rudolfo Anaya acknowledge the influence of Western European culture in their work, even though they reject many of its political premises. Paula Gunn Allen, Linda Hogan, and to a certain extent Jimmy Santiago Baca have dwelt in both the Anglo world and that of the multiracial "other" long enough to have developed a kind of street smartness about living on the margin. Only toward the end of the book, in Pat Mora, Denise Chávez, to a large extent Baca, and Luci Tapahonso, do we see Hispanic and Indian writers who acknowledge that their *primary* cultural endowment comes from their native tradition. In some sense these writers have made their own way, while in another sense they are indebted to those who came before. They are fortunate to have been enabled to fully celebrate their own cultural origins.

But even after we make allowances for so many specific cases, it is still possible to generalize *somewhat* about what happened here, and much of our generalization is rooted in commonplaces of our political history. The Anglo colonizers, broadly conceived from the soldiers, trappers, cowboys, and merchants of the 1850s to the anthropologists at the end of the nineteenth century to the technocrats of the Roosevelt administration, changed the shape of human behavior, as well as that of the land itself, within our region. The economic and technological shocks of the whole period, from attacks on traditional land holdings early and late to the detonation of the atomic bomb near Alamogordo, have informed the subject matter of all these writers for better or worse as they have shaped their stories.

Thus new voices are raised in response to the earlier voices, new explanations of reality challenge and finally overthrow the old, and new cultural imperatives emerge in this cauldron of place which is the Southwest. The voices that emerge in a constantly shifting discourse, over land and economics and culture, are both shaped by external realities and help to shape them over again. And our collection has captured them, as in an accidental snapshot. I am reminded of the photograph a tourist took a few years ago of his wife and child standing by a bush, looking out at a landscape. It wasn't until the vacation was over and the color prints came back from the drugstore that one could see the face of the cougar in the bush, not three feet behind the posing family. Wild, intractable, unafraid, these interviews are like that cougar: rooted in the past, but also real voices in the present, with the new power necessary to interpret the future.

The term "Spirit of Place" is used only once in the interviews in its original sense, at the very start, in the Frank Waters interview. But immediately Waters subverts the idea, first by translating it (into "karma of locality") and then by concurring that there can be *negative* as well as positive spirits residing in a place. He describes his sojourn in Las Vegas, Nevada, in the days of the early atom bomb tests—not by taking up the matter of the Bomb Culture directly, as he has done very well elsewhere, but by speaking plainly of the dangers of compulsive gambling: "I'm sure it is a compulsion to lose, and not to win." Subtly he thus links the Spirit of Place with something less than noble in Anglo culture.

Waters continues to tease our expectations and challenge our stereotypes in the rest of the interview. He tells this story with reference to his early days as a laborer in the Imperial Valley in California:

> At that time, there were few white men who could work in terrible heat out in the melon patches. So the big growers were bringing in Hindus, and Chinese, and also quite a few Negroes from the South. There was one cantina there predominantly frequented by the Negroes. I went in it frequently with The Deuce of Spades, a good fighter. I think that was the first time that I ever noticed what a terrible, rancid body odor a white person has. All those Negroes in there, sweating in that terrible heat, and drinking too, gave off a body odor which is a little on the sweet side. Then I noticed a strange impinging body odor, and I suddenly realized that it was my own. (Laughter) You feel yourself as a minority once in a great while, you know.

Though Waters repeats uncritically the myth of the white man who cannot work in the heat of the sun in the California fields, a story often used as a justification for the exploitation of migrant workers there, he goes on to subvert the racist stereotype of the dirty "colored" worker by regarding the scene from his own new vantage point as a stinking white "minority." This reversed angle of view is unusual, Lilliputian, though it is still somewhat disingenuous, since Waters could presumably opt out of a situation that the others could not. But, as is often true of Waters, it allows him some valuable room for ironic insight.

Waters touches on another theme that is important for what follows in our book: the survival of civilizations. Part of what he says comes out of his own metaphysical preoccupations, including his conflation of "eastern religions and mysticism and occult teachings of all kinds, and Jungian philosophy" with Hopi prophecy that "we are already beginning our emergence into a new world." But it is also a kind of Social Darwinism:

> *These tales of previous worlds, to me at least, are allegories for the different phases of mankind's cultural advancements, his evolutionary stages. I think we are approaching and already beginning a new step in a new direction. I think that the rate of breakup is so fast and we in this civilization are deteriorating so fast that we can't turn the clock back. We must accept the fact that it is plunging downhill; and the form of this civilization, as we know it, is bound to break up.*

Social Darwinism, of course, was an Anglo ideological prop during the "winning" of the West. A famous letter from Buffalo Bill Cody to Gen. W. T. Sherman, written near the end of Cody's life, expressed sorrow over the near extinction of the buffalo and the devastation of Plains Indian culture that followed it, with the "consolation" added—as victors share the spoils—that since all civilizations pass away, the weak succumbing to the strong, the white civilization too must die sometime in the future.

Here too, while not directly questioning the old myth, Waters shifts the ground from under it. Having prophesied our doom, he rescues us at the last minute, suggesting that the new culture will not simply overcome the dominant Anglo one, but will *contain* it.

> *. . . We must recognize our oneness with all of nature. Not only with all of mankind, but with the plant and the vegetable and animal kingdoms, with the earth itself, and with the planetary bodies which exert an influence on us too. We are not just Anglos, or citizens of Arizona or New Mexico or Nevada, nor of the U.S., but Citizens of the Universe.*

It is as if the Social Darwinism of the buffalo hunter has met up with the quietism of the Hopi, and in the aftermath the white man has been forced to sign a treaty with his conscience: he will sin no more, nor covet that which is his neighbor's, and in exchange he will be denied his tragic vision of his own fatal outcome. As the poet W. H. Auden once expressed it, "Your application to suffer has been refused."

Of course Indian writers have also meditated upon the death of whole civilizations and what is to follow them. These writers include Paula Gunn Allen, who uses the A-bomb as an apocalyptic plot element in her work in progress, the novel tentatively titled *Raven's Road*. In a manner reminiscent of Leslie Silko in her novel *Ceremony*, Allen sees the bomb as an enigma, both the creation and the potential source of destruction of the culture that made it:

> *The bomb is about cleansing the planet; it is about the voice of another power. There are reasons why I see it that way, some of which are metaphysical. . . .*

> But certainly, one of the things I can see right now is that a bunch of complacent colonizers are threatened with the extinction that they have visited upon everyone else. And, I don't know—I have a tacky sense of humor—I enjoy it. I think it is very funny watching them racing around trying to stop their own ultimate extinction.

Unlike Waters, Allen seems fairly certain that we will all have to go in such a wall of fire.

> We might find it very uncomfortable; I am sure that we don't want to go. But people don't like it too much when a mountain blows up and there is a volcano; they will have to get out of the way or perish. The Mother cares for us greatly, but not for us more than for herself.

Her grimly comic vision of poetic justice is echoed by a number of younger writers, among them John Nichols, Linda Hogan, Denise Chávez, Joy Harjo, and Jimmy Santiago Baca.

Even when it is not spelled out, the metaphor of the Spirit of Place dies hard, as we see when it is taken up by some of the middle writers, including Tony Hillerman, Edward Abbey, and Rudolfo Anaya, and the younger writer Denise Chávez. Here the land is sometimes still figured as something outside oneself, leaving intact the old subject-object relationship. And thus Tony Hillerman says, "I really think there is something about the Southwestern landscape and Southwestern culture and society that fosters creativity in a lot of people. . . . The view alone puts things in a different perspective." Edward Abbey puts it another way:

> I write to celebrate the beauty of nature, in my case the American Southwest. It's my favorite area on the planet not simply because of the desert, but because of the combination of rivers, forests, mountains, climate, sky, wildlife. . . . Writing is a form of piety or worship. I try to write prose psalms which praise the divine beauty of the natural world.

Rudolfo Anaya makes the landscape around the children's hospital in his novel *Tortuga* symbolic of hope:

> And even though the rest of the landscape alternates between the dead desert with the sandstorms and the frozen mountains on the west side, the springs of the mountain are still running—there is still hope, it's not too late, and you can go there and you can bathe and be made whole.

And Denise Chávez memorializes the land as her inspiration: "I am still very connected. When I am tired and have been writing, I go out and look at the landscape and it soothes me, particularly the mountains."

One might protest that these statements are not so special; they contain a universal rhetorical topic, recorded as far back as classical antiquity. But perhaps then we should ask what we mean by "recorded." In the oral tradition there appears to be a different view of "landscape," and that is what concerns us at the moment. Scott Momaday's image of "the remembered earth," for instance, announces a doctrine of memory rather than a celebration of landscape, to which the closest European analogy might be the neo-Platonism of St. Augustine. It turns out that this idea, that the land is *in* us rather than outside us, is repeated in different forms in many Indian and Mestizo cultures.

In this interview, Momaday barely responds to a question about landscapes, saying only that he doesn't paint them: "I prefer a closer focus in my painting." But Paula Gunn Allen gives the subject her full attention.

> *My work is all tangled up with landscape around here. But landscape for me does not mean "the landscape"; it does not mean something that great dramas are enacted upon. Maybe that's because so much of the drama in the Southwest is the land, not the people. We are, to me, the background against which the land enacts her drama. And by landscape I don't mean only the mountains and those vast plains, but the weather, the climactic conditions and rainstorms, the overpowering thunderstorms.*

Allen points out that people who maintain a close relationship with the land also keep a spiritual or metaphysical dimension.

> *I think that if you are really connecting with the land then you are going to have to connect with the spirits. So probably as a consequence of being with the land, I developed a spiritual dimension, because there is no way not to. I think you have to get away from the land and think of it as something you take pictures of before you can lose your spiritual connections. But if you talk to the tree periodically, which I do, you cannot lose your spiritual connection, because the tree talks back and so you know that there is a person in there.*

What has happened here phenomenologically is a negation of the "inside-outside" distinction as it exists in Western written culture. And with the power of the landscape now *inside* us, no longer *outside* us however much it is perceived sympathetically, we are but one step away from another important traditional idea, the point made by Luci Tapahonso in the last interview in the book: that identity itself comes from what is already inside the person, in this case beginning with one's relationship to her clan.

> *So when I identify myself . . . I think of myself . . . first as my mother and then as my father, and then my last name in Navajo which is Tapahonso, "edge of the big water." And so my identity is in terms of the clan which places the Navajo person in the world and define's one's relationships to other people and one's responsibility. It places me in certain waters. . . .*

The distinction which puts nature or landscape or place "inside" instead of "outside" expresses the dichotomy between what I shall call an *aesthetic of predication* and an *aesthetic of vision*. Predication is viewing from outside; vision is "seeing" from inside. Predication rests on what you say you will do; vision rests on what you *see* to do. Predication calls up the figure of speech; vision calls upon the thing itself.

We can perhaps understand this more clearly by noticing a problem that comes up between Tony Hillerman, generally acclaimed as an Anglo writer sensitive to the people he writes about, and Luci Tapahonso, a member of the Navajo Nation that is the main subject of Hillerman's detective stories. In describing his interest in the Navajo, Hillerman speaks of the "view" on the Reservation: "The view alone puts things in a different perspective." He goes on to say,

> *I identify with the Navajo. I like them. I like their philosophical position. The Navajo as much as anyone else is a product of his environment. I came out of the same kind of environment, poverty, trying to make a living from the land, hoping like hell it would rain and it wouldn't, always being at the bottom of the pecking order, socially. . . . So when I see these Navajos, I know where they're coming from. I can sympathize.*

In her interview, Luci Tapahonso responds, rather reluctantly, to a question about Tony Hillerman's work in the following way:

> *Again, it's a matter of perspective. He's so successful, but I think a lot of people don't even stop to realize it is fiction . . . it's all filtered through Tony Hillerman, bless his heart, his perspective and whatever kinds of intentions that he might have, and whatever sort of confidence he might have in his knowledge and his ability to write. But it would be very unfair in my mind for me to pretend or to presume to know so much about white culture or American culture in the Southwest that I would write something akin to "Murder She Wrote" from an Anglo perspective. But that's the difference between the way people are raised, and the way that people believe, and the way that people live. To me, it's a really crucial difference.*

A section of the interview with Jimmy Santiago Baca, of mixed Apache and Chicano descent, may help us understand the crossed purposes evident in the remarks of Hillerman and Tapahonso above. Baca points out that he uses the word "seeing" in a way that is different from ordinary Anglo usage.

> *The way the Indians say "seeing" is how close you can come to the way things really are, the way a deer sees a rock, or the way a frog sees water; we call that "seeing." Every human being has that "seeing" in them, and someone who gets up and writes every day, all he or she is trying to do is to get close to his or her capabilities; that's where the good poems come from, when you are able to see. . . .*

> *The English have a way of saying, "Find your voice," and that represents the egotistical sense of the English people. The Native American way is "to see." It does not entail a voice; someone like Black Elk, his seeing was very strong, nothing could boggle it. But the Anglo people always have this aggressive voice thing—"Your voice is very strong in this piece," right? While the Indians say, "Your seeing is very strong in this piece."*

Another way to discriminate between "saying" and "seeing" is to point out how different people view the bridging of differences. Perhaps the difference between cultures is so important to our new writers because so many of them come from more than one of those cultures: In our collection these include Momaday, Allen, Hogan, Harjo, and Baca, with other cases open to conjecture. Momaday subtly and carefully takes up this topic:

> *It seems logical to me that the mixed bloods are most naturally curious about their cultural identity. My father being a Kiowa and my mother being mostly European, I guess I had a sense of living in those two areas when I was a child and it became important to me to understand as clearly as I could who I was and what my cultural resources were.*

Allen treats her cultural conflicts humorously and at a bit of a distance.

> *I had a lot of questions about that when I was quite a bit younger. . . . I am Lebanese-American, I am Indian, I am a breed, and I am New Mexican and they have a lot to do with how I act and what I think and how I interpret things. . . . Certainly there are times when the Lebanese Paula and the Indian Paula come into awful conflict, because they are different. So certainly, there is intra-psychic conflict and stress that arises. And then I have a kind of overlaying or underlying American or Anglo culture that I mostly picked up in school. It is all me. It sometimes comes into conflict with itself, but it is still all me.*

Linda Hogan, a mixed blood Chickasaw, remarks, "How difficult it is for people to see difference. . . . What people look for is either similarities—or the shadow-self, as Jung says, so you can look for evil on the outside and not have to acknowledge your inner evil." On her own mixture, Hogan comments in an exchange:

> Smith: *I was just thinking about that poem where you describe yourself as having a Chickasaw hand in one pocket, and a white hand in the other . . .*
>
> Hogan: *Uh-huh!*
>
> Smith: *And sleeping on twin beds . . .*
>
> Hogan: *I know! And I've been living in the Twin Cities! This is it; this psychic split has gone too far! Time to get things together; I need to live in some place called Unity.*

Harjo does not address herself directly to mixed blood in her interview, but does concentrate on eradicating what she calls the dangerous "edge," in favor of "that place of no lies where we all understood each other." Baca argues that it seems to him the Apaches hated the Hispanics "because we were sleeping in their beds, and they were sleeping in our beds; hatred runs highest in the family, you know." On the other hand, he offers a compelling vision of unity between Hispanic and Indian peoples:

> *Yes, I am a Mestizo. I go up there to the Black Mesa behind us; the Indians go up there, that's their holy mountain—the Isletas—and I go up there with the Isletas; we sit up there and we talk. They tell me what they think of the yucca blossom—there are a lot of yucca blossoms up there—and I tell them what I think about it, and we find out that we both talk about it in the same way, we both see it in the same way. And it comes from that, you know, that we are really close to each other.*

When the topic of difference and unity comes up with the newer writers, frequently it involves a third term, myth and the making of myths. Momaday, Anaya, Allen, and Baca address this issue. All seem to relate their understanding of myth partly to their education in school and partly to their experiences at the feet of storytellers. Momaday makes a distinction between his cultural origins and his needs as an artist:

> *I'm not concerned to define or delineate American Indian experience, except to myself and for my own purposes. But I am very concerned to understand*

> as much as I can about myth-making. The novel I'm working on now is really a construction of different myths. . . .

Anaya speaks movingly of his first real teachers, "older people," the "fabulous *vaqueros* [who] would come in from the llano," and the *curanderas* of the village. At the same time, he credits the University of New Mexico, where as an undergraduate

> . . . we were guided to read Greek mythology. I wasn't really making the connections because I was looking at it as stories that had to do with another time and place. I think it wasn't until I turned more towards Native American mythology that I began to see that there are these points of reference that world myths have, that somehow speak to the center of our being, and connect us—to other people, to the myth, to the story, and beyond that to the historic process, to the communal group.

Allen focuses on the other end of the process, the writer's reception of the material, and claims that "as a writer I am not a creator of myths. As a channel I am."

> Eysturoy: How do you distinguish between being a writer and being a channel?
>
> Allen: Well, writers invent and I do it, too. But there are passages where, frankly, somebody else takes over. It is not me, and the reason I know it is not me is because they say stuff I wouldn't have said, and in fact some of it I disagree with.

Baca looks primarily at the social role of the myth maker. He sees myth as what ties together reality, and he works to create characters who embody community values within a mythical frame.

> Our history was so fragmented by colonialism that I have felt a mythology was needed, a putting together of everything in a modern sense. If you have a mythology then you have a place; if you don't have a mythology, you ain't got nothing. When I came back from prison, I decided to start writing about things I thought were as old as the earth, and so I started writing **Martin**, keeping in mind that I wanted to describe my experiences in New Mexico. . . .

Between the thinking of Anaya and Baca on myth there is an interesting relationship. Both go back to the land and the first human community as the ultimate source of myth. Anaya is willing to credit the institutions for preserving the myths of other peoples and tends to be a comparativist in this regard, combining stories for a certain effect. Baca seems unwilling to do this, for strategic reasons:

> I think there is an intermarriage [between the physical landscape and mythology] such that if it is ever broken then you will be broken. You can have all the mythology you want to learn in your English classes and not have the earth. You have got to find the beating heart of that which is you, and if you are able to find that then you are in business.

In terms of these interviews, it seems that a writer's personal sense of the state of that "intermarriage . . . between the physical landscape and mythology" helps form the writer's politics. The most radical writers revealed by these interviews are those who react with anger, shock and horror to the rupture that has been created between the person and the environment—what the young Marx would have called one's alienation from one's own species-being. Most of the writers express at least some amount of this response, but in several it is notable. Baca is outspoken.

> *I believe there was a violent, violent attempt by the authorities to bleed the Chicanos and the Indios and the Mestizos of any identity, any cultural remnants. There was a really strong effort at that, a most sophisticated effort. It was not outright "Let's go out and shoot them"; it was "Let's do it through education, let's do it through religion, let's bleed these people so they haven't got nothing left, so their only alternative is to become who we want them to become," right? And they accomplished that to a certain degree.*

We interviewed Margaret Randall shortly after the publication of her book *Albuquerque*, which was a report, mediated through journals and letters, of her return to the United States after twenty years of self-imposed exile. In the process of discussing how her photography had changed—from documentary work in Cuba and Nicaragua to more "artificial," nearly surrealistic work in the U.S.— she comments on the distortions of reality she experienced when she returned to North American society. For her, the situation here was upside down: unreality *was* reality.

> *I think it's not my photography that has changed, but the place [I'm working in]. I think of the meaning of this kind of photography in a place like the United States where our lives are contrived by media—who we vote for, how we dress, how fat or thin we are, what we eat, what we think we need, the kind of house we live in, who we pair with if we pair with someone, how we educate our kids, what we think of the world. And so it seems to me that my relationship to this place, in the kind of photography I am doing now, has exactly the same meaning as my relationship to Central America vis-à-vis the kind of photography I was doing there.*

John Nichols also views his role as a radical as central to the creation of his art. In an interview laced with fury at what he considers a bourgeois review, he attacks the convention that art must somehow be separated from politics.

> *It's been a long time since I've written anything I didn't consider to be propaganda. I feel that all art is propaganda, and that's an unpopular idea in a capitalist nation. . . . I worked with Costa-Gavras for four or five years trying to put together a couple of films about nuclear war and human survival in the nuclear age. The problem . . . is how to get the human imagination to imagine something which is basically so horrible it's unimaginable. To image it in a vivid enough way that people will be moved and will put energy into trying to avoid it. If you make it too palatable or too diverting, too "artistic," people can ignore it. If you make it too horrible, they can't watch it.*

I have the impression, rereading these interviews some time after their completion, that several of the Anglo writers—Frank Waters with his spiritualism, Edward Abbey the anarchist, and Margaret Randall and John Nichols the socialists—are especially courageous, because like the doctors who deal each day with a virulent disease, they are susceptible to the very cultural and political ailment they want to see eradicated from the earth. More "exposed" in this sense than the other writers in the volume, because they are following a political path unpopular with many people in their own community, these Anglos have often had to *invent* community where they felt the need of it. This puts them in contrast to those writers who work from *inside* their communities and thereby assure themselves a certain degree of protection.

Rudolfo Anaya, speaking with the insight of a veteran writer and organizer, proposes that

> the Southwest [is] a place going through a very interesting experiment—it has to do with how people can live with each other, can share—and this is as important to the whites and the Maori of New Zealand as it may be to the Catalonians and the Basques, the Nicaraguans and the Misquitos. . . . We can do something very positive with all the changes that are coming across this land, or we can blow it.

Images of unity and community appear in many other interviews as well. These range from touching private confessions, such as playwright Mark Medoff's that in New Mexico he has found a home that he never expected, to longer, more general statements from such writers as Pat Mora, Linda Hogan, Denise Chávez, and Luci Tapahonso. It is fitting, I think, to give the multicultural women the last word in this essay, because it is their collective voice that appears to be the strongest in our literature now.

Mora sounds an important cautionary note when she is asked to speak about her concerns as a regional writer and her sense of her audience.

> The whole sense of audience is always a difficult one and I have argued that minority writers have more trouble with it than non-minority writers. When I talk to non-minority writers they will say, "Well, you really shouldn't be thinking about any other audience than yourself, you know, write for the inner voices." While I understand that, on the other hand I think if you look at minority writers in this country, they do have a clear sense of audience. Yet I realize that one of the myths is to think that there is such a thing as a Chicano audience, or a Chicano community. One of the things that I have to have the courage to do is write the best I can at a particular time. There are going to be some people who like it and some people who may say, "Well, she is stuck with writing about the desert; she is stuck writing about the Southwest." It's a tension. . . .

Mora sees the writer's (and the human being's) world as one in which there is no end to struggle: "To me public space, almost all public space, is an area for conflict; it's just carefully veiled. There's that tension and that jockeying that's taking place all the time." She strongly endorses a "nonconfrontational approach," at least as her own means of responding to conflict.

Hogan, who appears to start from the same premises, has a parallel interpretation of both the writer's role in society and how to resolve conflict.

> In our human development we begin with ourselves and move outward

> *toward relationship, and in our written work it seems to be the same, that most writers begin with their own identity, with autobiography, and then move out towards family, friends, environment, country, world. I have noticed there's a return for many writers as they age . . . and I've noticed that for others the world expands outward more and more, never returning to self. . . . We need for writers to do both. We need the personal in its global context.*
>
> *I've often thought about how one of the things that was probably necessary for the women's movement—the dominant culture women's movement—was to break free of the duty of being a caretaker. But then, for women to return to being caretakers, because it's important to offer service to the living, and to the planet. . . . I see a direct relation to how we care for the animal-people and the plants and insects and land and water, and how we care for each other, and for ourselves. Part of our work here is to care for life.*

A similar degree of moral and ethical concern is evident in the work of the Chicana playwright, poet, and novelist Denise Chávez. While her orientation is perhaps even more "activist" than that of Mora or Hogan, the basic sense of spirituality underlying community values is much the same for all three.

> *This has been an oppressed culture and so the oppressed have to oppress as well, and it has usually fallen on women, or those who have dark skin, or the people who are laborers and so on and so forth. This cycle of oppression continues, and I am exploring a lot of those themes in my current novel.*
>
> *Our grandmothers did not have voices. My mother's voice was a cry, perhaps, a moan; it was a sad voice. Our voices are hopefully stronger, and we can sing our stories and other women's stories as well.*
>
> *We should not expect to be happy; we should expect to do our work, and I think that whatever happiness or state of contentment or peace one finally comes to—my characters are always looking for peace—it is a sad, lonely peace. But a strong peace. I think all human beings have to go through this because eventually, inevitably we are alone and there is that peace that no one can give you, really, other than you coming to grips with and confronting your own life and your own destiny, what work you have done and what you need to do.*

Luci Tapahonso, firmly grounded in her Navajo identity, has the last word. Asked about her "vision as a poet," she responds with a kind of doubleness, one side of which is the "seeing" that Jimmy Santiago Baca has already identified as a cultural strength of Indian and Mestizo culture.

> *I think it's real complex. It's the ways I think and the ways I react to all the situations that come to the Navajo people—the way that we talk, the way that we laugh, all those things that are part of the Navajo perspective. But I also know how to function in the world, in the professional and business and academic world . . . a whole different way of functioning. I can chair a meeting, I can organize events, I can raise money. So there's that perspective too. It's really interesting to think about.*

Finally, she lists projects she plans for the future:

> *Going back and building a home. I can see myself having a home that my children and I can go back to, and I can stay at, and I can go to in the summertime. Unless something miraculous happens, I don't see myself living there year round. But finally, when I retire, and I have no more reason to work for money, I'll go back and live there!*

There is a sense in which these writers come full circle, as Linda Hogan suggests writers do in their life cycle. Starting with their individual concerns, then addressing those of the world, they return at last to home, community, people or Nation, race, and vision. Taken all together, the interviews trace a kind of movement "into the interior," the "remembered earth" of those who have never forgotten their points of origin. If this is truly the condition of some of our best writers today in the Southwest, it appears that we are fortunate indeed to have visions so strong and clear and unmediated.

As one of the editors of this book, speaking in this case for William Balassi and Annie Eysturoy as well, it falls upon me to thank those who have helped us to make this volume possible. These people surely include Mary Dougherty Bartlett, the former director of the New America project, who conceived of the volume in the first place; Patricia Clark Smith, Louis Owens, and Tey Diana Rebolledo, who helped us begin the process of redefining and expanding the interviews to be included; Peter White, the present director of the New America project, who continued its support for this volume; and Barbara Guth of UNM Press, whose counsel has been both wise and generous. Finally, the many interviewers, who struggled to produce what you see here; and the authors, who endured us all. If this volume helps bring about a fresh look at the field we have learned to hold in awe and respect, we will all feel richly rewarded. But that outcome, reader, is at least partly up to you.

Photo by Cynthia Farah

chapter one
Frank Waters
Interview by Charles Adams

Southwestern novelist and essayist Frank Waters was born in 1903 in Colorado Springs, Colorado, of a genteel Anglo mother and a part–Cheyenne Indian father who had once been a boarder in her family home. Waters's father took his young son for a summer on the Navajo Reservation shortly before his early death from tuberculosis in 1914. This tragedy, brought on by working in the family coal mine, seems to have motivated Waters's quest for a reconciliation of the differences between "civilized" European and American Indian cultures. In 1927, after working as a telephone lineman in the Imperial Valley of California, Waters wrote the first draft of *The Yogi of Cockroach Court,* a novel of a young man's spiritual awakening in the California desert; he revised this work several times before its publication twenty years later. In the middle thirties, he moved back to Colorado to finish his semiautobiographical novels *The Wild Earth's Nobility* (1935), *Below Grass Roots* (1937), and *The Dust Within the Rock* (1940). When he went to northern New Mexico in 1940, his work took a new turn. Immersing himself in Indian lore, partly due to his new friendship with the Taos Indian Tony Luhan, he produced several novels contrasting the ways of Indian and white culture. *People of the Valley* appeared in 1941, *The Man Who Killed the Deer* in 1942. After brief service in the Army and as a propaganda writer in World War II, Waters published several important nonfiction works. In *The Colorado* (1946), a part of the Rivers of America series, he seemed to share the excitement over technical progress that marked the Roosevelt era. But *Masked Gods* (1950), ostensibly about Navajo and Pueblo Indian religion, challenges the Anglo view of progress and suggests instead an eventual Anglo-Indian unity based in Eastern metaphysics. For much of the next ten years, Waters pursued the story of Edith Warner, whose tea room was situated a short distance down the road from the Los Alamos laboratories. A novel with her as the central character, *The Woman at Otowi Crossing*, appeared in 1966. In 1971 he reedited his early autobiographical trilogy into a single volume, *Pike's Peak*. Since then he has studied Aztec civilization as another symbol of integration, in *Mexico Mystique* (1975). A historically important writer who has taken up the most pressing issues confronting three generations of Anglos in the Southwest, Waters has frequently been sought out for interviews. His talks with John R. Milton of the University of South Dakota in 1971 helped bring southwestern issues before a national audience. He has generously contributed this excerpt from the forthcoming *Talks with Frank Waters,* conducted with Charles Adams, Professor of English at the University of Nevada, Las Vegas, for the present volume. These interviews were made possible in part by a grant from the University of Nevada at Las Vegas Research Council.

Selected Bibliography:

The Wild Earth's Nobility: A Novel of the Old West, novel (New York: Liveright, 1935).

Below Grass Roots, novel (New York: Liveright, 1937).

Dust Within the Rock, novel (New York: Liveright, 1940).

People of the Valley, novel (New York: Farrar and Rinehart, 1941).

The Man Who Killed the Deer, novel (New York: Farrar and Rinehart, 1942).

The Colorado, nonfiction (New York: Farrar and Rinehart, 1946).

The Yogi of Cockroach Court, novel (New York: Farrar and Rinehart, 1947).

Masked Gods: Navajo and Pueblo Ceremonialism, nonfiction (Albuquerque: New Mexico University Press, 1950).

Book of the Hopi, nonfiction (New York: Viking Press, 1963).

The Woman at Otowi Crossing, novel (Denver: Alan Swallow, 1966).

Conversations with Frank Waters, edited by John R. Milton (Chicago: Swallow Press, 1971).

Mexico Mystique: The Coming Sixth World of Consciousness (Chicago: Swallow Press, 1981).

Adams: Frank, there are a couple of questions I'd like to ask first. They are about your being labeled a "regional writer" and specifically a "Southwestern regional writer." How important *is* region and, specifically, *your* region?

Waters: Well, it seems to me that all writers are regional writers, whether they like it or not. Good ones create works that go beyond their "local color," imbuing universal values. Most of my work reflects my native Southwest. If one of my books develops a life of its own, stays in print, is accepted in a variety of regions, it may be because it suggested a greater dimension.

Adams: This leads to a question some of my students brought up. In *Deer and People of the Valley* and *Otowi* there is a very strong spirit of place, and they know this right away; but they say, "Whatever you call it about the border town in *Yogi*, it can't be called a spirit of place." (Laughter) Many students see in it only external and negative influences. Could you say a location has a negative spirit of place?

Waters: Why not? It may imbue its own negative or evil karma of locality.

Adams: Any advice for young people growing up in Las Vegas under its bad influences?

Waters: I don't know that any advice would be different for them than it would be for young people in New York or Chicago or on the Mexican border. All big cities have both good and bad influences. Many young people in Las Vegas are students of yours in the university. Their interests lie elsewhere than in the bars and in the Strip hotels; they aren't always flocking to the casinos trying to get jobs. They are interested in other things.

Adams: They may want to work there because they have to get jobs.

Waters: Yes. They are different than the thousands of visitors who come for a high time. To a country boy or girl who comes to the city, its night life has glamour. Then they go broke and are disillusioned. I remember when I first lived in Las Vegas during the atomic test series. Our small staff would get off work at five o'clock and spend the evening in a Strip hotel. It was all very glamorous and exciting. But by the time we returned to Las Vegas for the second series of tests, we were so bored going to these places that all we wanted to do after work was to go some place for a quiet dinner and come back and read the newspapers or a magazine in our hotel. But occasionally we'd run into somebody who was really hooked. There was an officer in the Air Force who flew out there for duty during each atomic test. He spent every evening gambling away all of his salary and borrowing more money on his house in Albuquerque. Soon he could no longer afford a room out of his travel allowance, so we gave him a cot in our office. As he had no money to eat on, he would wait to get a cup of coffee during our coffee break when we would make a pot. So finally one day in the Golden Nugget he played a game like Bingo.

Adams: Keno?

Waters: Yes. He hit the Keno jackpot. I think he got something like five hundred dollars. He rushed up and grabbed me, saying, "Quick, save me from myself! March me right down to the Western Union office where I can telegraph some money to pay off the mortgage on my house which is due and my wife doesn't know about!" Well, you would have thought that this would have taught him a lesson, that narrow squeak he had. But, you know, on his next trip out there, he thought, "I won it once, why can't I win it again?" (Laughter) The Air Force finally transferred him to Alaska. I just don't know what the compulsion is behind gambling. I am sure it is a compulsion to lose and not to win.

Adams: It's either a desire to lose or a kind of frantic attempt to somehow be in control of your own destiny when everything else about you is wrong—with of course the illusion that money can fix it.

Waters: This is strange. I haven't known enough gamblers. When I was living in Imperial Valley, one of my roommates for a short time was a dealer, a young Mexican fellow, very handsome, with long turquoise eardrops, who thought that I should make a good gambler. So every evening he tried to teach me how to shuffle and to deal cards. And after a while, he said, "Frank, give it up. Maybe you can get your hands so you can handle the cards, but you just don't have the temperament."

In Mexico, you know, the national lottery is strictly controlled by the government. In every town there is a building or at least quarters on the main plaza where the winning sheets are posted. Everybody goes there to check up their lottery tickets and see if they have won. It's a national industry that provides an interest in life the poorer people don't have. But when they buy a little lottery ticket, then they are equal to the richest guy in the world that buys one.

Adams: Your chances are as good as his.

Waters: Yes. When they walk up to see if they have won, they may stand there in the same building with the business man who drives a big car; a poor shoeless guy can walk right up and stand right beside him; he's got an equal chance.

Adams: Do you have any more observations about Tai Ling in *Yogi?*

Waters: I can't say very much more about Tai Ling. I guess he's the only major character who's a real person. Barby and Guadalupe and Sal were all fictitious or composite, but Tai Ling was a real person, and the shop is very much as I described it. I used to go down there quite often, and I not only enjoyed wandering around looking at all the cans and bottles and tanks of strange fish that he had but also his tremendous collection of herbs for every possible illness you could think of. Somebody would come in with an illness or a stomach ache or want an eye wash or anything, and he would prescribe the herb for them. So he had quite a reputation as an herbalist in addition to selling fish and lottery tickets. I loved to watch him mark lottery tickets, too.

Adams: I noted from several of the early reviews of *Yogi* that it got worse reviews than anything else you have written.

Waters: Oh, it was a complete flop from the start. My agent sent a copy to England to get an English printing, and the publisher or the London agent sent it back with a comment that this was a very foul, salacious book, and she would not offer it to any reputable publisher in England. It went out of print very quickly.

Adams: Well, I noticed that so many of the reviews had the same thing in common. Tom Lyons in his book quotes one of them as referring to "nauseating detail." And yet it really is one of the favorites with my kids. I suppose times have just changed.

Waters: Yes. Those were the days I guess before Henry Miller and literary sex became popular.

Adams: "It's not literary. It's not pretty."

Waters: Well, it seems to be having a good sale.

Adams: In any other work, you don't really deal as nakedly with the problems of duality, unresolved dualities, as in *Yogi*.

Waters: Not in fiction. The trilogy has something in there, but this really puts it on the line.

Adams: I think that might be one of the reasons my students like it. It seems to be strangely relevant to students in Las Vegas. As they point out, even the visitors to Las Vegas are polarized. Visitors have one code of behavior for at home and another code for Las Vegas.

Waters: I think that's true.

Adams: You get a weird mixture of the typical tourist revealing his dark side to an employee who is catering to it, who knows what he is doing, and then is caught in the trap of either staying in it or finding some strange way of getting out. And a lot of the kids do this by going to college. Or they develop a very personal technique of dissociating themselves from their jobs. In *Otowi*, Jack had no trouble at all in handling Las Vegas. He just took it in his stride, very easily. And yet that was quite a different adventure for him really. Is it just because of Jack's personality? Or did he have a big city background?

Waters: No, I think he was a sensual, outgoing kind of aggressive, extroverted guy.

Adams: I've always liked the touch that it's Gaylord who winds up listening to Helen.

Waters: The least to be expected, you see, and not Jack. Gaylord turned out to be a good character. I suppose I had in the back of my mind to make him a heavy; but as he kept going on and developing with all his trouble, he began developing into a good guy. Much more sensitive than Jack.

Adams: In quite a few of your articles you mention the witches that are supposedly still in Taos. Any comment there? Is witchcraft as much of a problem in Taos as it used to be?

Waters: I don't think it is. I think all the older people still believe in witches, and they still tell witch stories; but I think the great fear of it, and witchcraft itself, is probably not as prevalent among this current generation as it was. I think among the Hopis, however, it is probably *more* prevalent than it was.

Adams: Is this due to a negative force . . . ?

Waters: This point has been disputed by good authorities, but I believe that witchcraft is just the obverse side of religious ceremonialism; and as ceremonialism begins to break down, the witchcraft side comes up. I think that is what is happening among the Hopis.

Adams: Certainly that idea has historical support. For centuries this seems to be the way that things tip.

Waters: Marc Simmons's book on witchcraft [*Witchcraft in the Southwest* (Flagstaff: Northland Books, 1974] doesn't have as much to say about witchcraft *per se* as it does cataloging all religious beliefs and practices throughout the little Spanish villages and some Indian pueblos in New Mexico. He mentions in there that in the little Indian pueblo of Nambé, which was at one time a site of strong religious ceremonialism and a thriving pueblo, the hold and fear of witches got so strong, so many women were put to death for being witches, that the population of Nambé decreased so rapidly it was practically extinct. I believe this probably occurred at the time of the early Anglo and Spanish influence when their church was dominating Indian religious ceremonialism. Here was the problem of evil.

Adams: Another question that my students always ask, and I make no attempt to answer it, is the extent to which *Pike's Peak,* or the trilogy in separate volumes, is autobiographical.

Waters: It's not an autobiography by any means, and yet I've used much of my own and my family's experiences. It's not completely fiction. But I'm like all novelists; we're congenital liars. Take an incident and dramatize it, you know, to the point where we actually believe our own dramatization rather than the actual incidents. And I think that is probably true with me.

Adams: Now, how about, for instance, the flood scene, which appears in both?

Waters: Well, that flood actually occurred. And it can be documented.

Adams: One of the questions, which is really quite minor, but always piques the students' curiosity, is about the ghosts.

Waters: The whole ghost thing is true.

Adams: We always assume that it is. Each class assumes that it has to be.

Waters: I'll tell you. It's so fabulous that no one could make that up.

Adams: That's pretty much the class reaction.

Waters: And before they all died off, whenever all my family got together, that was always the question. What became of the Kadles? The ghosts.

Adams: That's it . . . where *did* they go?

Waters: Our old house is still standing, in pretty good shape. I saw it a year ago. But my sister Naomi, many years before, was in town and drove down there. She found it had been converted into a rooming house, with a couple of apartments and single rooms for rent. Wanting to see what the place looked like inside, she asked the landlady, "Any vacant rooms?" The woman showed her through the house. When they walked up the stairs, Naomi said, "These stairs are awful squeaky." And the woman said, "Oh, I don't know what's wrong with those stairs. There was a fellow who lived here a long time ago, I understand, and wrote a book about these squeaky stairs. Said it was ghosts. I don't know what it is." Naomi was delighted. She thought maybe the Kadles were still sticking around.

Adams: Maybe they are still there.

Waters: I hope so!

Adams: As I remember, those stairs squeaked for no particular reason.

Waters: Oh yes. They drove my poor grandfather nuts. He had his carpenters replace the stairs with good seasoned timbers, but they still kept squeaking. So, he just gave it up. (Laughter)

Adams: Let the Kadles stay. If they like it, it's theirs. Oh, one thing a student wanted me to ask you, and I think it is as personal a question for him as it is for you. He wanted to know, "How fictitious is Barby, really?" He said, "I know he is a fictitious character, but I also know that Mr. Waters did some border prize fighting, and there has got to be some of him in there somewhere."

Waters: When I first went to Los Angeles, I used to hang around a sporting club on Main Street. It was quite a famous place, and sometimes I'd work out with some of these boxers. I got to know the fellows pretty well. Then when I was transferred down to Imperial Valley, where there was a small ring for mixed prizefights, I met some of these fellows from Main Street brought down to fight with the Mexican and Negro boys there. I think Barby probably is a composite of some of these "fight toughs" down there. And that other one . . . Deuce of Spades. I knew him well. At that time, there were few white men who could work in terrible heat out in the melon patches. So the big growers were bringing in Hindus, and Chinese, and also quite a few Negroes from the South. There was one cantina there predominantly frequented by the Negroes. I went in it frequently with the Deuce of Spades, a good fighter. I think that was the first time that I ever noticed what a terrible, rancid body odor a white person has. All those Negroes in there, sweating in that terrible heat, and drinking too, gave off a body odor which is a little on the sweet side. Then I noticed a strange impinging bad odor, and I suddenly realized that it was my own. (Laughter) You feel yourself as a minority once in a great while, you know.

Adams: And that is a pretty personal way to feel it.

Waters: Well, the way the world is going I think the white race is going to find itself a stinking minority among the rest of the world.

Adams: It looks that way. I think of all the other evidence you cite in various works. It indicates we whites are inevitably going to be outnumbered.

Waters: If you believe in racial karma as well as individual karma, then we've really got a lot to pay off.

Adams: I'm afraid so.

Waters: Our assumption of superiority is a horrible thing to look at. There again is the transference of our own evil. I made a talk some time ago at Arizona State and the question was asked, "Don't we have any morality play that is unique to America?" I said, "Yes, we have one just as traditional and indigenous to America as the Russian ballet is to Russia, and that is the Cowboy-Indian morality play." One of the women in the audience jumped on me, and said, "Yes, and now you are contradicting yourself because you were just talking about how terrible and how cheap the Cowboy-Indian thing is and why don't writers write good Western literature without adhering to this stereotype." And I said, "Well, it is our good vs. evil morality play, and whether we like it or not, we are still adhering to it in actual fact." She wanted to know why, and I said, "Our good cowboys are still killing off the evil Indians in Indochina and Cambodia."

Adams: Whether you call them "Redskins" or "Gooks."

Waters: Sure, it's the same thing. We have just transferred our traditional anglo hatred of redskins to the colored races throughout the world . . . the black, brown, and yellow.

Adams: And we are still the virtuous whites.

Waters: This is our tragedy. Sometimes I am inclined to be pessimistic about the ways things are going. I think our western civilization is going downhill so fast, there is no arresting its plunge. It has got to hit bottom before the decks can be cleared for new growth.

Adams: That's not really a pessimistic point of view.

Waters: Well, I guess not.

Adams: Because you're counting on that regrowth, aren't you?

Waters: Yes, you bet. And I think the way these young people are looking at things, becoming interested in eastern religions and metaphysics of all kinds, indicates that the movement is growing in the right direction.

Adams: I've certainly noticed a change in my students over the years. They are much more aware and alert and concerned and involved.

Waters: When I was at the age of the students that I talk with nowadays, none of *us* were interested in what was going on. All we wanted was the security of a good job by which we could climb to the top as fast as possible.

Adams: The Horatio Alger story.

Waters: Yes, we were all incipient Horatio Algers. Marry the boss's daughter, inherit the business.

Adams: And live happily ever after. (Laughter)

Adams: On a completely different topic, my wife wanted me to ask you, since you have had some contact with the Nevada Test Site, if you have any reaction to using Nevada as the dump for nuclear waste. It is a rather hot issue locally.

Waters: Where would the dump site be? North and east of Las Vegas?

Adams: Probably.

Waters: Well, the reason Nevada was chosen for the Test Site was that all of the winds in this country come from the west and sweep to the east. The physicists tried to pick out a spot in the United States where the radioactive fallout would fall over an area that is the least inhabited, most sparsely inhabited region in the United States. That is why they picked an area just a little bit east of Death Valley, the most sparsely inhabited area of Nevada. But even with so few people, there was a great deal of flack. Because ranchers found that the radioactive fallout had blinded many horses, and when the horses had fallen on their backs, it had turned the hair on their backs white. But I don't think that you could ever entirely get rid of these radioactive wastes. I suppose if the stuff would be buried in the earth, it would not be safe forever, would it?

Adams: We've really created a Frankenstein.

Waters: This doesn't solve the nuclear problem. A book came out a while ago by a young physicist at Los Alamos, who was hired to design the smallest bomb possible. His book shows that the atomic bomb is really not a complicated "gadget" at all. Now that the secret of its construction is known, a man can go to a drugstore and a hardware store, buy all of the material, and in his little carpenter shop make an atomic bomb for about one hundred dollars.

Adams: It's frightening.

Waters: It's not a question of a few countries having the secret of the atomic bomb. Everybody, even these "primitive" nations, with a few smart people, can make their own. And where is all this stuff going, if it ever gets spread?

Adams: One of the objections raised about the nuclear waste dump was that any kind of guerilla or rebel activity could set off an explosion that would release what was in the dump.

Waters: All of this is beyond my comprehension, as it is to most of the people in the world.

Adams: Any reactions on your part to the totality of your books? I'm thinking particularly in terms of what it means for me as a teaching experience, but also what it means for you, because you're really teaching that course.

Waters: Well, I've never thought much about all of my books taken as a whole. What *do* they amount to? This is the question. As I was writing, book by book, I think I was approaching the psychological problem of the dualities. Without knowing it, I took it up in one aspect and then in another. In that early trilogy, the boy March, part Indian, part white, suffered the conflict of the forces of his dual nature. In *Masked Gods* as a whole, I discussed that same problem rationally and philosophically. In *Yogi*, there it was again between the boy and the girl, and the problem of possibly superseding it; and then again in the *Otowi* book it came up. Well, that's a problem everybody has got to solve for himself.

Adams: I think your books help students an awful lot. While they may not constitute answers, they constitute a direction.

Waters: I think that is a good answer. This unconscious projection of the problem of dualities and writing it in the books has brought this up into focus in the consciousness so that the attempt of working on it has helped me a great deal, I'm sure.

Adams: Well, you've been successful.

Waters: I hope so.

Adams: I suppose you have already given the answer: it's individual.

Waters: It's the two trying to get into a three, and then trying to accomplish a four, but it is just an expression of a one again, you know . . . in numbers.

Adams: And we come right . . .

Waters: Come right back.

* * *

Adams: Well, what hope?

Waters: In *Mexico Mystique*, I have a little bit on this in the back, where I am speaking of the Mayan idea of the beginning of our present world. As they conceived it, it began around 3,000 years B.C. and that will end around 2,000 A.D. As I see it, there won't be a worldwide fatal catastrophe—so that the poles will be exchanged, Japan will sink into the sea, the whole East Coast will be under water, and earthquakes will destroy most of South America—I just don't believe that there will be such a worldwide cataclysm that the human race will be destroyed. To be sure, there are catastrophes and they are happening every day, and, at the end of a precessional period, there is bound to be a great change. This is the end of the 25,920 year precession of the equinoxes. This is also the end of the Piscean age, the last of the twelve zodiacal cycles, each lasting about 2,100 years. The twelve zodiacal cycles comprise a total of 25,900 years, which is the precessional period when the revolving earth completes that circle. So astronomically and astrologically it's a tremendous period of change. But these tales of previous worlds, to me at least, are allegories for the different phases of mankind's cultural advancements, his evolutionary stages. I think we are approaching and already beginning a new step in a new direction. I think that the rate of breakup is so fast and we in this civilization are deteriorating so fast that we can't turn the clock back. We must accept the fact that it is plunging downhill; and the form of this civilization, as we know it, is bound to break up.

But at the same time, these indications of a new threshold of consciousness being reached are very much in evidence. I think the young people's attitude toward this fusty world has completely changed. They just don't care for making money like their forefathers did, or even their own fathers. They don't want to make a lot of money; they don't want to live on this rational-materialistic level. They are searching for something. They don't know what they are searching for, but they are done with the old. They are searching for what's new. Now what the new is, they don't know, but they are searching through all kinds of eastern religions and mysticism and occult teachings of all kinds, and Jungian philosophy has come very much to the front in the last few years, so they're going inward for what they are searching for, instead of going out. And I think these are all indications of a complete change in our mode of thinking, of our expanding consciousness. Therefore, as the Hopis say, I think that we are already beginning our emergence to a new world. I am not really too pessimistic.

Adams: Actually it's optimistic.

Waters: Yes.

Adams: If you listen to any newscasts or pick up any newspaper, you are automatically depressed.

Waters: Yes. There is not a spot on the earth that is not in a turmoil of some kind because of our constant fragmentation. Division of countries, of people, of races, of sex. Constantly being divided into ever smaller units of every kind—physical, material, religious, ideological. And it is this that has to be changed, in the shrinking one world, into a one-world unity of peoples. We must realize our spiritual solidarity, and put it into practice. I don't think this can be achieved by political and economic expediency. I think the United Nations has proved this.

Adams: The kids are right then; it comes from the inside out.

Waters: It comes from the inside; that's where it's got to come from.

(Long pause)

But, I think, to attain that feeling of unity, of solidarity, we must recognize our oneness with all of nature. Not only with all of mankind, but with the plant and the vegetable and the animal kingdoms, with the earth itself, and with the planetary bodies which exert an influence on us too. We are not just Anglos, or citizens of Arizona or New Mexico or Nevada, nor of the U.S., but Citizens of the Universe.

Photo by Cynthia Farah

chapter two
Frances Gillmor
Interview by David Johnson

Born in 1903, the daughter of a coal company owner in Buffalo, New York, Frances Gillmor has crossed a number of important boundaries in her life. She worked as a journalist in Florida in the twenties while on leave as an undergraduate from the University of Chicago; finished her B.A. at the University of Arizona in 1928; and completed her first novel in 1929. By 1931 she had traveled by herself on the Navajo reservation, completed her second novel, and written a master's thesis on two Navajo Indian traders. She produced a collaboration on Navajo myth and legend with one of the same traders, which was published by Houghton Mifflin in 1934. She traveled and studied extensively in Mexico, collecting and publishing Mexican folk drama in the early forties. She published a fictional biography of Nezahualcoyotl, the great Mesoamerican king and poet, in 1949, received a doctorate from the National University of Mexico in 1957, and published a biography of the first Moctezuma in 1964. During this time, after a brief teaching stint at the University of New Mexico in 1932–34, she held a continuous teaching post at the University of Arizona, until she retired as a Professor Emeritus in 1973. She was interviewed by Professor David Johnson of the University of New Mexico English Department in 1985.

Selected Bibliography:

Thumbcap Weir, novel (New York: Minton Balch, 1929).

Windsinger, novel (New York: Minton Balch, 1930; republished Albuquerque: University of New Mexico Press, 1976).

Traders to the Navajos: The Story of the Wetherills of Kayenta, with Louisa Wade Wetherill (Boston: Houghton Mifflin Co., 1934). Reprint, University of New Mexico Press, 1965, 1983.

Spanish Texts of Three Dance Dramas from Mexican Villages (University of Arizona Bulletin, Vol. 13, No. 4, Oct. 1, 1942).

The Dance Dramas of Mexican Villages (University of Arizona Bulletin, Vol. 14, No. 2, April 1, 1943).

Flute of the Smoking Mirror: A Portrait of Nezahualcoyotl, Poet-King of the Aztecs, historical biography (Albuquerque: University of New Mexico Press, 1949; republished Tucson: Arizona University Press, 1968).

The King Danced in the Marketplace, historical biography (Tucson: Arizona University Press, 1964; republished Salt Lake City: Utah University Press, 1977).

Johnson: What first brought you to the Southwest in the late 1920s?

Gillmor: Well, to go back a bit. I took my first two years of college at the University of Chicago, but I had a cold and the flu every winter, so I went south to Florida and got a job as a reporter at a newspaper in Palm Beach.

Johnson: How long were you in Florida?

Gillmor: I was there for that winter and went back three different winters, working on three different papers.

Johnson: How then did you finish college?

Gillmor: When I decided to finish my degree, I wanted warmer weather since I had never had flu in Florida. So I came to Arizona. I loved the University of Arizona, so I stayed put and here I still am.

Johnson: Had you been in Arizona before?

Gillmor: No. It was my first visit to the Southwest.

Johnson: Did you start writing in high school?

Gillmor: Yes. I was the editor of the high school magazine.

Johnson: Was there any particular teacher or someone that gave you a boost?

Gillmor: They all encouraged me, but ever since I was a little girl I've been writing. Now, I wish that I hadn't thrown away so much. I threw away all those childhood things I wrote once—poems, as well as stories—in a notebook.

Johnson: So you were writing fiction and articles before the later scholarship?

Gillmor: Yes, absolutely. My first novel came out in 1929, the year after I graduated; I'd been working on it between my seasons of reporting.

Johnson: How did you get into teaching? Did you go right on for a graduate degree?

Gillmor: After receiving my bachelor's degree in 1928, I was given a fellowship, which nowadays they call a teaching assistantship, here at the University of Arizona while I was getting my master's. And later an instructorship. They used to say that the fellowship was the academic trap, that once you started teaching, you stayed with it. And I did. I've loved it, except for examination time and giving grades.

Johnson: Did you develop an interest in Navajos in Arizona or during the two years you taught at the University of New Mexico?

Gillmor: That really stemmed from the problem concerning what I would write for my master's thesis. By that time I had published my first novel and I wanted to do another. But you couldn't do a novel for a master's thesis. So the head of the department here, Professor Sidney Pattison, suggested the Wetherills, Navajo traders as living people about whom I could do a biography. Since it would be from interviews and not from library sources, I would then meet the problem of dealing with living material, not with material already fixed in print. So I first went up to Kayenta at his suggestion. And that's what started me on Navajos.

Johnson: How did your thesis become a book?

Gillmor: After it was my thesis, but before any thought about its publication,

I had written *Windsinger,* my second novel, and it had come out in 1930. The Wetherills had liked it; I was glad of that. The Houghton-Mifflin western sales representative was a Mr. Leussler—salesmen very often are scouts, as you know— and he was. His office was in San Francisco. He got a copy of the thesis and came to see me about it, and also went to Mrs. Wetherill, because I had included material from her collection of Navajo myths and legends which she had personally recorded. The Houghton-Mifflin people thought that the general public was not interested in Indian myth and legend as such. They didn't think that Mrs. Wetherill's collection of myths would be publishable—she had tried publishers before. They wanted me to do a book that would incorporate that material but be based in its general approach on my thesis. I went up to Mrs. Wetherill and we talked about it, and she was in favor of the idea. So that's what I did— a collaboration between us.

Johnson: Where did the title, *Traders to the Navajos,* come from?

Gillmor: That's a good story. Mr. Leussler, who had made the connection with Houghton-Mifflin, had a concern for the book, of course. They didn't like the title we had given it, *Around Hogan Fires.* They said the general reader, looking at that, would think it was about Paddy Hogan and a peat fire in Ireland. So just to have something to refer to—explaining that it was not necessarily the permanent title—they substituted *In the Lodges of the Navajos.* I wrote back that, of course, it couldn't be that because the Navajos did not have lodges—Plains Indians did—and it would completely confuse the contents of the book. As the publication date approached, Mr. Leussler got into the elevator of his San Francisco office building one day and was chatting with a man whom he met in the elevator now and then, but didn't really know, and idly said to him, "What would you call a book that was about a family of traders on the Navajo Reservation?" And the man said, "Why not 'Traders to the Navajos'?" and stepped off. Mr. Leussler liked it and wrote an airmail letter to me. I liked it and wrote a letter to Louisa Wetherill on the Navajo Reservation—mail came twice a week to Kayenta from Flagstaff by truck. She liked it, and that was it. I still don't know who the man was who gave the book its title.

Johnson: When you first began to travel among the Navajo, did you ever go by horse?

Gillmor: Sometimes to ceremonies. But to Kayenta, where the Wetherills lived, I went on a truck from Flagstaff that carried groceries, mail, and passengers. I was the only non-Indian passenger. There were Hopi passengers and Navajo passengers. It took two days for that 150 mile trip, with sections of the road where everybody got out, pushed, and dug through the sand—near the Elephants' Feet, for example, just beyond Tuba City. It was difficult back then. Now, of course, you can do it fast—a different world.

Johnson: Maybe too fast.

Gillmor: At Monument Valley I remember a time during the Second World War when there were geologists scouting for uranium in a low-flying plane. They stayed at the Gouldings. I had my meals with the Gouldings and the geologists, and at the table one day I remarked that I was surprised to see Navajos living in tents in Monument Valley. The Gouldings explained that the last movie that had been made there left the tents, part of the equipment, as a gift to the Navajos. And now the Navajos were using the tents. The young geologists had no idea that tents were that recent, that there were only hogans and brush *cha'os* or shelters before. Of course, tents kept things dry in the summer rains, but they were very modern to me.

Johnson: And that was during the war?

Gillmor: Yes. There is a wonderful story that Mr. Goulding told about the uranium mines in the area. It was late autumn, and the mines had been running about a year, I guess, and the Navajos were interested in knowing why the government wanted to buy uranium. So one time Mr. Goulding picked up a rock with the uranium in it—it looked like yellow powder on top—and said, "You see this? This is pollen, and as you know, pollen has great power. The government plans on dropping that on the enemy and thus winning a victory." Winter came, the snows were deep, and a letter arrived from the FBI. The FBI man said he was very anxious to talk to Mr. Goulding; he had tried to fly a plane in but couldn't find a landing place because of the snow, and when did Mr. Goulding expect to be coming off the reservation? Mr. Goulding was a friend of the sheriff at Fruitland, Colorado, and said that he was planning to go up there on such a date. The FBI man met him there and said, "Now, what is this I hear you're telling the Navajos about uranium?" Mr. Goulding couldn't think what it was, and then it dawned on him, and he explained what he had said. The FBI wanted it stopped right away. Mr. Goulding said that it would be stopped much more quickly if no issue were made of it. It would be repeated a few times from Navajo to Navajo; then it would no longer be a story and no one would think to tell it. He finally convinced the FBI man that that would be the best way to handle it, but he still did not know why the FBI man was upset. He didn't find out until the bomb dropped on Hiroshima.

Johnson: How quickly it got to the FBI!

Gillmor: Yes, and Mr. Goulding knew nothing about the bomb.

Johnson: That makes you believe in the unconscious, doesn't it? Or intuition. Did you find anything unusual about the Navajos when you began to learn about their culture?

Gillmor: They were the first Indians I had ever known, and I was vitally interested in everything, their mythology and ceremonies. I read everything that I could about them. The Wetherills had a fine library of their own, because all of the geologists and anthropologists who had worked up there had sent their publications to the Wetherills, usually with printed acknowledgments of their help.

Johnson: Did you learn to speak Navajo?

Gillmor: No, just simple things like asking for directions. I knew all the parts of the body; so if a man's arm was done up with a cast, I could ask if his arm hurt. And if I was talking with a woman and she had a baby on a baby-board beside her, I could ask whether it was a boy or a girl and say it was a pretty baby. I would always ask about roads, whether they were sandy, whether it was far to a place. Anything more complicated and I would have to use an interpreter. Even years ago, people often answered me in English, and now on the Navajo Reservation there are very few young people who don't speak English.

Johnson: Did you find something in the Navajo view of life that was different from what you had known before?

Gillmor: I suppose so, but it was also universal. For example, the events in

Windsinger, which I've always thought of as being a highly symbolic book, were events witnessed by the Wetherills and recorded in *Traders:* the flu epidemic, the deep snows, the singer struck by lightning, his prophecy about a flood and the people moving to high ground. I used these events in *Windsinger* in terms of the quest by any person, the artist or religious person, seeking or finding the way.

Johnson: The religious quest?

Gillmor: Yes. And I was impressed by the space. The women coming in to water the sheep at the windmill at Kayenta. When I first went up there, and a car went by on the road, everyone dashed out to look at it. If two cars went by in a day, that was a lot. There was a sense of remoteness and distance.

Johnson: Was it difficult for you to be accepted?

Gillmor: No, everybody was always very kind to me. Of course I had the Wetherills's introduction, so that was fine. When I went to ceremonies I always went with somebody I knew. During the period of the Second World War and the uranium thing, when I camped with my own bedroll, I stayed near traders and field nurses, and once near the Gouldings. I was told that I should always do that and not camp by myself.

Johnson: Did the Navajos know about *Windsinger*?

Gillmor: There's a story I'll never forget. I was at a ceremony out from Kayenta, at Marsh Pass. I went with a girl who was working at the hospital. The ceremony was given for her younger sister, a girl about fourteen or so who had Saint Vitus's dance. We went in my car and were there through the afternoon and far into the night. During a break in the ceremony, when people were going in and out, we got ready to leave, but her mother urged us to stay and have a little lunch before we left. She had goat ribs for us, which were very good. So we sat in the brush shelter where the cooking was being done, with the light of the fire. Over in the shadows people were sitting. Except for my young friend, who was interpreting for me when I needed an interpreter, I hadn't heard any English spoken from about noon to midnight. Suddenly, while we sat in the firelight eating our goat chops, a girl's voice spoke out in the shadows, "Are you the one who wrote *Windsinger*?" I was startled no end, but I didn't want to lie and say, "No, it must be somebody else," so I said, "Yes, I was the one." It turned out that she had read it in school and had liked it very much—I felt very much relieved. She's the only Navajo I knew who had read it.

Johnson: That's a wonderful story.

Gillmor: After *Windsinger* came out, and I was going east—by train in those days—I was talking to a man who had been on the Navajo Reservation. I had just been there myself, and we were talking about the reservation when he said to me, "You know, there is something that happened when I was on the Navajo Reservation that I've always remembered. The most surprising thing. Somebody ought to write about it sometime." He then said, "Somebody had prophesied that there would be a flood. And all the Navajos rode by to get to high places, moving their goods, their household pots and pans and flocks. It was a whole migration." And I said, "Yes! I've written about it." And it was *Windsinger.*

Johnson: Carl Jung called these unexpected connections in one's life "synchronicity."

Gillmor: Does he? Well, this man hadn't known about the book, and it was very interesting to have that come to me on a transcontinental train from somebody sitting across the aisle that I didn't know at all!

Johnson: Did you learn Spanish while teaching in New Mexico?

Gillmor: No. I went down to Mexico to learn it in order to use it in New Mexico. And then I got so wedded to all the things I was doing in Mexico that I never got back to New Mexico, which I still love.

Johnson: How did you plan to use Spanish in New Mexico?

Gillmor: While I was at the University of New Mexico, I was very much interested in the Pueblo Indians, and at that time in the Pueblos young people could speak English, while the old people could speak Spanish. Of course, they all spoke their own, native languages. So in order not to have to learn the languages of several different Pueblos, I thought that if I learned Spanish I would have an open sesame to the people that I really wanted to talk to—the old people. Young people never trust a newcomer to the village. They don't know whether they should talk to that person or what they should say; they don't know whether to talk about ceremonies, or in Mexico, fiestas. They might say things they shouldn't be saying. That's true everywhere, in the Southwest and down in Mexico.

Johnson: What were some of the plays you recorded in Mexico?

Gillmor: My first script of the "Moors and Christians" play came from a village just out of Mexico City at Ixtapalapa. It was about 1938, a time when all the churches were closed; and when I went there and got the script everyone was very cordial and very kind.

Johnson: How did you get a copy of the script in the first place?

Gillmor: I happened to see the Moorish King who had a long false beard for his costume and dark glasses—they wore dark glasses to indicate they were Moors. He fell out when he had a period when he didn't have lines and sat down in the shade of the churchyard wall. He had got an ice cream cone, so he shoved aside his beard to eat the ice cream and study his lines in a little notebook that he had. If he had continued to wear his beard, I wouldn't have dared to speak to him—he was a Moorish king—but when he put the beard aside and ate an ice cream cone, he looked less formidable and I could see that he was one of the villagers; I asked him if he would let me see the notebook. He was delighted to show it to me. Then I asked him if I could copy it, and he said yes; after he was through with his part, he would be very glad to have me copy it. So I sat right there in the shade of the church wall and copied it, but he only had his own part. The Christian ambassador, who was the real director of the play, had all the parts—but separated, not put together in sequence. He lent them to me and I took them into Mexico City and I copied them. I brought them back and sat with him while he gave directions about putting them together with paste and scissors. There was a Frenchman, Pierre Verger, taking pictures on that occasion, and after chatting a bit he asked if he could have a copy of the script. I said he could, and he said that he would give me copies of his photos, which he did in due time. So he came along to an appointment with the maestro; the two of us sat and laid out the speeches on a mud floor—though our host had electricity—and pasted them all together. And the French photographer copied it. Before the script was published I wanted to be sure that it was all right for me to use his photographs—he was a professional photographer who had published books of photographs from different parts of the world. I tried to get in touch with him, but the war had come along by that time. So I wrote to his agent in the United States, and she wrote back saying that he was in the Western Hemisphere and that she was sure it would be all right to publish the pictures—that she could authorize it.

Johnson: It is difficult to imagine all the problems.

Gillmor: Another time involved quite a different situation with a *La Conquista* play from Oaxaca. I had borrowed the script and had it copied by xeroxing—times are easier now, if you're close to a xerox machine. But still there were different pieces of the script, different parts, etc., and I had to go to the director of the play and have him put it together: "Now the king, now Santiago, now is the time for the Moors to go to the camp of the Christians, now time for the Christians to go to the camp of the Moors," and so on.

Johnson: And these scripts were then published.

Gillmor: The University of Arizona published as a Bulletin three of the scripts I had collected. They showed the shift from the "Moors and Christians" play, which had come from Spain, to the "La Conquista" dance-drama, where the battle was between Spaniards and Aztecs, to "The Dance of the Plumes" from Oaxaca, where the two sides were French and Mexican at the time of Maximillian.

Johnson: So the pattern evolves and the plots and speeches remain essentially the same?

Gillmor: More or less. The same speeches are made more appropriate to the historical setting, as, for instance, an attempt to convert to Christianity, and so on, with elaborate costumes from the period. By the way, I published the script as it was, with all the mistakes in spelling and grammar. There are two theories about that and I'm not committed to either one. I have been praised by people working in the field; they said it made it possible to use them. But on the other hand, some people say it makes it very difficult to read, even for a Spanish-speaking reader, and they think it is better to modernize and correct the spelling.

Johnson: When did your interest turn to Mesoamerica?

Gillmor: Through living down there in Mexico, and learning Spanish, and when I started going out to these fiestas. I began to take courses at the National University of Mexico. Eventually I put my work from the National University together and received my degree, Doctora en Letras, in 1957.

Johnson: When did you decide to write *Flute of the Smoking Mirror?*

Gillmor: That was quite early. I got interested in Nezahualcoyotl, the fifteenth-century poet-king, and not many people in the United States knew anything about him. He was a good subject for an article, but it grew and grew until it became a book, and then it was published. At the same time I was getting interested in Montezuma the First, Motecuzma Ilhuicamina, the great-grandfather of the Montezuma who was ruling when the Spaniards arrived.

Johnson: Nezahualcoyotl and the elder Montezuma were friends.

Gillmor: Well, they were relatives, allies, and yes, friends also. They were allies in the various conquests throughout the tribute area of the Aztecs—actually of the Nahuatl-speaking people. I use Aztec because most English speakers would not know what is meant by Nahuatl; very strictly speaking, the word "Aztec" applies to the Nahuatl-speaking people of Tenochtitlan, what is now Mexico City.

Johnson: How did you decide to do *Flute of the Smoking Mirror* as a kind of recreated history?

Gillmor: Well, it isn't really created, except for the market scene at the beginning just after Nezahualcoyotl was born. They are talking about his birth in the market, and that is a created conversation, though everything they say is from historical sources, exactly. After that point, the conversations come directly from the original sources. This history comes to us mostly from the sixteenth century, and there are conversations all the way through. In that century that was the way they wrote history. And I used direct translations of those speeches.

Johnson: But you put it together in such a way that there is a kind of chronology that one doesn't find in just one source.

Gillmor: Every time I put anything in, I gave its source. There are long conversations in the sources as one person talks to another. Years ago Paul Radin wrote about these conversations and their authenticity. He said that these were undoubtedly not the words that the people actually used, but they were words that the chroniclers put in their mouths. Nevertheless, they expressed the policies and viewpoints of those people, of each ruler, of the peace party and the war party, and what the viewpoint was in each case. So the conversations are an essential source of information.

Johnson: The linking of information to the spoken words of a living person gives that viewpoint a kind of validity and power.

Gillmor: The Spanish conquerors used those conversations to understand the cultural traditions, because there were people still living who knew Nezahualcoyotl. There were three short reigns between Montezuma I and Montezuma II, so there were people living in 1519, the time of the Spanish conquest, who could remember Nezahualcoyotl's death in 1472.

Johnson: Some of these speeches seem to represent the height of their culture in terms of ethics and beauty.

Gillmor: That was the high period of Aztec culture.

Johnson: There are suggestions in *Flute of the Smoking Mirror* that Nezahualcoyotl was unique in some respects, that he was a loner who was not caught up in human sacrifice like the others.

Gillmor: All the sources talk about the fact that he built a temple to *Tloque Nahuaque,* the God of the Near Vicinity, the With and the By, as Father Garibay translates it. There is a great deal in the sources about this god, and both Father Garibay and his pupil Miguel Leon-Portilla go into a great detail about the God of the Near Vicinity being the source of all creation.

Johnson: Was this like a separate religious route leading almost to monotheism?

Gillmor: No! No! Not at all. Not even apparently for Nezahualcoyotl. He didn't deny the existence of the other gods. He simply disliked human sacrifices, so he built a temple to the God of the Near Vicinity who demanded no sacrifices.

Johnson: While looking through your two Mesoamerican biographies I was impressed with the beautiful job of editing: the maps, notes, text, bibliography, and illustrations—a great deal of work.

Gillmor: Which of those two do you like better?

Gillmor: In some ways, I prefer *Flute of the Smoking Mirror* because of the person who emerges; he's full of human complexity. There is a thoughtful, creative person behind his portrait.

Gillmor: Yes, that's true. And of course, Ilhuicamina was not an attractive person; he was more austere, more remote. So much of the decision making was left to Tlacaelel, who was his councillor—actually the councillor under three Aztec rulers. Tlacaelel was like an alter ego. His name runs through the Aztec histories; they teem all the way through with his ideas, his plans for military rule. But when the time came for a new election, he always refused to be the new ruler. Quite extraordinary!

Johnson: There is something very fascinating about these people, isn't there? Is it because of all the contradictions?

Gillmor: I think that's part of it. There was a kind of hard and terrible beauty to the period. It was a cruel civilization. All the human sacrifices; of course, it was considered an honor to be sacrificed. There is the story about a warrior from Tlaxcala, who was captured. He had a great reputation for military ability and they wanted to incorporate him into the Tenochtitlan army. They even brought his wife from Tlaxcala to make him contented in Tenochtitlan. But he refused the offer; he considered it an insult not to be sacrificed.

Johnson: The history of the Aztecs is quite unusual when you think of how few years it was between the period when they were wandering nomads and when they became regional rulers.

Gillmor: Yes, the whole period was 150 years or so.

Johnson: I wanted to ask you something. They talked about blood being necessary for watering the earth or feeding the gods, but there's a sense in which all cultures have talked that way.

Gillmor: Oh yes, that's true.

Johnson: But other cultures tended to evolve from the literal to the symbolic. In other words, rites took on a metaphoric dimension; so now, instead of pouring a person's blood, you take a pitcher of special water from a particular ceremony and pour it on the image of the god. It becomes then a symbolic act, but it seems that the Mesoamericans did not have enough time to move from the literal to the symbolic. Would you agree?

Gillmor: I think that's an interesting, good analysis of it; they might have evolved, and then again they might *not* have. That came up, oddly enough, in my oral exams for my doctorate. Somebody wondered whether it was a terrible thing that the European civilization broke off and crushed an indigenous one, and then a comparison was made between Christianity and the Aztec religion. I said that the emphasis on blood and human sacrifice among the Aztecs made it a cruel civilization—that, of course, was true. And I said that the Spaniards were also cruel and shed much blood in warfare, but there was a difference. When we consider the Spaniards as Christians, we look upon war as a failure of Christianity; whereas the Aztecs looked upon war as the fulfillment and objective of religious activity—that constituted a fundamental difference. Of course, the Aztec culture was stopped; whatever might have become of it in the course of a few more centuries, nobody knows. It would have been men like Nezahualcoyotl who could have had a great influence on the future. Now there are many more poems credited to him by Nahuatl linguists like Miguel Leon-Portilla than when I wrote about him. I would have used more of his poetry had I been certain that he composed them.

Johnson: Did you learn Nahuatl? Did you study it?

Gillmor: Yes, not so that I could go out to a village and speak it, but I took courses in it, from Professor Wigberto Jimenez Moreno. He likes *Flute of the Smoking Mirror* better than *The King Danced in the Marketplace.*

Johnson: I was going to ask you which you liked better.

Gillmor: I think I really like *The King Danced in the Marketplace,* in spite of the fact that the leading person in it is not a *simpatico* character. I like it because the book gives a wider spread with more detail of the ceremonial and governmental procedures.

Johnson: It is fuller.

Gillmor: Yes, it's fuller in terms of background. That was partly necessary because Moteczuma Ilhuicamina could not stand alone in the book; he needed more background, but that became an advantage for the book itself.

Johnson: Each has its beauty. Both are written beautifully. There is a great deal of poetry in your prose. That goes way back, doesn't it?

Gillmor: People say that about my earlier books. But in this case I deliberately picked the most poetic portions from the Nahuatl sources.

Johnson: The Germans are very strong in Mesoamerican studies, aren't they?

Gillmor: Yes, like Edward Seler, who translated Nahuatl into German. Seler's pupils in Germany could come to a Nahuatl-speaking village in Mexico and actually speak to the people. Seler was very good. And then of course Father Berard Haile's early studies of Navajo on the Navajo Reservation produced a series of grammars and so on, and all were published in Germany. At that time no scholarly press in the United States would publish them.

Johnson: I didn't know that.

Gillmor: His Navajo dictionary was published in Germany. You know, during the war I wondered about something: We had Navajo army men on the radio talking to each other, to transmit messages, because nobody would know what they were saying. And yet the Germans were the people who were specialized in Navajo and had published Navajo materials.

Johnson: I've never made that connection before.

Gillmor: But of course, that doesn't mean that two Navajos wouldn't be talking Navajo slang. Also, publishing those things doesn't mean that anybody was actually studying Navajo at the time in Germany, but Seler's pupils could come and speak Nahuatl in villages. So if somebody wanted to study Navajo in Germany, they had a lot of stuff to start with right there.

Johnson: Those Navajos in the army were called Code Talkers. Every once in a while the local paper says they've had a reunion. I don't know how many are left, but they made a real contribution.

Gillmor: That's interesting. Of course, there are lots of people who don't speak anything but Nahuatl, but I think that is getting to be less and less true.

Johnson: Were your Aztec biographies translated into German?

Gillmor: No. The only one that was translated was *The King Danced in the Marketplace*, and that was translated into Spanish and Polish.

Johnson: Is it out of print now?

Gillmor: Yes.

Johnson: Does international copyright protect you in Poland?

Gillmor: Yes, but I'm not terribly happy with how they handled the book. A young man in the library here, whose first language is Polish, said it was an excellent translation, but they only translated the text, and they didn't put in any of the notes, and without the notes it looks like a novel. And instead of the tracings from Mexican codices, they put in photographs of Aztec sculpture.

Johnson: That takes away from the flavor, doesn't it?

Gillmor: I'm sorry they left out the notes, which were close to my heart.

Johnson: The Spanish translation seems almost identical to the English version.

Gillmor: Yes, except that Ilhuicamina means the Archer of the Skies, and they reversed that on the cover by putting the arrow into the earth. But if the world is round, then you can move the book in a circle, and it's all right.

Johnson: When you first went down to Mexico, how did they feel about a woman studying in Mexico City? Did they welcome that?

Gillmor: Yes. In fact, there were woman doctors and lawyers with their signs up all over Mexico City. They were graduates of the National University and sometimes had added training elsewhere.

Johnson: Were they more supportive of women going into the professions than here in the States?

Gillmor: I always thought so, from the great number of women that were in the professions; but on the other hand, I'm not so sure now. I knew a woman briefly who was a pediatrician, though she had specialized in endocrinology. She'd given papers in the U.S.; her graduate work was in the U.S., but she said it was awfully difficult to break in down in Mexico. Yet you saw signs all over the place.

Johnson: Didn't you interview Lazaro Cardenas, the President of Mexico, in the late 1930s?

Gillmor: Yes, I interviewed him. I was gathering material on the villages that had been swamped by the lava and ash when Paricutin erupted in 1943, and refugee villages were set up. I was interviewing people in those refugee villages, interviews which I still have and which would make a small, very interesting book. One woman in particular talked in sheer poetry. At that time Cardenas was like the patron saint, and still is, of those new villages. They would point to a footprint made in the cement of the school that was being built, and that was Cardenas's footprint. So I interviewed him mainly on those villages and the things that were being done there. They were close to his heart; he was no longer President of Mexico, but there were other things, including Wycliffe Bible translators, that he admired.

Johnson: How were Wycliffe translators involved with campesinos?

Gillmor: Well, it was against the law in Mexico for foreign missionaries to come in as a group, but the Wycliffe translators did more than translate the Bible to various indigenous languages—work known all over the world. They actually performed agricultural extension work, like those that we have in the United States: providing agricultural information, home economics, and the like. Cardenas would drive from Mexico City to his home in Michoacán and notice a certain area that looked very prosperous; the crops were good and all sorts of interesting things were being done there. He found Wycliffe Bible translators were doing these things, so while he was President he made an exception to the rule about foreign missionaries. So I asked him, "How did it happen that they can be here?" and he said, "They have made a place for themselves."

Johnson: Have you been to Mexico City recently?

Gillmor: No. I don't go to Mexico City quite as much; many of my old professors are now dead, sadly, and besides I was getting involved with all the plays in the Guadalajara area. I'm doing this work in cluster fashion because you can't possibly cover everything in folk drama in all of Mexico. On the day of Santiago, for example, there will be hundreds of plays given in different forms; you can be in only one village and will have to wait to the next year to see the drama again. So you really can't cover all the ground, only a sample.

Johnson: Are you currently working on these plays?

Gillmor: Oh yes: where the plays are given, the village fiestas, the people, the village background of the plays, the variations in the texts. I hope that the book will include a number of the texts.

Johnson: Do you have a publisher for the book?

Gillmor: No. I always peddle. I've never had a publisher committed ahead of time. Each one has been a separate risk, and sometimes publishers keep the manuscripts a long time.

Johnson: Do you see the end for this work?

Gillmor: Yes, but I keep changing things around. Actually I presented the last chapter in so many ways now that it's a wonder that I don't go cold on it, but I haven't. I've been giving papers on the plays, drawing threads together. The last one, not long ago, was at the International Congress of Americanists held in Vancouver, and I was invited to give a paper there in a symposium—it's my addiction to go to meetings in anthropology and folklore. The paper in Vancouver was on the symbolic aspects of the play, "Los Tastoanes," which is the play that is pulling everything together for me. It has elements from Shepherd Plays, Passion Plays, and "Moors and Christians."

Photo by Cynthia Farah

chapter three
Tony Hillerman
Interview by Sue Bernell and Michaela Karni

Tony Hillerman was born a Catholic in Oklahoma in 1925. After a fitful start in college at Oklahoma State University, he was drafted and served in World War II, where he received the Silver Star, Bronze Star, and Purple Heart. On his return, he took a B.A. from the University of Oklahoma in 1946 and started his professional life as a reporter for the Borger, Texas, *News Herald* in 1948, working his way up to the post of political reporter for United Press International in Oklahoma City in 1950 and bureau manager for UPI in Santa Fe in 1952. Subsequently he was editor of the Santa Fe *New Mexican* from 1954–63. He decided to abandon journalism for a try at his own writing, and moved to Albuquerque where he began graduate studies in English at the University of New Mexico. He received his M.A. in 1966. Of his first novel, *Blessing Way* (1970), it is solemnly reported in *Contemporary Authors* that "Hillerman, who had Indians as playmates and friends, says that he is interested in what can be done, in the literary sense, with the contrast of cultures." Hillerman himself claims his first novel was a stepping stone to a more ambitious effort, *The Fly on the Wall* (1971). But in subsequent fiction, mostly dealing with crime and detection, he returned to the Indian setting: His principal heroes have been Joe Leaphorn and Jim Chee, Navajo sleuths of Hillerman's creation. Today Hillerman is one of the most popular and widely read authors of Southwestern background. He still lives in Albuquerque, where until recently he taught at the University of New Mexico. This interview was conducted at his Albuquerque home in the spring of 1986 with local mystery writers Sue Bernell and Michaela Karni.

Selected Bibliography:

The Blessing Way, novel (New York: Harper and Row, 1970).

The Fly on the Wall, novel (New York: Harper and Row, 1971).

The Boy Who Made Dragonfly: A Zuni Myth (New York: Harper and Row, 1972). Reprint, University of New Mexico Press, 1986.

Dance Hall of the Dead, novel (New York: Harper and Row, 1973).

The Great Taos Bank Robbery and Other Indian Country Affairs, stories (Albuquerque: University of New Mexico Press, 1973).

The Spell of New Mexico, nonfiction (Albuquerque: University of New Mexico Press, 1976).

Listening Woman, novel (New York: Harper and Row, 1978).

People of Darkness, novel (New York: Harper and Row, 1980).

The Dark Wind, novel (New York: Harper and Row, 1982).

The Ghostway, novel (New York: Harper and Row, 1984).

Skinwalkers, novel (New York: Harper and Row, 1986).

Indian Country: America's Sacred Land, nonfiction (Seattle: Northland Press, 1987).

Thief of Time, novel (New York: Harper and Row, 1988).

Talking God, novel (New York: Harper and Row, 1989).

Hillerman: I really think there is something about the Southwestern landscape and Southwestern culture and society that fosters creativity in a lot of people. There are some who feel oppressed by vast distances, the space. But others, and I'm one of them, are stimulated by this. It's simply—you look out at a countryside that doesn't seem as if it were designed for human occupation, yet here we are. The view alone puts things in a different perspective.

Bernell: Along with different perspectives of the same view.

Hillerman: No question about it. When I was in Santa Fe, editing the *New Mexican*, I had two men writing for me. One was Oliver Lafarge, who won the Pulitzer Prize for *Laughing Boy*, and the other was Winfield Townley Scott, who won the National Book Award for poetry. Both of them were New Englanders, born and bred. Both of them had come out here and just been captured by the Southwest. Lafarge was fascinated by the Hispanic and Native American cultures. His interest in the landscape was only in terms of how it affected the people. Scott was totally enamored by the landscape. He wasn't at all interested in the people.

Karni: While you incorporated both, by writing about the Navajo, how they adapted to the setting and made it part of their traditions.

Bernell: And turned the concept into a very original and successful series of mystery stories. How did that evolve, the journalist moving to fiction?

Hillerman: With a little more planning than how I became a journalist. I'd never considered it until I was discharged from the army after World War II. Before that I'd attended Oklahoma State University, to study science. I was going to be a chemist, of all things, and I was busily flunking out of my freshman year when the draft board offered me an opportunity to get out with some . . .

Bernell: . . . with some degree of dignity.

Hillerman: (Laughter) Right. Some degree of dignity. Then I returned from overseas with no vision in one eye and another that was damaged, so I couldn't work in a chem lab. Besides, I already knew that wasn't my forte, though I wasn't sure where my talents lay until somebody told me. During the war a woman on the *Daily Oklahoman* had done a feature story about me. She'd gone to my mother and gotten all the letters I'd written home, describing my experiences, my feelings. She said that when I got back from Europe she'd like to talk to me. So I went down and talked to her, and she told me I should be a writer.

Karni: Then you returned to college, studied journalism, and were hired immediately by a newspaper.

Hillerman: No, my first job was with an ad agency in Dallas, writing pig chow and coffee commercials for radio. (Laughter) It was dreadful, dreadful. The hardest thing I ever did. The Purina Company sponsored a morning newscast, six days a week. There were three commercial breaks during the show, and the copy for each spot had to be different. I had to come up with eighteen different ways to sell pig chow every week. I didn't last much longer than a week, as I recall. Then I went to work for a newspaper in Borger, Texas as a police reporter.

Bernell: Your first connection with crime. (Laughter) Did you like reporting it?

Hillerman: Oh, I loved it. And Border was a great little place for crime. It was boomtown in the middle of oil country, carbon-black from oil and gas wells, overcrowded with drillers, plenty of fights, and no decent housing. Marie and I were newlyweds. We lived in kind of a box on an alley, behind a frame bungalow. The town practically sprang up overnight, and it was surrounded by private ranches so there wasn't much room to expand. With all that teeming humanity crushed together, violence was inevitable.

Karni: How did you make the switch from journalism to fiction?

Hillerman: After the job in Texas, I went back to Oklahoma and worked for United Press International, then moved to Santa Fe where I was editor of the *New Mexican*. By then I'd been in the newspaper business for seventeen years, had five children, and a book I wanted to write that wasn't getting written. Marie and I decided that if I ever was going to get past the first chapter, I'd have to break away from journalism and re-pot, so to speak.

Bernell: You began chapter two by quitting your job?

Hillerman: And moving the family down to Albuquerque where I enrolled in the graduate program at the University of New Mexico. This was to get the background I'd missed as an undergraduate. I'd never studied Shakespeare or Milton, and I'd heard great things about the staff here . . . Edith Buchanan, Katherine Simons, and Ellen Spolsky, the young woman who taught Chaucer. Before writing, I wanted to study literature at its roots.

Karni: Is that when you started teaching in the journalism department?

Hillerman: Not that early. I was just a student then, though I did go to work at the university, as sort of a handyman for Tom Popejoy, the president of UNM. My job was to do whatever needed to be done, and there were times he needed some pretty unusual things done. As an example, one day he said to me, "Tony, you're going to get a call from a county sheriff. He's got to have twenty-four mattresses in a hurry without any publicity." Well, I'd been around New Mexico politics for quite a while. I knew this particular sheriff was also a brother of a county chairman who had considerable influence with a couple of state senators. When he called, I told him we had what he wanted, just send a truck over. Later we cashed in those mattresses on two crucial legislative votes for establishing a medical school at UNM.

Karni: Tom Popejoy was an amazing politician, brilliant at getting what the university needed from the state legislature.

Hillerman: He was a very savvy fellow.

Bernell: So was the sheriff. Why did he need those mattresses?

Hillerman: They'd had a little jail riot and burned up all his. He didn't want it known, and he didn't have the money to buy any more because his budget was overspent. So we gave him twenty-four old Peace Corps mattresses that had been stored in the basement of Hokona Hall.

Karni: Is that when *The Great Taos Bank Robbery* was published?

Hillerman: All the short pieces in there had been published separately before the collection came out in book form. They were written for Morris Friedman, my M.A. chairman. We decided that my master's thesis would be a series of essays aimed at a popular audience. Meanwhile, I was trying to sell them to magazines, which I did, one by one, thanks to Friedman. He was an excellent teacher, a fine writer. I learned a tremendous amount from him, the skills I needed. Technique. His encouragement meant a great deal to me in terms of confidence. When Friedman accepted me as an equal and said I was talented, I knew I was talented.

Karni: Didn't you know it before? You'd been making a living as a writer.

Hillerman: I'd been doing a certain kind of writing. I knew I was a competent journalist, but for someone of his caliber to say I was good in another area was very reassuring.

Bernell: Enough for you to tackle the book that wasn't getting written?

Hillerman: Not just yet. *The Fly on the Wall* was my second book. That was my second book. That was going to be The Book, the big important novel, the story I really wanted to write.

Karni: About the role of the media in elections, the way reporting affects the outcome. It's a controversial issue. How objective a newswriter can be. Or should be. And you had an inside scoop.

Hillerman: A lot of it was based on personal experience. After I was a police reporter, I became a political writer, and more so than in any of my other books, the characters in *The Fly on the Wall* were derived from people I'd known. One of the reporters in the story was modeled after a man who worked on the *Oklahoma City Times*. He helped break me in and taught me about covering the state capital.

Bernell: Why was that your *second* novel?

Hillerman: Because I still wasn't sure I could write it. I'd never written anything that long, and I hadn't written any fiction except for a few short stories. I knew I was good at description. I could move narrative along, do dialogue. But I didn't know if I could develop characters or plot. So I decided to start with a shorter book. Then, to give myself an ace in the hole, I'd set it in an exotic locale, a place that was interesting in itself. I was interested in the Navajo, and I thought other people would be too, so I thought I'd try it and see what happened. I'd practice first.

Karni: With *The Blessing Way*. Nice practicing. It was a finalist for the Edgar Allan Poe Award as best first novel. Wasn't it your third book that won the award for best mystery?

Hillerman: Yes. *Dance Hall of the Dead* won. *The Blessing Way* was beaten out by *The Anderson Tapes*, a really good book which I thought deserved to win. *The Fly on the Wall* was beaten by *The Eagle Has Landed*.

Karni: Other than prize-winning, how were these books about the Southwest received? Were you classified as a regional writer, or did you break through that kind of labeling by virtue of originality?

Hillerman: I never worried about being pigeonholed, though for some writers it's a problem. I tend to have two sorts of fans, anyway. And I notice it most dramatically when I go out of state on a book-signing tour. One kind are the mystery readers, who care more about plot. The other kind I call "desert rats." They're the people who were raised in the Southwest or have spent some time here. A lot of them are anthropologists or Indian buffs. They want to talk about the details of the ethnic materials. They say things like, "I did my dissertation on Navajo sweat baths, and the description you wrote is unfamiliar to me." Then there are the people who tell me, "When my wife and I are on vacation, we always take along one of your books and drive over the reservation, following the route you describe."

Bernell: After you wrote the novel about the newspaper business, what drew you back to writing mysteries set on the Navajo reservation?

Hillerman: I identify with the Navajo. I like them. I like their philosophical position. The Navajo as much as anything else is a product of his environment. I came out of the same kind of environment, poverty, trying to make a living from the land, hoping the hell it would rain and it wouldn't, always being at the bottom of the pecking order, socially. Not only were we poor, we were Catholic, living in Oklahoma and surrounded by Fundamentalist Protestants, which really set us apart. So when I see these Navajos, I know where they're coming from. I can sympathize.

Bernell: I've always been struck by the respect with which you treat Navajo customs and rituals. As an Anglo writer, you could have taken a more critical approach, stressing the conflict between traditional beliefs and twentieth century practices. Instead you created a positive combination, where a college-educated Navajo policeman uses his knowledge of ancient ways as an advantage in solving modern crimes.

Karni: It also seems to me that your theme is tolerance and respect. All ethnic roots have a commonality in that they spring from man's effort to create an orderly system of living, a moral standard, a code of ethics to preserve life. So many civilizations have been wiped out because of religious intolerance that you have to admire a people who've survived the test of endurance.

Hillerman: I do. I admire the Navajo for keeping their ways—a "living tradition." Where I grew up in Oklahoma, there wasn't much tribal identity. Around us were Potowotamies, some Seminoles, a few Blackfeet, but they were just people who lived on the next farm and played baseball with us. They knew very little about their cultures. They were pretty well assimilated, maybe too assimilated. When I was working on the paper in Santa Fe, one of the linotype operators came to me for help. He said, "I've got to fill out this form for the government. I'm a Potowotamic, but I don't know how to spell it. How the hell do you spell Potowotamie?"

Karni: So the newspaper reporter from Oklahoma came to New Mexico and became an editor, a novelist, a university teacher, and a noted authority on Navajo culture. You do everything very thoroughly, don't you?

Hillerman: Not without a lot of research first. When I decided to continue writing Navajo tribal mysteries, I found I didn't know as much as I thought I did. All I really had was superficial knowledge, and it wasn't enough. For instance, how do you pick names for your characters? That was one of the things that intrigued me about the Navajo. Their real name is known only to themselves and very, very intimate family members. That is who they really are, and it's secret. They only use the name when they're going through a cure or a religious ceremonial. The rest of the time, they operate on a nickname basis, some characteristic that can identify them, or an event that happened in their lives. A woman on the tribal council was called Ozzie's Mother. That's how she was known.

Karni: How did you choose Joe Leaphorn's name? By an event?

Hillerman: No, by mistake. That was one of my early blunders. He was a minor character in the first book, and at the time I was reading Mary Renault's *The Bull from the Sea*. In it is a ceremony with a bull where they leap over the horns.

Bernell: Then your hero has Cretan ancestry.

Hillerman: Not by intention. And from that point on, whenever you meet a Navajo in one of my books, the name comes out of the Shiprock telephone book or the graduation list of Red Rock Demonstration School, or from people I know. They're all real Navajo names other than that one single unfortunate exception.

Karni: Does that have anything to do with why you dropped Joe Leaphorn and developed a new series character? Or will you be bringing Joe back for more guest appearances the way you did in *Skinwalkers?*

Hillerman: Possibly, but I didn't abandon him because of his name. I realized after a while that he was too old, too sophisticated and knowledgeable of the white man's world to ask the kind of questions I wanted him to ask. To show more contrast, I needed a younger guy, a more traditional Navajo who didn't have all that experience, that exposure. In the first book, I sealed Joe Leaphorn's doom at the Enemy Way ceremonial when the singer looks at him skeptically and asks, "Do you believe in witches?" Joe answers, "I believe in evil."

Bernell: While Jim Chee isn't so certain there would be bad without a mystical influence.

Hillerman: On one level he's afraid of it, but on another he recognizes that if he conquers that fear, he's rejecting his religion.

Karni: So you had to learn more in order to frame his questions realistically.

Hillerman: I spent a hideous amount of time in the Addison Room at the Smithsonian, researching background. Anthropologists have recorded every detail of puberty rites, so the information is there if you want to find it. Trouble is, you also begin to find discrepancies.

Bernell: And disagreements.

Karni: Research is important in most kinds of writing, but for murder mysteries technical details have to be right to maintain credibility. Preferably they're little known details, so no one will be able to dispute them.

Hillerman: There's a theory about that. I heard some guy claim that you can't be wrong about a fact if the plot turns on it, but otherwise it doesn't matter.

Bernell: That's quite a stretch of poetic license. If you can make up your characters and actions, you can invent the facts too. Sounds fine for science fiction, but I wouldn't try it in a police procedural.

Hillerman: Neither would I. Definitely not in a tribal police procedural. I want my facts right, and I want people to respect their being right. I'm always checking up on myself too. When Navajos come to a book signing in Farmington or Gallup, I ask if they caught anything I'm wrong about. Once in a while they do, and when they tell me my mistake, I don't make it again. One thing you run into, though, is that what a Navajo considers proper on a checkerboard reservation is not accepted procedure for Navajos over in Tuba City.

For example, when they built the Chinle Clinic, the Indian Health Service went to great pains to make it hospitable for the Navajos. They built a healing room on one end, shaped like a hogan with a fire pit on the floor in the middle, so the shamans could have ceremonials in a proper setting. Then the health service asked the medicine people in Chinle to check that everything was right. It was. But when the shamans from the eastern side of the reservation come to the clinic, they won't go into the healing room. The outside is landscaped with lava rock, and where they live, the black rock around Mt. Taylor is considered the blood of the Walking God, the first of the monsters that was killed. It carries an evil connotation.

Karni: So the health service people didn't do all their homework.

Hillerman: They didn't check all the Navajo origin stories.

Karni: Then if you write one particular version of a ritual, there would be people who think you've made a mistake unless they're aware that so many variations exist.

Bernell: If you're concerned that all the Navajos might not realize and assume it's your error, you could always have one of your characters explain.

Hillerman: I do that once in a while. I try to make the point that things aren't the same in Tuba City as they are in Crownpoint, as far as theology goes.

Bernell: A moral for the BIA and writers. Always go directly to the source.

Karni: What made you decide to work in the mystery form?

Hillerman: Because it has so many possibilities. Look at what people have been able to do with the form. Chandler makes it political sociology. Graham Greene gives you the dark side of the soul. Ambler plays whatever tune he wants to on it. Everybody can use the mystery form to do their own thing. It's a superb format for telling a story, and I wanted the flexibility to tell a story and say my own thing.

Bernell: Sometimes they aren't the same. Often a writer's viewpoint is judged by the words he puts in his character's mouth when it's just the character talking, not the writer.

Hillerman: That's true. In my mysteries I'm trying to write from the viewpoint of a Navajo who is conditioned to his beliefs, his customs. Jim Chee's judgments of the world are based on his value system, not mine. I understand the influences that motivate his thinking, which enables me to express them. But I don't necessarily share his opinions. Any judgments I make in a book come from his head. My personal viewpoint is contained in how I write about it.

Karni: In your books the physical landscape of the reservation alone is a clue. Description doesn't only explain what an area looks like; it poses questions.

Hillerman: That's true. I couldn't have written a book anything like *The Dark Wind* if it weren't set on the border of the Navajo and Hopi reservation. We have to have that isolation, that desert, the geography of the mesa, or the story wouldn't come off. And since the sense of place is an integral part of my books, I need to go out there and refresh myself before writing about it. I always go to the area I'm describing and spend time taking in the atmosphere, smelling the wind, watching how it blows across the mesa. In a book like *The Listening Woman*, for example, the whole first chapter is simply involved in establishing the place. There's a long paragraph leading in that tries to give you a feeling of the remoteness of the setting, and the remoteness is important to the plot.

Bernell: There are times when the fertile imagination tries to graze on not-so-fertile pastures, and that blank page stays blank. How do I get from A to D? Yesterday the creative juices were flowing and I was on a streak. Today I'm striking out.

Karni: Sometimes it seems easier to dig ditches than to write.

Hillerman: Do I know it. Look at me right now. Look at all three of us right now. (Laughter)

Bernell: At least we're talking about writing.

Hillerman: Maybe it will help. I've got to do a seven-thousand-word text for a photo book, and I'm in one of those sticking places where I have to find a clever transition—one of the hardest things to do—so that the seam doesn't show. And I just hope to go back in there and apply the kind of concentration I need to review all the things that lead up to it, get the tone again, clarify where I'm going. I'd much rather sit here and talk about what I'm not doing. Somebody once told me that a good way to avoid running dry is to stop when it's going well. Don't wait until after you've finished a segment or until you're stuck.

Karni: Good point. Stop in the middle when you know what's coming up where you left off.

Bernell: Any other suggestions on creative continuity?

Hillerman: Actually, the biggest help for me is working on several projects at the same time so I can switch when I need to. While I'm writing mysteries I'm still doing articles, short pieces, nonfiction. I do a lot of reading too.

Karni: What's on your agenda now, along with the seven-thousand-word text?

Hillerman: I'm trying a mainstream novel, two of them in fact. One is a coming-of-age during the Depression, sort of a redneck *Catcher in the Rye*. (Laughter) It's a typical first novel in some ways, a personal revelation. The other is set in the Philippines, in the aftermath of the Viet Nam War. The older brother of a soldier who had been killed in action is sent by his dying mother to find her newly discovered Vietnamese granddaughter. The story isn't a mystery, though it involves a search for the girl that leads from Manila to Thailand. The conflict is the older brother's relationship with his mother and his prejudices about a foreign place and a people who are alien to him. I want to finish this book first to see if I can write a mainstream novel. Then I'll get back to the coming-of-age book. I've got a draft, but I'm not ready to go on with it yet.

Karni: You want to practice first, the way you did before writing *The Fly on the*

Wall. What approach will you take with the mainstream novel? Even if you travel extensively in Southeast Asia, you won't achieve the familiarity you have with New Mexico, to capture the essence of the place so completely.

Hillerman: I'm going to take a trip there, but that book will be much more a novel of characterizations, of people. The only thing that will be important about the place is the brother's feeling of alienation from it.

Bernell: Perfect research. He doesn't have to know any more about it than you will.

Hillerman: Right. All he needs is a visitor's view. His relationships with people will be the main focus.

Bernell: Are you planning to write in the humorous vein again, Tony? Some of the stories in *The Great Taos Bank Robbery*, including the title story, are among my favorites.

Hillerman: I love comedy, but it's a difficult technique to carry off. I've mainly used it in short pieces, though I've got a novel I started years ago that if I ever get good enough to write it, will be a comic novel.

Karni: The coming-of-age book?

Hillerman: That's the one.

Bernell: I detect a note of humor in your mysteries, little touches of farce such as the scene where Joe Leaphorn is bringing back a jail escapee and removes his handcuffs so the fellow can help him go after a killer. When the smoke from the gunfire clears, so has the escapee.

Karni: Humor is a wonderful way to break into sudden drama so the change has a surprise element. There's the traditional comic relief for tension and the comedy of using tension to create a predicament that abruptly becomes unfunny.

Hillerman: That's the trick of using humor in a mystery. It has to accomplish certain tasks, and like any recipe when you're cooking, you've got to be careful what you add. The first ingredient is making the character sympathetic, establishing a bond between the book and the reader. After that you can do marvelous things with comedy. Donald Westlake's books are intended to be funny, and they are. But some people go overboard. When I read mysteries to review them, a lot of the problem writers have with comedy is turning it into burlesque. They make the character such a jackass, you don't care what happens to him.

Bernell: Are you ever tempted to add a comedic note where it doesn't belong? Do you find you have to pull back sometimes?

Hillerman: Oh, sure. I see absurdities in all kinds of situations. It's easy for me to go off on a tangent, but in a mystery once you break the spell, it's gone. You can't recapture suspense. You have to build it all over again.

Karni: Now, that's *not* funny.

Hillerman: You know, I think you kind of write at the limits of your abilities, or I do. And the better I try to get, the harder it is.

Bernell: That's true. You stretch to the point of wondering, "Am I capable of this?"

Hillerman: And "Can I maintain this?" It's so doggone tiresome.

Karni: Don't get too tired before you finish the coming-of-age book.

Bernell: He won't. Remember what he said about the Southwest being so inspiring? Stimulating his creative juices? He'll probably finish it before we get this tape transcribed.

Hillerman: Pick up your coffee cups, ladies. We're going to have to drink to that.

Photo by Cynthia Farah

chapter four
Edward Abbey
Interview by Kay Jimerson

Edward Abbey was born in Pennsylvania in 1927. When he was seventeen, on the way to serve in the army, he took three months to hitchhike across the country. His first sight of the Rockies, he later wrote, "struck a fundamental chord in my imagination that has sounded ever since." After the end of World War II he studied philosophy at the University of New Mexico, then spent years traveling in the southwest desert, working sporadically as a park ranger and fire spotter. He settled in a succession of western locales through the mid-1960s. Several of his early novels, *The Brave Cowboy* (1965) and *Fire on the Mountain* (1962), depict anarchistic heroes in doomed defiance of the authorities. Jack Burns, the brave cowboy, tries to free a draft resister from jail; John Vogelin of *Fire on the Mountain* fights the U.S. Air Force when it seeks to buy out his ranch for a test site. Abbey's first work of nonfiction, the popular *Desert Solitaire* (1968), compresses three years he spent as a park ranger into one in a vision of wilderness that recalls Thoreau's *Walden* and Krutch's *The Desert Year*. *Appalachian Wilderness* (1970) also includes trenchant commentary on technological intrusions into natural settings. The novel *Black Sun* (1971) is perhaps his most cerebral: The hero's search for his lost love culminates in the Grand Canyon with buzzards circling above, surely an allegorical journey to the underworld. By contrast, the lively satiric novel *The Monkey Wrench Gang* (1975) has ecological activists brazenly attacking machinery wherever it challenges the land. The essays in *The Journey Home* (1977) and *Abbey's Road* (1979) again interrogate man's apparent impulse to destroy nature. His most recent novel at the time of the interview, *Good News* (1980), shows the West after the holocaust. Critics have noted these works' increasingly darkening vision. Abbey himself tended to stay apart from public view. When he appeared for this interview at the small, noisy Mosaic Cafe on the west end of Tucson in November 1987, according to Kay Jimerson, "We took the interview out to my car in the parking lot, away from the chatter of the jukebox." Abbey was "polite and well-spoken, but nevertheless seemed relieved when the interview was over." He noted that while he then summered in Moab, Utah, and wintered in Oracle, Arizona, he might have to move again soon, "maybe to Colorado, maybe to Australia," to escape an encroaching civilization. Abbey requested and was given this already short interview to edit, whereupon he condensed it considerably. It was one of the last interviews he gave; he died a year and a half later, on March 14, 1989.

Selected Bibliography:

The Brave Cowboy, fiction (New York: Dodd Mead, 1956).

Fire on the Mountain, fiction (New York: Dial Press, 1962).

Desert Solitaire: A Season in the Wilderness, nonfiction (New York: McGraw Hill, 1968).

Black Sun, fiction (New York: Simon and Schuster, 1971).

The Monkey Wrench Gang, fiction (Philadelphia: Lippincott, 1975).

The Journey Home: Some Words in Defense of the American West, nonfiction (New York: Dutton, 1977).

Abbey's Road: Take the Other, nonfiction (New York: Dutton, 1979).

Good News, fiction (New York: Dutton, 1980).

Slumgullion Stew: An Ed Abbey Reader (New York: Dutton, 1984).

Beyond the Wall: Essays from the Outside (New York: Henry Holt, 1984).

Confessions of a Barbarian, fiction (dual edition, Santa Barbara: Capra Books, 1986).

One Life at a Time, Please, essays (New York: Henry Holt, 1988).

Fool's Progress, novel (New York: Henry Holt, 1988).

Jimerson: Your motives for writing are listed in *Abbey's Road:* to record the truth, to defend mankind from techno-industrial tyranny, for money, for pleasure, etc. Have you additional reasons?

Abbey: Yes, there is also an aesthetic one: writing as an art. One book might be strictly polemical, another, fun—but all are meant as literary art.

Also I write to celebrate the beauty of nature; in my case the American Southwest. It's my favorite area on the planet not simply because of the desert, but because of the combination of rivers, forests, mountains, climate, sky, wildlife. . . . Writing is a form of piety or worship. I try to write prose psalms that praise the divine beauty of the natural world. Humans are part of that beauty, too, though we foul up the world and make a mess of human affairs.

Jimerson: Much of your language has spiritual associations. Are you religious?

Abbey: I'm not religious in the orthodox sense. I don't belong to an organized religious group. On the other hand, atheism and agnosticism are too limiting. If I have a religion, it's pantheism, the belief that everything is in some sense holy, or divine, or sacred. Everything—even human life.

Jimerson: It seems paradoxical that you, whose livelihood is words, would say as you did in one of your books that naming things amounts to "verbal reduction." Could you explain?

Abbey: We have a tendency to name things, then settle for words as a sufficient description. Names are useful and necessary, but names are not enough. There is far more in a flower or a forest than we can capture in a name. We must go beyond names, beyond words; we must look at and understand a flower or a forest in and for itself.

Jimerson: Do you write for an audience?

Abbey: No, I have no particular audience in mind, though I have a vague idea of millions of people thinking as I do. Out there somewhere, they will be receptive to and understand what I am writing, I hope.

I write also because no one else has written what I want to write exactly the way I want to write it.

Jimerson: Do you think fiction should have a purpose other than to entertain?

Abbey: Entertainment is a good and sufficient reason to write. However, the writers I most admire have some moral purpose in mind. Samuel Johnson said it is a writer's duty to make the world better. I'll go along with that. It's a lot to ask but still worth shooting for.

Too many American writers labor over the nuances of personal relationships, as if nothing else interested them. Frivolous, tedious, irrelevant soap operas—how much more do we need? How many books do we need about marriages? Divorces? Love affairs? Misunderstood teenagers? Jane Austen took care of that pretty well.

I admire writers willing to make fools of themselves, a little crazy, willing to stick their necks out on something controversial. John Nichols, for example, is one who cares about social injustice, and one whom I like because he cares. I don't think much of his simple-minded literary Marxism, but I like his emotions, motives, and courage.

Good writing can be defined as having something interesting to say and saying it well. And you have to care about life deeply and passionately in order to have something interesting to say. Most contemporary American writers are cautious temporizers—eunuchs. They write trivial little books about trivial subjects.

Jimerson: I'd like to hear more about your feelings for animals. You have said that only boys kill for sport, but that hunting out of need is justified. Yet many people live on vegetarian diets, and so it would seem hunting is never defensible.

Abbey: To kill anything merely for fun is contemptible. I don't even like to swat flies myself. The older I become, the more squeamish—or tenderhearted—I get. But hunting is morally justified if the game is abundant and the need is genuine.

I still eat meat occasionally. If I visited a slaughterhouse, though, I'm sure I would give it up. I do a lot of things I don't morally approve of—out of sloth, habit, and convenience. I am not very consistent. Never have been. I don't always practice what I preach. Probably never will.

Jimerson: Readers often see you or your characters littering the highways with beer cans. In *The Journey Home* you claim, "It's not the beer cans that are ugly; it's the highway that is ugly." Surely we aren't to take this justification at face value. What is the point you are making?

Abbey: Littering highways is a trivial matter compared to what our industrial culture is doing to nature and to human nature. People who get upset about littering really aren't aware of what's going on in the world. They're the fiddlers on the deck of a sinking ship.

Jimerson: One of your favorite themes is damning the damming of the Colorado River. One might argue that the creation of Lake Powell makes possible enjoyment of canyons by many who are not able-bodied; the splendors of nature should be accessible to all.

Abbey: Glen Canyon is now a stagnant reservoir. The splendors of nature are buried beneath it, no longer accessible to anybody.

As for "able-bodied," you didn't have to be an athlete to float down the river; anyone could do it. It was easy, safe, and cheap. Nowadays to enjoy Lake Foul, you have to buy a cabin cruiser or a houseboat. Those who think the lake is beautiful didn't know the area before it was dammed.

Even if recreation on the river were a privilege only of the young and healthy, damming the river was still a crime. Everyone is young at some point in life. I have no sympathy for old people who had the opportunity for adventure when they were young and strong. I'm getting old, too; I can't climb rocks and mountains as easily as I used to.

Jimerson: "That which today calls itself science gives us more and more information, an indigestible glut of information, and less and less understanding." That is a quotation from *Down the River*. What is the relationship between knowledge and understanding?

Abbey: Knowledge can lead to understanding, but knowledge alone is not sufficient for understanding. Science is mostly an accumulation of facts, mere information. Clever people can make useful knowledge out of it. But for understanding, we need knowledge *and* love.

Jimerson: Then you disagree with Plato, who thought knowledge is the highest good we can pursue.

Abbey: Plato was wrong about almost everything. Most philosophers consider knowledge their specialty, and so they think knowledge is the highest good. That's vanity and arrogance.

I'm in favor of science as the search for knowledge. I'm opposed to science when it's corrupted, a tool for industry, commerce, and war.

Jimerson: Are you a proponent of space exploration?

Abbey: I'm in favor of it as a human adventure. But space exploration should be supported through voluntary contributions rather than taxes. Masses of people are forced to pay taxes to support the games of the scientific elite. Space exploration is interesting in itself, but doesn't deserve compulsory support. Science should be a free enterprise supported by those who care about it, not by the public at large. I contribute ten percent of my income to worthwhile endeavors, mostly conservation groups, and I would contribute to science and space exploration too—but not under threat of imprisonment or death. That is, by taxes.

Jimerson: Tell me about your job at the University of Arizona. What do you get out of teaching?

Abbey: Teaching keeps me from becoming a hermit. My job takes two days a week for fifteen weeks, one term a year, so it doesn't interfere with writing. Or living. If I taught full-time, I wouldn't write. Writing means sitting indoors at a desk, thinking about words and ideas. It must be balanced by doing something entirely different, out of doors; otherwise, literary death occurs. And spiritual death. And physical death.

Jimerson: Can creative writing be taught?

Abbey: To some extent. But the essential love of words and ideas comes from something deep inside us—too deep for teaching to reach.

Anyhow, student writers are best off staying away from creative writing workshops. Although the workshops can provide some useful training, it would be better to spend that time studying science or history or languages, or working at some sort of job, acquiring real knowledge of the world. Experience is far more important than formal training. The best American writers didn't even go to college: Hemingway, Faulkner, Steinbeck, Dreiser, B. Traven, Walt Whitman, Mark Twain, for example.

Jimerson: Do you have a favorite book of your own? That you wrote, I mean.

Abbey: All my books are my children; I love them all, the trashy and the classy both. *Desert Solitaire* and *The Monkey Wrench Gang* are the most popular, but I think *Black Sun* is the best of the fiction so far, while *Abbey's Road* contains the best essays. My next book, due for publication in the fall, is the best—or it better be: *The Fool's Progress*, I call it—*An Honest Novel*. Don't ask me what the subtitle means—I'm merely hoping to annoy the critics.

Photo by Cynthia Farah

chapter five
N. Scott Momaday
Interview by Louis Owens

N. Scott Momaday was born in Lawton, Oklahoma, in 1934, the son of artists Alfred Momaday and Natachee Scott Momaday. He defines himself first of all as "an American Indian (Kiowa) . . . vitally interested in American Indian art, history, and culture." Between 1935 and 1943, Momaday lived with his parents on the Navajo Reservation, an experience that would create a deep affinity for Navajo culture in the half-Kiowa child. In 1946 the family moved to the Jemez Pueblo in New Mexico, where Momaday would spend the formative years of his youth and where he would set *House Made of Dawn*, the Pulitzer Prize-winning novel published in 1968. Momaday received a bachelor's degree from the University of New Mexico in 1958 and immediately accepted his first teaching position at Dulce, on the Jicarilla Apache Reservation in northern New Mexico, where he began a long poem that would eventually evolve into *House Made of Dawn*. Lured by poet and professor Yvor Winters away from Dulce to Stanford University in 1959, Momaday completed his M.A. in creative writing at Stanford after one year and his Ph.D. in English from the same university in 1963. Since receiving his Ph.D., Momaday has taught on both the Santa Barbara and Berkeley campuses of the University of California as well as at Stanford University. He is currently Professor of English at the University of Arizona, where he teaches courses in the Native American oral tradition. Momaday's first published book was a revised version of his doctoral dissertation, *The Complete Poems of Frederick Goddard Tuckerman* (1965). In 1967 Momaday privately published *The Journey of Tai-Me*, a collection of Kiowa oral literature, which was republished in significantly revised form in 1969 as *The Way to Rainy Mountain*. When Momaday won the Pulitzer Prize for *House Made of Dawn*, the publishing world—seemingly ignorant of such important earlier novels by Indian authors as John Joseph Mathews's *Sundown* (1934) and D'Arcy McNickle's *The Surrounded* (1936)—was, in the words of Henry Ramont, "stunned at the selection."

Momaday has spoken often about his concern to avoid stereotypes of what "Indian" is assumed to mean in twentieth-century America, and he has spoken just as often about the crucial place of landscape in Indian lives. A passage from his autobiographical work *The Names* (1987) recalls "the long wall of red rocks which extends eastward from Gallup" beneath which are "cattle and sheep, rabbits and roadrunners, all delightful to a child." In his most recent work, *The Ancient Child*, a novel published in 1989, Momaday's protagonist is, like the author, a painter who "sees the world in a particular way, in terms of lines, and shapes, and shadows, and forms." The "inner eye" that Momaday invokes in both of these passages extends throughout his work as a principal motif. In this interview, conducted by Louis Owens on April 3, 1986, Momaday speaks eloquently of his concern for ecology and reflects, once again, upon what it means to be an American Indian writer today.

Selected Bibliography:

The Complete Poems of Frederick Goddard Tuckerman, edited by Momaday with foreword by Yvor Winters (New York: Oxford University Press, 1965).

The Journey of Tai-Me, Kiowa oral tales (Santa Barbara: Privately printed, 1967).

House Made of Dawn, novel (New York: Harper and Row, 1968).

The Way to Rainy Mountain, autobiographical reminiscence, Kiowa oral material and history (Albuquerque: University of New Mexico Press, 1969).

The Gourd Dancer, poems (New York: Harper and Row, 1976).

The Names: A Memoir, autobiography (New York: Harper and Row, 1976).

Ancestral Voice: Conversations with N. Scott Momaday, Charles L. Woodard, ed. (Lincoln: University of Nebraska, 1989).

The Ancient Child, novel (New York: Doubleday, 1989).

Owens: I'll begin by asking what it means to you to be included in a volume focusing on "Southwestern Writers." Do you consider yourself a Southwest writer?

Momaday: Well, I think of myself as being a native of the Southwest. I've spent most of my life in the Southwest, so I identify with it very strongly.

Owens: Living in the West and Southwest, have you ever felt isolated from the publishing center in New York?

Momaday: Oh, no. I'm very much involved with the publishing houses in New York. I get to New York often enough, and besides, that's the sort of thing you can do by mail and telephone.

Owens: Well, let me shift to a different kind of question. How do you approach the act of writing, the mechanics of putting words on paper?

Momaday: I generally do my work in the morning. I like to write before noon, and when I'm really on a good schedule I start pretty early. I like to get going by eight o'clock or even earlier, if possible, and I find I can work for maybe six hours at the outside. I try to get up early and get to work early and then by noon I'm through.

Owens: During the past several years you've been spending a good deal of time with your painting, I understand. When do you paint?

Momaday: When I paint, it's generally afternoon.

Owens: You achieved early, impressive success as a writer, winning a Pulitzer Prize nearly two decades ago for *House Made of Dawn*. How successful has your painting been in recent years?

Momaday: Quite successful, actually. I have paintings currently in several galleries—in Santa Fe, in Scottsdale, and here in Tucson. And I have shows coming up in May and June of this year in Basel, Switzerland, and Heidelberg, West Germany. I've been very pleased.

Owens: I can think of no one who has written more eloquently about the landscapes of the Southwest, what you call in "The Man Made of Words" and *The Way to Rainy Mountain* "the remembered earth." Do you respond differently to landscape in painting than in writing?

Momaday: I don't paint landscapes. I prefer a closer focus in my painting. Lately I've become very interested in painting Indian shields, for example.

Owens: You've mentioned that you plan to spend time in Europe writing in between the shows in Basel and Heidelberg. How important is place to your art, particularly your writing? Do you find that you can write anywhere, or is a particular environment important to you?

Momaday: It's not the place so much. It seems that I *can* write almost anywhere. I don't know what the circumstances have to be for me to write, but I will say that I have been very productive in Europe. I've spent quite a bit of time in Europe in the last several years, and I seem to work there pretty well.

Owens: Since we're on the topic of Europe, do you have any thoughts as to why there is currently such a strong European interest in American Indian writing, perhaps a stronger interest than we find in this country?

Momaday: I don't know that it is only currently; I think there has consistently been a strong interest in Native American culture in Europe. This has been my experience from the first time I went there. There are a lot of factors. I think that Europe being older and having developed the land so long ago, there is a kind of deep appreciation for what we think of here as the frontier experience. They identify with that, and the American Indian represents to the European a kind of freedom, a relationship with the wilderness that is no longer practical in Europe so that it becomes a kind of vicarious experience.

Owens: You stated a long time ago, in "The Man Made of Words," that "Ecology is perhaps the most important subject of our time." Do you still feel this way?

Momaday: Yes. Today, of course, we think much more of nuclear war—that, too, is ecology.

Owens: Do you find a different ecological sensitivity in Europe, one that might be more sympathetic to an American Indian attitude toward the earth?

Momaday: I think so. For the reason I gave a moment ago, the fact that there is very little wilderness left in Europe, the European has a sense of loss where wilderness is concerned, and the fact that there is still wilderness somewhere is important to Europeans in a way that it may not be to Americans. I think this is becoming true all over the world.

Owens: It sounds as if you also may be talking about a need for a psychic wilderness.

Momaday: I think so.

Owens: The sixties, which saw what has been called a renaissance in Native American writing, also was a time of tremendous new interest or revitalized interest in ecology. How do you feel about our attitudes toward ecology today?

Momaday: I think a much-needed and real interest in ecology came about in the sixties, and I applaud that awareness. I think not nearly enough is being done to protect the earth from exploitation, but there is a greater awareness, certainly, and maybe one can be sanguine about that. Maybe we will take the steps to preserve the environment eventually. It's one of those things you just can't know. Sometimes I think the interest is waning and that we've passed the critical point. I hope that we all have become ecologists in a way, and there I think the American Indian stands to set an example.

Owens: When we spoke earlier this year, you mentioned the light pollution around Tucson.

Momaday: That's interesting to me. It's something I never thought about until I moved here, and something I understand at first hand now. Just seeing the stars is a very important thing, something I took for granted growing up in the rural Southwest. It's a moral issue now. I want my kids to see the stars, and their kids, and so on, and there's a possibility they won't.

Owens: Given your own sense of relationship that you bring out so well when you discuss the Kiowa myth of the sisters who ascended to the sky to become the stars of the dipper, there would seem to be a kind of dangerous "mythic" loss in being cut off from the stars.

Momaday: Oh, yes. I see it that way too. It's something that threatens me at my center. The stars are very important to me mythically. To think of losing the stars represents to me a very deep wound.

Owens: Do you see your own writing as political?

Momaday: Political? No, I don't think of it as political at all. That's not my disposition somehow. I'm not a political person. A lot of people I know will read my work as a political statement, and it can be read that way I suppose, but so can anything.

Owens: On a different subject, you have a Ph.D. in literature from Stanford, one of your first publications was an edition of the poems of Frederick Goddard Tuckerman, and you've taught at such universities as Berkeley, Stanford, U.C. Santa Barbara, and now Arizona. Still, you are known worldwide as primarily an American Indian writer. How has this education and training in very conventional Anglo-European scholarship affected your approach to American Indian materials? How have you been able to achieve a synthesis?

Momaday: I don't know that I can answer that. I think that the formal training that I had at Stanford under Yvor Winters was extremely important because there was an awful lot that I didn't know about traditional English poetry and I learned a lot about that when I was a graduate student at Stanford. As to how I might have applied that learning to my work in American Indian tradition, I really don't know.

Owens: A large percentage of those writers identified from very early on as Indian—people like John Milton Oskison, John Joseph Mathews, D'Arcy McNickle and others—have been very highly educated, most having completed graduate as well as undergraduate study. Do you see this high level of formal education and corresponding affiliation with academia affecting what the general public perceives as "Indian" writing?

Momaday: I really haven't thought about that. I have a difficult time understanding what "American Indian" writing is. I know that I've read things on American Indian culture and American Indian experience by both Indians and non-Indians, and I'm not able to make for myself any important distinctions.

Owens: You were one of the few early positive reviewers of Hyemeyohsts Storm's *Seven Arrows,* as I recall, a novel that was controversial because of questions concerning Storm's identity as a Northern Cheyenne and his use of traditional Indian material. This whole question of identity becomes a rather troublesome one. Do you have difficulty with someone such as Gary Snyder assuming an Indianlike role, what has been called "white-shamanism," in his poetry?

Momaday: I don't see anything intrinsically problematic about that, though I think that someone who writes about an experience who does not himself have that experience runs a certain risk. That's just, I think, completely up to the writer. I've read non-Indians who have written about Indian matters and done it very well, and of course that works the other way around too. I've also read some things that were very bad because the writer was simply writing outside his experience.

Owens: During your recent reading at the University of New Mexico, you were asked by someone in the audience whether D'Arcy McNickle had been an influence on your writing and you replied that he had not because you had not read very much of McNickle's work. Have any American Indian writers been influential in your own work?

Momaday: I can't think of any who were a particular influence. I don't know many Indian writers who wrote early enough to be an influence on me. I keep up now with Jim Welch and some writers of my own generation and younger writers, but I think that when my literary intelligence was being formed I wasn't reading Indian writers. I just didn't know about them.

Owens: You weren't aware of such writers as John Joseph Mathews, Oskison, Mourning Dove, or McNickle?

Momaday: No.

Owens: Am I simply imagining the echoes of Hemingway and Faulkner in *House Made of Dawn*, or were you aware of such influences when you wrote the novel?

Momaday: I don't know of any such influences. I certainly read Faulkner when I was an undergraduate and before I started writing seriously. Hemingway is less likely, I think. I knew one or two things by Hemingway well, especially *The Old Man and the Sea* and *A Farewell to Arms*, but that's about it. I don't particularly care for Hemingway. I admire Faulkner now and then. He exasperates me but there are things about Faulkner that I admire very much.

Owens: Given your own fascination with totemic bears, how do you feel about Faulkner's *The Bear?*

Momaday: I think that's very good. I read that very early on and I admire it.

Owens: What about D. H. Lawrence?

Momaday: Lawrence was a man I liked as an undergraduate and read widely, and I still admire Lawrence very much. He is more likely to have been a kind of influence on me than either Faulkner or Hemingway. And, of course, I admire the work of Isak Dinesen very much.

Owens: When you were studying at the University of New Mexico and later at Stanford, it was nearly impossible to specialize in American Indian literature as a legitimate area of study. Given the opportunity, do you think you might have preferred to have completed a Ph.D. with, say, an emphasis upon the American Indian oral tradition?

Momaday: Oh, if such a thing had been possible I might have. But it wasn't possible, so I didn't even think about that. I did draw upon my experience of the Indian world when I was doing graduate writing at Stanford, and I was encouraged to do that. But, you know, I took the Ph.D. in American literature and got interested, of course, in the oral tradition very soon after I left Stanford. I've been able to develop that interest, but as a teacher rather than student. As you know, at the University of Arizona I teach a course in the American Indian oral tradition every year.

Owens: I seem to recall that you taught a course in Dickinson while at Santa Barbara? Is that so?

Momaday: I don't remember, but it could be. In fact, it probably is so. I had a Guggenheim Fellowship while I was teaching at Santa Barbara, and I spent that year reading Emily Dickinson in manuscript.

Owens: Your essay "The Man Made of Words" contains your splendid definition of what an American Indian is. You say that "an Indian is an idea which a given man has of himself. And it is a moral idea. . . ." And you also say that "We are what we imagine. Our very existence consists in our imagination of ourselves." Would it be valid from your point of view to suggest that *The Way to Rainy Mountain* is your own act of imagination, a personal quest for identity?

Momaday: Yes. I would not argue with that. I think that's certainly true.

Owens: And I suppose *The Names* would be a continuation of this quest.

Momaday: That's right.

Owens: In *The Names* you write of yourself as a child curious about what it means to be Indian. How does this question of identity affect Indian writing as you see it, given the fact that so much of what we identify today as Indian writing is written by mixed-bloods, people of both Indian and European ancestry? Does that complicate the question?

Momaday: It seems logical to me that the mixed-bloods are most naturally curious about their cultural identity. My father being Kiowa and my mother being mostly European, I guess I had a sense of living in those two areas when I was a child, and it became important to me to understand as clearly as I could who I was and what my cultural resources were. And I daresay that's probably true of other people who are of mixed-blood. It seems to me that's where you would be most likely to find this business of identity being worked out in writing.

Owens: Would it be correct to say, then, that most contemporary Indian fiction represents a kind of identity quest? I'm thinking of writers like Janet Campbell Hale, Louise Erdrich, Leslie Silko, and so forth.

Momaday: I think so.

Owens: And then I think of someone like Jim Welch, who is a full blood and writes a novel such as *The Death of Jim Loney* about a young mixed-blood caught between Indian and white worlds.

Momaday: Well, Jim is also Gros Ventre, and maybe it can be a tribal division as well as a cultural one. I've never talked to him about that.

Owens: Given the fact that most of what is published as American Indian literature is written by people of mixed Indian-European ancestry and culture, is this giving the reading public a slanted view of what it means to be Indian today?

Momaday: I would reiterate that it's probably the people who have some possibility of identifying themselves in more than one way who are most interested in the question. And maybe they're in the best position to write about Indian culture, those who have an investment elsewhere as well and can bring a certain objectivity to bear.

Owens: Let me ask you a question about *House Made of Dawn*, something that's intrigued me for some time. You once said that Tosamah is your favorite character in that novel.

Momaday: Far and away. I think he's the most intricate. He's much more interesting because he's more complicated and has many more possibilities. He has a strange and lively mind, and I find him, and did at the time I was writing the book, fascinating.

Owens: My students have almost always been fascinated with Tosamah. In addition, however, he also strikes me as the most displaced character in the novel.

Momaday: I think so. He's a kind of riddle, and he's extremely skeptical, but has the kind of intelligence that makes the most of it. But I think of him as being in some ways pathetic, too. He's very displaced.

Owens: He's a poignant figure.

Momaday: I think so.

Owens: I've read that one of your Kiowa names can be translated as Red Bluff, is that true?

Momaday: Yes, that's true.

Owens: Does the name John Big Bluff Tosamah play on your own identity, and is Tosamah a kind of self-portrait?

Momaday: Well, no, it's not a play upon the name. He is called Big Bluff, but that's not the meaning of his name. I invented the name Tosamah. There are names very much like it in Kiowa, and in Jemez for that matter. There is a Tosa family in Jemez and a Tonomah family in Kiowa, so I think the name just came about.

Owens: But Tosamah does appropriate some of your own language.

Momaday: Oh yes, I used him. I took great advantage of him.

Owens: It seems as if he takes great advantage of you in some ways as well.

Momaday: (laughs) He acts as my mouthpiece here and there.

Owens: He's a wonderful trickster figure. I'd like to ask about your own peregrinations. Have your repeated movements from New Mexico to Stanford and Santa Barbara, Berkeley, Arizona, Europe, and so on affected what you have described as a "tenure in the land," a sense of intimacy with place?

Momaday: I don't know the answer to that. I still think of myself as having deep roots in the Southwest, and belonging in that landscape. But I have not been really rooted to that landscape in my adult life. I come and go. I get into it now and then but I've traveled widely. I sometimes wonder. In one sense I have driven a kind of wedge between myself and the ancestral land, but in another I've fulfilled the nomadic instincts of that culture, and I'm not sure what it all means.

Owens: Let me ask another question about identity. So much contemporary Indian fiction—that is, fiction written by people who identify as Indian—is very syncretic. Leslie Silko, for example, writes *Ceremony* using her knowledge of the Laguna Pueblo and of Pueblo and Navajo mythology, weaving a kind of tapestry. You yourself, who identify as Kiowa, write a novel set in Jemez Pueblo, and again you weave different cultures together. Could all of this be achieving a kind of synthesis in the American imagination of what an Indian is, so that it obscures the diversity of American Indian cultures?

Momaday: Well, it may be. I think the effect of such writing is a working towards a synthesis of some kind. Maybe all writing is a working toward a similar synthesis. I'm not concerned to define or delineate American Indian experience, except to myself and for my own purposes. But I am very concerned to understand as much as I can about myth making. The novel that I'm working on now is really a construction of different myths. I've taken a Kiowa myth to begin with and am bringing it up to modern times. I don't know how much I've told you about this, but my main character, Set, is the reincarnation of a boy who figures in Kiowa mythology, a boy who turns into a bear. And I'm also working with Billy the Kid in the same novel. And there will be other elements like that, other mythic elements that will inform the story in one way or another. I regard what I'm doing as an inquiry into the nature of myth making.

Owens: The portions of the new novel that I've read or heard you read are very powerful. Is the Kiowa boy you mention the same boy who figures so prominently in the Kiowa story about Devil's Tower?

Momaday: That's the basic myth, the one that I start with. That myth is very important to me personally, and I have thought about that story a lot and now it seems that it's time for me to expand upon it, to follow through on some of the possibilities that I've seen in it.

Owens: This myth-making impulse, which seems to be at the center of *The Way to Rainy Mountain* as well, seems to be an impulse that leads us in the direction of an imagining of identity, a realization of who we are.

Momaday: I would say so.

Owens: What you've just been describing sounds like a synthesis of the quest for a personal identity that I see in *The Way to Rainy Mountain* and *The Names* and a larger concern for the myth-making impulse in general.

Momaday: That's something that I'm working on and it's important to me. I think you're right about that, and that's really what I'm concerned to do.

Owens: How do you explain the hiatus between the two novels? You won a Pulitzer Prize for *House Made of Dawn* in 1969, and you must have had tremendous pressure from your publishers, agents, whomever to come out with another novel quickly, yet here it is almost two decades later.

Momaday: (laughs) A lot of people have suggested to me that I should come out with another novel, but I don't think of myself as a novelist particularly. I happen to have written a novel, but I'm more concerned to write well in other forms as well as the novel. I've been fairly productive over the years—besides the one novel, I've also written a number of poems and prose pieces that are nonfiction.

Owens: You've certainly been productive, but what prompted you to move away from the novel and now back to it almost twenty years later?

Momaday: I think I wanted to see what writing in other forms was like, so I took my turn at autobiography and poetry and what have you, even travel literature, which I really like. I find myself very interested in writing about travel. I'm doing a piece on Bavaria now for the *New York Times*. But I think that the only way I can pursue this myth-making business is in the novel form now. It's possible to get at it in poems and to write about it in terms of scholarship perhaps, but the heart of it is a matter for fiction.

Owens: Could you say something about the novel form—what insights have you gained since your first novel?

Momaday: I don't know that I've ever really come to define the form of the novel to my own satisfaction. I think of a novel as a story first of all and therefore a narrative, and I believe that it should have a perceptible shape to it—a beginning and so on—but beyond that, I think there's a lot of room for experimentation in the novel form. Obviously a lot of other people do as well.

The novel I'm working on is experimental in certain ways because it deals with ancient matter, which has its own form; and it's an expansion of that form, a kind of reworking of it, and I hope to come up with perhaps new ideas of reflection or amplification or expansion. I think it's an unorthodox kind of novel.

Owens: Since you refer to it as experimental, are you very conscious of the experimental fiction of the last couple of decades by people like Robbe-Grillet?

Momaday: Really not at all. Every time I hear contemporary critics talking about fiction I'm completely confused. They're using terms that they weren't using in my day, and I just haven't kept up.

Owens: So your experimentation is not an impulse that rises in part from awareness of people like Donald Barthelme, Robert Coover, and that sort of new-fiction crowd?

Momaday: No, I'm well outside that camp. I was at the Salzburg Seminar in American Studies last summer, and I met such people. Deconstruction was very much in the air, and I must say that I wasn't understanding what was said. I'm not a critic.

Owens: There's a great sense of play in the portions of your new novel that I've seen. Will that element be consistent throughout the entire work?

Momaday: I think it's going to, though I won't know that until I get around to the final revisions. It certainly informs what I have down so far. It's going to have a kind of playfulness to it that I haven't really tried before.

Owens: It's something that seems characteristic of recent publications by Indian writers. There's a rich vein of black humor in Jim Welch's writing, and there's a great deal of playfulness in Louise Erdrich's *Love Medicine*. Of course, it was even more true of Gerald Vizenor's *Darkness in Saint Louis Bearheart* in 1978. Do you have any sense of writing by American Indians having matured since your seminal work in *House Made of Dawn*, with a new sense of confidence perhaps?

Momaday: I think so. I think that's what ought to happen and what probably is happening. With every new step, with everything written by an American Indian now, I think there is a growing confidence. It will be a very important literature, probably is already, but it's certainly going to become more and more confident and secure.

Owens: Could you compare what has happened in American Indian writing during the last two decades with the Harlem Renaissance in black writing?

Momaday: I think of *Bury My Heart at Wounded Knee* as a kind of breakthrough. It seems to me that with the publication of that book there was a sudden disposition to understand the experience of the American Indian. The kind of burgeoning that we're talking about really happened in the publishing world rather than in any sort of social or political arena. It was really a willingness to look back at history and to say, "No, this isn't necessarily how it was." It seems to me that's what Dee Brown accomplished.

Owens: You've mentioned Jim Welch. Are there any other contemporary writers in particular whose work interests you?

Momaday: There are writers who interest me. But I don't find myself keeping up with any particular writer completely. I don't read contemporary fiction in great depth; I'm too busy with other things.

Owens: I recently came across a reference by Yvor Winters to you as a "post-symbolist," and elsewhere I've seen you described as a "lyrical imagist." You may not want to do this, but how would you describe your own poetry if you had to attach a phrase to it?

Momaday: I don't know that I'd want to do that. Post-symbolist is a term I heard a great deal as a graduate student, and I fail even now to understand it. I see my poetry as being also cross-cultural in a sense. When I was exercising my earliest knowledge of traditional English forms, I was doing a lot of very closely controlled writing, and I came to understand the value of such control. But at the same time I was concerned to develop my voice as a projection of the oral tradition. So I keep the two things going, and I think probably that it's good for me to work across those boundaries.

Owens: As a final question, do you have any overriding sense of what Native American fiction is today as opposed to 1969, when you won your Pulitzer for *House Made of Dawn?*

Momaday: Well, I think that it's very secure, that writing by Native Americans has certainly caught the attention of the world at large. There can be no doubt that now a good many people across the globe understand that there is an experience that is important in itself. I feel very good about so-called Native American literature.

Photo by Colleen McKay

chapter six
Margaret Randall
Interview by John Crawford and Patricia Clark Smith

Born in New York City in 1936, Margaret Randall grew up in Albuquerque, attending public school there. She completed a year and a half at the University of New Mexico in 1955, returned East in 1960, and left for Mexico in 1961, where she edited the magazine *El Corno Emplumado* with her then-husband Sergio Mondragon until the time of the student massacre of 1968. She emigrated to Cuba, where she spent the next decade, and then to Nicaragua where she worked under the Ministry of Culture following the Sandinista revolution of 1978–79. She returned to the United States in 1983. She is the author of numerous volumes of poetry, oral history, reportage, and photography, those in English published mostly by small presses in the United States and Canada. Her best known works include *Part of the Solution: Portrait of a Revolutionary* (1972); *Cuban Women Now* (1973); *Carlota: Prose and Poems from Havana* (1978); and *Sandino's Daughters* (1981). Her most recent works at the time of the interview were *Albuquerque: Coming Back to the U.S.A.* (1986) and *This is about Incest* (1987). She was interviewed in Albuquerque by John Crawford and Pat Smith of the University of New Mexico in the summer of 1987, before leaving to teach for a year at Trinity College in Hartford, Connecticut. At the time of the interview, Randall was living under threat of deportation by the Immigration and Naturalization Service, growing out of her having acquired Mexican citizenship in order to find work in Mexico in the 1960s. In the summer of 1989, the Board of Immigration Appeals ruled that she had never lost her U.S. citizenship. At present Randall expects to remain in Albuquerque, supporting herself with visiting professorship appointments from time to time.

Selected Bibliography:

Part of the Solution: Portrait of a Revolutionary, poetry and prose (New York: New Directions, 1972).

Cuban Women Now, interviews (Toronto: Women's Press, 1974). Republished in Spanish editions in Cuba, Mexico, Venezuela, and Columbia.

Carlota: Prose and Poems from Havana, poetry and prose (Vancouver: New Star Books, 1978).

Doris Tijerino: Inside the Nicaraguan Revolution, interviews (Vancouver: New Star Books, 1978).

Sandino's Daughters: Testimonies of Nicaraguan Women in Struggle, interviews (London: Zed Press, 1981).

Women in Cuba: Twenty Years Later, interviews (New York: Smyrna Press, 1981).

Editor, *Breaking the Silences: An Anthology of Twentieth Century Poetry by Cuban Women* (New York: Pulp Press, 1982).

Christians in the Nicaraguan Revolution, interviews (Vancouver: New Star Books, 1983).

Risking a Somersault in the Air: Conversations with Nicaraguan Writers, interviews (San Francisco: Solidarity Publications, 1984).

Women Brave in the Face of Danger, photography and interviews (Freedom, Calif.: The Crossing Press, 1985).

Albuquerque: Coming Back to the U.S.A., autobiography (Vancouver: New Star Books, 1986).

This Is about Incest, photography and autobiographical prose (Ithaca: Firebrand Press, 1987).

Memory Says Yes, poems (Willimantic, CT: Curbstone Press, 1988).

The Shape of Red: Insider/Outsider Reflections, letters with Ruth Hubbard (Pittsburgh: Cleis Press, 1988).

Crawford: It seems to me that things have changed a lot since your early days in the East Village. If you were to write a book on America now, say, called North American Women Now, how would you characterize the way women function as artists in this society?

Randall: I've certainly given it a lot of thought. I think the changes were radical in the twenty-three years that I was out of the country. The world has changed completely vis-à-vis the different responses to racism: there was no such thing as an American Indian movement, a black movement, and there certainly wasn't a women's movement when I left this country. Specifically about women writers and artists—I remember, in the late fifties and in 1960 in New York City, there weren't very many of us. Obviously there were lots I didn't know, but certainly compared to the men there weren't very many.

Crawford: You must have felt like pioneers.

Randall: I think we felt more like groupies. (Laughter) I mean, we *were* really groupies, in the grossest and most disgusting sense of that word. I freely say this about myself and about some other fine women writers I know, though not about everybody. But certainly the pressure to be groupies was on everyone . . .

Smith: That would enable you to be tolerated and perhaps even give you a chance to read a poem of your own . . .

Randall: That's right, we lapped up praise from the male poets, we went to parties where the male poets talked to each other, and we sort of looked at them and fixed dinner. I remember a couple of years ago, shortly after I came back to this country, I was at a party in New York City and Hettie Jones was there. She had been married to LeRoy Jones (Amiri Baraka) in the fifties, and he is the father of her two children. We went off in a corner and talked for several hours about how we had never really known each other, although we had been in the same room, at the same parties, and the same readings in the same crowd for several years in New York City. After we talked, Hettie looked at me and said, "You know, you coped with it all by leaving and I coped with it all by staying," and I really knew what she meant. I don't think we could have articulated those things back then. One of the great changes is that feminism killed our shame in some ways; we are not ashamed to be strong and we're not ashamed to be vulnerable, and we're not ashamed to write as women and not "as well as a man." All of these things seem to be cliches, but certainly behind those cliches is a very important set of considerations.

Smith: Do you remember the way you felt about other women—your fellow groupies—during your New York days? Were *you* ever with those women in a corner talking about your work?

Randall: No, I just assumed that I preferred talking to men. Even though it was a fiction, that's what I assumed. I had some friends among the women, certainly—Diane DiPrima, Carol Bergé, Diane Wakoski—but we weren't real close at that time; there were Rochelle Owens and Rosalyn Drexler, who both wrote plays.

This is another interesting thing—most of my close friends in those New York years were not poets or writers, but artists, painters. There was a number of such women—Elaine DeKooning was my closest friend, and Pat Paslof was a very close friend. The poet Susan Sherman and I became close a number of years later, after I had gone to Mexico. Susan is probably my oldest friend and tremendously important to me.

Smith: Was there someone like Susan with whom you have kept pretty constantly in touch all the time you were out of the country?

Randall: Yes, more than one. I have a very peculiar—unpeculiar to me, but peculiar to other people—thing that I do, that I've done all these years. I keep a sort of journal, which is not a totally private journal; it is xeroxed and sent off. I send it about once a week, I'd say, and I might write ten pages a week, I might write one page; there might be a week that I write twice, or don't write at all, but that's about it, and I share that with about twenty-five people, maybe twenty women and five men, and they haven't varied very much over the years. Susan Sherman is one of them. Many of them are writers, and some of them are painters.

Smith: Were you doing that even when you first left?

Randall: Yes. I've done that most of my adult life. It's a very, very important communication to me, extremely important, and in fact the book *Albuquerque* is based on that, with some rewriting and some rearranging and a lot cut out, of course.

Crawford: Not only is the exchange of letters an intimate relationship, but in a way, with so many people involved, it's an objectified one, also; you have some distance because you're not writing just to one person.

Randall: It has a lot of qualities that are really interesting. I will, for example, send a draft of a poem that is not finished and that I would never show or send to an editor or read in a reading, you know—and then another draft of the same poem, and then someone will comment on a change that he or she liked or didn't like . . .

The people have different ways of relating to it; a few of them do something very similar to what I do, send a journal once a week or once every two weeks or so, and others communicate only by phone. And with other people, we just have to see each other periodically, which is the case with Susan and myself.

One of the people, Stan Persky, is a poet in Vancouver and an ex-editor for New Star Books, and he and I are extremely close. When I was getting *Albuquerque* ready for the publisher, I was really stuck at a particular point around a certain issue, and Stan just says, well, I guess I'll just have to get into my little red car and drive down to Albuquerque, and he did. Stayed here for four days and four nights and we just . . .

Smith: Untangled . . .

Randall: Yeah. And, you know, he and I work very well together. I once ran into him in Nicaragua, and in a thirty-six-hour unbroken span in which we did not sleep, either one of us, we batted out something like fifteen articles about Nicaragua. He was sitting at the typewriter half of the time and I was dictating, or I was sitting at the typewriter and he would dictate; there are certain ways of being or working that just work. And so with some of the people in this journal group, it's a matter of thrashing out ideas, feeling that there is a safe place to talk about things that are not going to be misunderstood.

Crawford: This makes me think of the reading you and Judith McDaniel did at the American Booksellers Association in Washington in May 1987. What were you feeling about that reading?

Randall: It really excited me, and I know it excited Judith, too. I had never heard Judith read her poetry, and she had never heard me read mine. In fact, although we have a pretty intense connection, it actually came out of her stopping by here in Albuquerque one afternoon on her way to Tucson, to the Sanctuary trial a couple of years back, and the letters that we've written one another, sharing our work. And now the fact that we both have the same publisher at the same time—Firebrand.

Judith is a lesbian feminist pacifist, known for her novel, *November Passage*, and for her poetry, and for writing about issues that some people in this country would consider too "personal," such as alcoholism recovery, the issue of pacifism in the anti-nuclear movement, and so forth. And I am more known for "political" work; I put both the "personal" and the "political" in quotes. And so, since I had written a book about incest and she had written a book about Sanctuary—which right away situates each of us in a place where people who put labels on things would be surprised to find us—we decided to try to do this reading.

Judith and I met the night before in Washington, had dinner and said, well, how shall we do this? I really don't think that Judith had given much thought to it before that dinner; I know I hadn't. But suddenly we looked at each other and said, you know, it doesn't really make sense for just one of us to read and then the other, since there are so many things in each of the books that touch on important points in the other book. We both deal with risk taking; with memory and the obliteration of memory; with how the system works us over in a political sense, i.e., keeps people poor and uses racism and sexism and so forth to keep people separated, and how it deals with people in Central America et cetera.

Smith: And the way the family system works, too, the way a family can be structured to keep memory out and . . .

Randall: And danger. How people face danger. So we decided that we would read in bits and pieces, sort of work off each other's readings. It was very exciting. At the end we decided that we would trade poems and we would end with Judith reading a poem of mine and me reading a poem of hers. We picked those the night before, and we talked a bit about why and so forth. We left one another really excited about this, but I think both of us were still wondering how it would actually work, because I know I was nervous before the reading and rarely am. Then at three o'clock in the morning I woke up in my hotel room and said, "Oh, the first part of it just isn't going to work like that," and I redesigned it, using completely different materials, and interestingly Judith, on the other side of Washington, D.C., also woke up and did the same thing.

So we got together at the reading and we just did it. I think it was extremely successful; we felt very, very good about it, and I think from the comments I got the audience thought it was really a powerful reading. So we're planning on polishing it a little more and seeing if we can do it in other places.

Smith: That's wonderful, as opposed to that whole competitive spirit surrounding so many readings.

Randall: Well, I'm sure that's true sometimes, but I wonder if it's not due to certain circumstances. This past weekend I took part in a reading in Philadelphia, which Temple University put on and Sonia Sanchez actually organized; it was extremely interesting, in that there was a powerful connection between the poets and none of that sense of competition. There were six of us, three men and three women—Miguel Algarín, Miguel Piñero, and Haki Madabhuti, and June Jordan, Sonia Sanchez, and myself. It was an all-day activity; the visiting poets did two workshops with inner city high school kids, four hundred of them, so that we each had sixty, thirty in the morning and thirty in the afternoon. When we got together to do the evening reading, I was stunned by the fact that although I was the only one who was not a person of color in the reading, which made it an extraordinary honor to be included, the issues we were dealing with in our poetry were so very similar.

In the morning something very interesting happened. Miguel Algarín is a black Puerto Rican poet from New York City who has been teaching the Shakespeare course at Rutgers for about twenty years. When we were about to go into the first session of the workshop, he said, "I'm kind of wondering if I should broach the subject I want to with the kids, whether it would be too hard for them." And I said, "What subject is that?" and he said, "Incest." And I thought, does this man know that I just wrote a book about incest? And he didn't know. It was the last thing I expected from a male poet, not that men are necessarily marginal to the problem of incest, because they certainly aren't, but—. So I said, "You know, I think incest exists in a lot of lives. I wouldn't hesitate to do that if I were you." And he did and got extraordinary responses from the kids.

I happened to find other things to talk about with them and they with me, but it really did amaze me how powerful the sense of togetherness and the connections were, not just in the work with the students, but also in our readings.

Smith: What kinds of things do you do if you're just walking in and this is a bunch of kids that you're seeing for one time only?

Randall: Well, it depends. At Temple they asked us to spend the morning reading three or four of our own poems very slowly, and then talk to them about how those particular poems had been made. I did that part of the time, and part of the time I just wanted to know what their concerns were; that led to such a fascinating discussion that there wasn't much time for anything else. In the afternoon we were supposed to get them to write. You know, there's a big difference in working with kids that age whom you've never seen before and kids you have on a regular basis. It takes awhile, and clearly they were kids whose backgrounds were very different from mine. I didn't know what they would think of me or how well we would be able to connect, so in the afternoon I gave them news clippings on three subjects. One was about the little boy who had just been mauled to death by polar bears in the zoo in New York, one was about Contragate, and one was about Operation Move, which was something that, being from Philadelphia, they probably had some pretty strong feelings about. I just asked them if they wanted to use one of those articles to stimulate the writing of a poem. I also told them that if they had a poem that they wanted to write that had nothing to do with any of the three subjects, that was fine, too. I felt like I had to do that because I didn't know where they were at. In the morning I had asked them all why they were there and, you know, clearly half of them were there because they really thought of themselves as writers, they were beginning to write, and it was real exciting for them to be there; the other half were there because that way they wouldn't have to write the last short story of the year. So not all of them were really into being there.

Crawford: One comment about Judith McDaniel. With so many Americans who have gone to Central America, their writing seems to start at the point of trying to shed some of the North American ideology, especially alienation, and then comes full circle into self-discovery at the end. You probably went through some similar process when you first were in Mexico and Cuba. But one thing interesting about that reading you did is that Judith was going in that direction and you were coming back, so that in a way you met in the middle.

Randall: Of course I went through that period that you talk about, separating myself from what I might have imagined was American ideology at that point in my life. I think that, especially if you're white and middle class, you go to a place like Latin America and you want to separate yourself because you're so different. But I think that the power in Judith's book for me—and I would hope that someone could say this about me as well—is precisely that she does *not* separate herself from an American ideology and that she's able to discuss Sanctuary or being captured by the Contras in the context of the recovering alcoholic, visiting a shelter for homeless women precisely on Liberty Weekend and watching with these women, you know, the unveiling of the Statue of Liberty on a little old black and white TV. I think that her consciousness is also very informed by North American issues and North American concerns like Big Mountain, for example. Her book ends with the interview at Big Mountain, which is very, very powerful to me; it's all in there together, and it's a way of making a connection.

There are other ways of making those connections. One can make them by proving politically that the same interests are being served by sending money to the Contras as by cutting back social services in this country. An economist or a social commentator can make those connections. But those connections are being made in art today, in poetry, and with a tremendous power, and I think that's precisely because there isn't that leaving of part of yourself at home. The whole person is looking at the issues.

Crawford: In this connection too, it seems as if the difference between 1961 and 1984 is that there's an enormous, almost collective voice of American women, which really crystallized about the time you came back; I'm thinking of the meeting at the nuke site in Seneca, New York, which was around that time . . .

Randall: 1983.

Crawford: Have people around that experience been the community that you've identified closest with since you came back?

Randall: Well, Judith was there and she writes about this in her book. I'm not sure I know a lot of those women. Certainly when I think of that encampment I think of the spirit of the people like Barbara Deming; I admire her greatly, although I have differences with her. I would say that many of these women tend to be pacifist in a way that I'm not, or nonviolent in a way with which I don't completely identify. I don't think that anyone who has lived through Latin America or Third World countries anywhere in the world during the years that I've lived there tends to embrace that kind of nonviolence. I would certainly like to see a nonviolent world—it's not that in theory I would prefer to be violent—but we tend to come to some issues differently. We may strategically agree but tactically disagree in certain areas—and I am speaking politically now, not as a poet or as an artist.

Crawford: That brings us to such poets as Mila Aguilar of the Philippines or Nancy Morejón of Cuba, and some of the other poetry coming out of the Third World, which seems more flatly dialectical, more overtly revolutionary. It seems to me that that's a Third World perception of social change, and that in the United States we don't have that same focus on it.

Randall: Well, I think that the level of economic production in a society really informs those issues more than most people realize. And the level of production in American society is very high, in spite of the fact that if you're Native American or black or white and come from Appalachia you may have an economic level not that different from many people in the Third World. But the level of production *in general* in the society informs our political work in some way, so that the issues we face here may seem to people in many Third World situations as luxuries, but are not luxuries for us here, because they are the real issues.

Crawford: You have mentioned that you use and even perceive photography differently when you are abroad than in coming back to America.

Randall: Yeah. There is a difference. When I started doing photography in Cuba and Nicaragua, I simply did what seemed absolutely essential, most urgent—chronicle what was happening. That took the form of what in this country at this particular moment is called documentary photography or photojournalism. So what I did was observe with my camera; sometimes it took the form of having to shoot it into a fifteen-year-old kid's coffin; sometimes it was the giving out of land titles; sometimes it was in the market or women doing different things, or people working, or whatever; public demonstrations of one kind or another, the way people live.

I came back to this country and found that I had gotten something of a reputation as a documentary photographer, and my first big project in this country was a continuation of that. I had always wanted to do a calendar of women and talked about it with Crossing Press, and it turned into a book, *Women Brave in the Face of Danger.* I had with me thousands of images of women from Cuba, Nicaragua, Mexico, but very few from the United States, so I made a trip around the western part of the United States, up to Washington state and along the California coast, and on to some of the eastern cities, Buffalo and New York and so forth, and got a sizeable number of images of women in this country. That book is still photojournalism; it has bits and pieces of letters and testimony and poetry by other women and photography by myself from North and South America.

It was sort of impenetrable at first, but as I began to photograph more in the direction that being home led me in, I began to be drawn to a very contrived studio type of photography, which has very little to do with photojournalism in most people's minds, or any other kind of documentation. I did a project called "She Answers Back" that was my first of that type, in which I tried to tell the story of a young woman who grapples with her identity (those pictures I actually have ready for exhibition here).

People have remarked how my photography has changed, and that set me to thinking whether in fact it has; I think it's not my photography that has changed, but the place. I think of the meaning of this kind of photography in a place like the United States where our lives are contrived by media—who we vote for, how we dress, how fat or thin we are, what we eat, what we think we need, the kind of house we live in, who we pair with, if we pair with someone, how we educate our kids, what we think of the world. And so it seems to me that somehow my relationship to this place, in the kind of photography I am doing now, has exactly the same meaning as my relationship to Central America vis-à-vis the kind of photography I was doing there.

Smith: Would you say that your subjects are essentially the same?

Randall: Yes, the subjects are the same; it's the treatment that's different.

Crawford: A friend of mine is writing about her year in Honduras and El Salvador. She says she has suffered something like stress syndrome returning to this country, and that as a journalist she tries to write about this, but it's being rejected because the news media doesn't want to hear about it.

Randall: There is one very good and astounding piece about that that the news media did accept, but I've never seen another since. It was in *Esquire Magazine* about two years ago. There was a piece in there by Gloria Emerson about Susan Meiselas that talked about Susan's dealing with stress in the kind of work that she is doing. And it was so real to me; it was the only thing I ever read that really pinpointed the way stress operates in those situations, and I totally identified with it.

I deal a little with this in *Albuquerque*. You would think people would be much crazier in a place like Nicaragua, and yet the fact is that the craziness is something that people share, and the symptoms are something people understand. I remember that in my office where I was working in Nicaragua, at one time seven people working together got a disease where your gums hurt a lot and bleed. It comes from sleeping with your teeth clenched. We all had different ways of showing our anxiety during that period, but that was something that we hadn't taken into account.

I've thought of it a lot since I've come back, in relation to young people. It came up again during these two workshops I did with these inner city high school kids in Philadelphia last weekend. A lot of them just said to me "Our world is not the same as your world. We are facing nuclear annihilation, teenage suicide; teenage pregnancy and drugs are our daily bread—you know, it's not just something that happens to somebody in another place." There is a kind of anxiety that comes from that sort of helplessness, the impotence—there are kids in Nicaragua who may die tomorrow and who are bombed, or even in battle, but there is a sense of purpose. I'm not saying that one would want that to happen to them or it is better that way, but they do have a *sense* of greater connection with what happens in their lives; whether or not that is really true is something else.

Crawford: There is in the Nicaragua workshop poetry the sense that we are all human beings, and the shared feeling that the enemy is a technological giant.

Randall: That's right. There is David and Goliath—there, in a country as steeped in the Bible as it is—the sense that the human is always more powerful, and that it is still possible to do and make and be and change.

Smith: Whereas, even really fine and basically healthy kids here talk freely about that sense of helplessness that I think is different from the teenage *angst* that we grew up with.

Crawford: It seems like the world you were experiencing in the Southwest when you were a teenager had one set of problems and now there is one that is different. But in both cases there has been a kind of American alienation, not simply between genders or social classes or whatever, but even from one's own future.

Randall: Yeah, I certainly think back to my high school and junior high school years in New Mexico, and I don't really know how I turned out to be the person I am.

Smith: What was Highland High School like then? What was the racial composition there at that time?

Randall: There were two high schools in Albuquerque at that time—Albuquerque High and Highland. All the Hispanics and I would say most of the Indian kids and probably also most of the blacks—there were very few blacks—went to Albuquerque High, while the racial composition of Highland was almost exclusively white. I think there was a single black girl in my graduating class, a single Japanese American, and maybe one or two Hispanics. So probably in a graduating class of five hundred there were less than a dozen kids who were not Anglo. We were all from the Heights, we were basically paternalistic in our attitudes toward racism. I wanted to be cheerleader and homecoming queen during my high school days. It's true that I also wanted to be, and was, editor of the school paper and took a creative writing class. But I think I was a pretty ordinary white middle-class provincial North American young woman, who, you know, wanted and expected pretty much the same things as she had been taught to want and expect by society. That changed a lot immediately after I left high school.

Crawford: Your rearrival in Albuquerque must have been fairly stark; all the images of western America, this sense of separateness and aloneness—it must have been a shock to see that again after twenty years.

Randall: Yeah. But I think that was a lot of what I brought with me, also. I think I might have felt that even if I had gone back to the East. Certainly, I was surprised by things I shouldn't have been surprised at, because you know, these seemed like leaps to me, and they had been the result of the interminable and endless struggle of people who remained here. But the surprise was not only in terms of what we, people, had done, in different movements, but the technological advances. When I came back here I had never had a credit card.

Crawford: In leaving Albuquerque now, at least temporarily, to go back East, do you feel you have unfinished cultural business in the Southwest?

Randall: Oh, I don't feel like I am leaving the Southwest. This is my home, and for as long as I am able to appeal and/or win the case, this is where I want to be, and it is absolutely where I feel I belong. I guess that, yes, I have a lot of unfinished business, because where you belong is where your unfinished business is.

Photo by Cynthia Farah

chapter seven
Rudolfo Anaya
Interview by John Crawford

Rudolfo Anaya—novelist, short story writer, oral historian, editor, and college professor—has spoken frequently of his relationship to the *llano*, the harsh rangeland of eastern New Mexico, and his role as a groundbreaking Chicano novelist of the 1970s. Born in 1937, he grew up in Santa Rosa, New Mexico, where he attended school through the eighth grade. He moved with his parents to Albuquerque to complete his schooling at Washington Junior High and Albuquerque High School (1956), and then went on to the University of New Mexico, where he received a B.A. and M.A. in English literature. After graduation he wrote laboriously. He borrowed the backdrop of his best-known novel, *Bless Me, Ultima* (1972), from his early years in Santa Rosa. "Part of the land structure, the river, the llano, the hills, are there. Some of the church, the school, and the bridge is there. It seemed the major symbology that I work with was there but it had to be extracted, distilled through the creative process." Hailed as one of the first major Chicano novelists, he went on to write two more books in succession: *Heart of Aztlan* (1976), a story of a family's hard migration from the llano to Albuquerque, and *Tortuga* (1979), the tale of the recovery of a paralyzed boy in a children's hospital deep in the desert. He also began to produce an ongoing series of anthologies, marking him as uniquely generous towards younger writers. He still lives in Albuquerque, where he is professor of English at the University of New Mexico and edits the literary magazine *Blue Mesa Review*. This interview with John Crawford took place in his office in May 1986.

Selected Bibliography:

Bless Me, Ultima, novel (Berkeley: Tonatiuh International, 1972).

Heart of Aztlan, novel (Berkeley: Editorial Justa, 1976). Reprint, University of New Mexico Press, 1988.

Tortuga, novel (Berkeley: Editorial Justa, 1979). Reprint, University of New Mexico Press, 1988.

The Silence of the Llano, stories (Berkeley: Tonatiuh: Quinto del Sol, 1979).

Editor, *Cuentos Chicanos* (Albuquerque: New America, University of New Mexico Press, 1980). Revised Edition, Editor with Antonio Márquez, University of New Mexico Press, 1984.

A Chicano in China, nonfiction (University of New Mexico Press, 1986).

Editor, *Voces: An Anthology of Nuevo Mexicano Writers* (Albuquerque: El Norte Publications, 1987). Reprint, University of New Mexico Press, 1989.

Anaya: One of the most interesting experiences about coming to Albuquerque in the fifties was coming from a very small rural town into a big city *barrio* and being thrown into a completely different life-style. Recently, while attending the Writers of the Purple Sage Conference, it occurred to me that almost every writer there had shared a similar experience. No one lives in a small town any more; nearly all of us are city writers. Although I had all my upbringing in that small town, the majority of my life has been spent in the big city now. That's kind of shocking—we write about our roots that are close to the land, and then we get slapped with this new reality.

Crawford: In your novels there's a double move, from the llano to the small towns and then to the big city.

Anaya: I think it's a progression that has happened in New Mexico. Historically, after World War II you have that exodus from the small towns into the metropolitan areas, especially from the Mexican working community. The new professions were being opened up, the GI Bill was sending some of the veterans to the university, and my writing reflects that historical pattern.

Crawford: In *Heart of Aztlan* it sounds like the small factories were opening up in New Mexico and they were exploiting cheap labor where they could find it, and that would be a reason also.

Anaya: Absolutely.

Crawford: One particular way I remember you writing about the space you grew up in had to do with interior space: the public library in Santa Rosa.

Anaya: I would visit it periodically, starting at an early age, when I was in grade school. It was a little one-room library actually placed on top of the fire house on the first floor, where there was an old beaten up fire truck used on a volunteer basis when there was a fire in the town. We climbed up those rickety steps to the little room that was the library. That interests me too, you know, looking back at what was formative in my love of books.

Crawford: In your novels the formative influences seem to be the figures who represent wisdom and knowledge, like Ultima and Crispin. Were there real people like that in your life who would serve such a function, or are those characters a sort of metaphor or composite?

Anaya: I think it was a little bit of each. In our Hispanic culture there is a great deal of respect given to older people—and growing up in the forties as I did, the relationships that we had with older people were ones of trust. We listened to what they said and we learned from them. And there were specific people that I knew and held in awe. These fabulous *vaqueros* would come in from the llano and my father or brothers and I would visit them; to me, they were almost mythological figures, bigger than life. I think I felt the same way about teachers, because it was normal in our culture to be taught by anyone who was older and to give him or her respect. So when I came to write my novels, which basically have to do with a search for meaning or an archetypal journey, the person who can guide the hero turns out to be the older person not only out of the structure of myth as we know it but out of my background, out of my life. Those older people played very important roles. We believed that *curanderas* could cure; we saw them do it. We believed that there were evil powers that came to be represented by witches, because we lived in the universe where we saw those powers work.

Crawford: And also that things were animated with life, like Tortuga the mountain. There were places that had power.

Anaya: Most definitely. I think it's Clemente in *Heart of Aztlan* who recalls, "I remember there were times and certain places in the llano where I grew up where I would stand at this place and have a feeling of elation, a feeling of flying"—that's interesting, because there are *cuentos* or folk tales where you get these little stories about people who can fly—so in your mind you think, where does this power come from? Is it the power of imagination that we as a communal group are given by those older, wiser people, or can it actually be? So it was very interesting to deal with the power that the earth has to animate us—we *are* animated by the power of the earth—it is in Native American terms our Mother—it nurtures us, it gives us spirit and sustenance, and I guess if we're attuned enough or sensitive enough it can give us different *kinds* of powers. And so, coming out of that kind of complex universe where I grew up thinking of all these places, the river and the hills, having this life to them, this animation, it was very good not only for my growing up but for the imagination, getting fed by that very spiritual process that was in the natural world around me.

Crawford: That must have come to you first in the *cuentos* themselves, the stories you would have heard while growing up. When did you start taking an interest in myth outside your own culture—was that in college—and where did this interest lead you?

Anaya: It was probably when I was an undergraduate here at UNM. We were guided to read Greek mythology. I wasn't really making the connections because I was looking at it as stories that had to do with another time and place. I think it wasn't until I turned more toward Native American mythology that I began to see that there are these points of reference that world myths have, that somehow speak to the center of our being, and connect us—to other people, to the myth, to the story, and beyond that to the historic process, to the communal group.

Crawford: You have a way of making the myths take on very specific roles in the novels. I'm thinking of the incredible way that the mountain and the boy interplay at the beginning of *Tortuga*, where the mountain actually moves and something in the boy moves. It must have taken a great deal of trial and error to find out artistic ways to make the myths connect up with the plots of the stories you were working. They seem highly integrated, in *Tortuga* especially.

Anaya: I would hope that by *Tortuga* they would seem integrated, because it was my third novel and I had been consumed by that process long enough, and possibly also had learned a little bit about how to write a novel.

I have been told, when I travel around the country and read, that there haven't been that many American writers interested in the role of myth and in making myth work in contemporary settings—but I think now we see more and more writers doing that. All the Native American writers tend to do that, fuse their sense of myth into their stories, but at least for awhile it's been rather new to people.

The other thing that people seem to remark on is that not too many writers are lyrical novelists—you know, *Ultima* opens with a great deal of lyricism, a song of invocation almost, if not to the Muse then to the Earth, because Antonio says "In the beginning she opened my eyes and then I could see the beauty of my landscape, my llano, the river, the earth around us."[1] There are other examples in American literature when that happens, but certainly it's been one of my preoccupations. I think the sense of diction and syntax and rhythms of language that come out of having grown up in a Spanish-speaking world, and the act of transferring that to English, creates a "fresh ripple" in people's sensibilities as they read this new language, this conversion of Hispanic language and world view into English. They may be a little shocked at the onset, but most people who get past it find it's refreshing, it's new.

Crawford: I was especially struck by the freshness of the language in the Christmas play scene in *Ultima* and when the children go to the theater in *Tortuga*—partly, I think, because these are scenes of rebellion against the norms of authority and partly because these are children in their spontaneity. There is such vitality in these scenes, where one set of cultural and social expectations crosses another. I suppose when you were writing *Ultima* there wasn't much like that in prose, even in Chicano prose.

Anaya: No, there wasn't—actually, I had read absolutely no Chicano prose during all my school years, including my university years. There were a few novels out there, and I suppose if you were into research you could have found diaries and newspapers, or in folklore you could have read the *cuentos,* but contemporary Chicano prose wasn't born until the mid-sixties during the Chicano movement, and so I think in a sense what we did in the sixties was to create the model itself, or as I have phrased it elsewhere, we set about to build a house and in the sixties we built a foundation. From that comes what we're seeing now in the eighties, an incredible amount of production and writing and unique forms and styles of writing. But all of that was new; it was new to me. In fact, in the sixties when I first began to work, I used Anglo American writers as role models. But I really couldn't get my act together until I left them behind. They had a lot to teach me and I don't underestimate that—you're learning whether you're reading a comic book or Hemingway or Shakespeare or Cervantes—but I couldn't tell my story in their terms. And it wasn't until I said to myself, let me shift for myself, let me go stand on my earth, coming out of my knowledge, and tell the story then and there—that's where Ultima came in. She opened my eyes as she opens Antonio's eyes at the beginning of the book, for the first time; so I sat down to write the story *Bless Me, Ultima,* thinking in Spanish though I wrote it in English. And it worked, because I was creating what to me was a reflection of that real universe that I knew was there.

Crawford: It seems tremendously integrated—not only as to myth and plot, as

---

1. The first paragraph of *Bless Me, Ultima* begins
    Ultima came to stay with us the summer I was almost seven. When she came the beauty of the llano unfolded before my eyes, and the gurgling waters of the river sang to the hum of the turning earth. The magical time of childhood stood still, and the pulse of the living earth pressed its mystery into my living blood. . . .

we were just discussing, but the style. I know you said you put it through several drafts; it looks as if it just sprang out of heaven that way. That must have taken an enormous amount of work.

Anaya: At least seven drafts *is* a lot of work. And then there is a concern for what you just said, that integration, that consistency that you don't want to give up in any one place, and a kind of conscious/subconscious working and interrelating of the myths and the symbols so that they all make a consistent pattern, like weaving a beautiful Navajo rug, you know? It's consistent because it reflects not only the particular person who does the weaving, but all the communal history that went into those symbols and those colors.

Crawford: There also you have the sense of the llano, probably best described there of the three books—and also the farming communities and the towns. And there's a juxtaposition of one against the other, shown in the conflicts of the two families. Was that from your own background? Were both sides of that conflict present within your own family?

Anaya: Yes, in fact, my mother is from a farming community and my father did most of his work as a *vaquero*—what you would call a cowboy or a sheepherder—out on the llano in the ranches; so there was the antagonism between the *llaneros* and the farmers in my family.

Crawford: I love the way the farmers are people of few words. When they are talking to Antonio they will communicate in a few sentences what they have been thinking about all day. That seems to be true of farmers everywhere.

Anaya: Yeah, I think it is a characteristic, isn't it, of people who work with the earth to have imbued in them a sense of patience. On the other hand, they also have their own storytelling, and I remember visiting those farms along Puerta de Luna, where my grandfather had a farm, and late at night people would gather around and begin to tell stories. But the tradition was kind of different. The *llaneros* (*vaqueros* to me) would always be the loud men; they made a lot of noise, they were rough, they were gruff, they laughed more and probably drank more, so what you learned from the respective groups was very different, had its own flavor. . . .

Crawford: There's a strong sense in *Ultima* that the life experience cuts against some of the aspects of traditional Catholicism, so that there seems to be a sort of striving to supplant or transform it into a kind of world religion based on experience, especially mystical experience. Am I right about this? And did you encounter resistance from traditional Catholics for that message in the book?

Anaya: I've never felt there was any resistance or opposition. I think quite the contrary, a lot of readers who are Catholic have seen an accurate portrayal of the church at least as it was in those times—you're talking now about forty years later, and things have changed. But I think it's fair to say that what goes on in the novel also reflects my attempt to get an understanding of the Native American tradition and those other religions that are not Catholic and not based in the Christian mythology.

Crawford: Especially from the *indio*.

Anaya: Especially from the *indio*. And again, not to give up the one tradition for the other, but to see if those points of reference I talked about can be reached, whether from my Catholic world I knew as a child or my exploration of the Native American world that is also part of me or the worlds that I read of in other mythologies, such as Buddhism. And so I think for me to look only in my Catholic background was too limiting, and *Bless Me, Ultima* begins to explore new ground.

Crawford: I was struck by the richness of choices that Antonio has at the end of the novel. He has many things to think about, reconcile, bring together.

Anaya: Well, his universe begins to get constricted. I think Antonio's life is— as he begins to see that he is losing the innocence of childhood—it possibly reflects the life of the Hispanic community in New Mexico, in the sense that we too began to lose that age when the only thing that affected us happened within our family or our village. The world was changing around us and was going to bring a lot of new and positive things to us, but also some threats. And we had a lot of decisions to make. Pretty quick.

Crawford: There's a thread of continuity in the books—literally, the same family is mentioned first in *Ultima*, is the whole subject of *Aztlan*, and the boy carries on in *Tortuga*—but also, there is the thread of another kind of continuity. It seems to me that the three books are a trilogy, and in the third book is an overall interpretation you can bring—what the boy is going through personally somehow involves the whole culture, and his success, his survival, is a very important thing: an achievement for everyone.

Anaya: It's strange that no one has ever said that, you know. And I agree with your interpretation, because it seems to me that one of the important things I was doing in *Tortuga* was taking the main character and trying to make him well again after he had been crippled by life, by the circumstances that occur in *Heart of Aztlan*. And I felt that as much or more than any other character I had ever created, Tortuga was Everyman of the Chicano culture, that indeed the culture was under assault, and that the paralysis reflected in Tortuga was that paralysis that had set on the community. Tortuga has not only to get well, he has to perform still more heroic tasks in the future; not only that, the Mexican American community has to find ways of breaking out of its bondage, its paralysis.

Crawford: It's also true that there are people from other cultures in the hospital who are also afflicted. . . .

Anaya: Yes, and in this respect I think the novel should acquire some kind of universal meaning, because what we have created of our modern society can paralyze all of us—those of us from minority groups get displaced more and used more, but I think if we are not careful the same forces that cripple us can do it to everyone. So you have in the hospital, even if they are never completely identified by ethnic group, representatives of all of them.

Crawford: In all three novels, the power of love is the redeemer in some sense. In *Tortuga* it's very much a literal one: It's sexual love, it's also working together— there's a wonderful sense of the people pulling together in a more collective spirit within the room he's in; there's real affection between the boys there—in fact, that seems to be the dominant message that your novels carry. . . .

Anaya: I think you're right. Though I have lived in and explored the existential universe, I have come back to a communal universe. I grew up in that tradition, I left it in some of my wanderings, and I returned to it; and what the tradition of the community has to teach us is what I've already alluded to—respect, love for the family and for the village that is the community. I think that's where the power of love comes in. I feel it has sustained all those Indian and Mexican pueblos that have occupied this region for such a long time; they must have had it as they came together and formed their bond—a bond not only of tradition and language and culture and heritage, but of love. That's how they were able to survive, and that's how they will be able to survive in the presence of all those powers that can cripple and kill us, you see.

Crawford: In *Heart of Aztlan* there is also that spirit of coming together, within the community established in Albuquerque, in the various parts of the *barrio* whatever the difficulty of the circumstances.

Anaya: One of the things that some critics have viewed as a failure in *Heart of Aztlan* has been that no structure, no political structure with a given political ideology, is put into place. But I guess my feeling is that while those structures may come into being, if they're not shored up by some common respect and a common goal that we have as human beings, they don't last long. And I do see their importance—they're the way we get things done in today's world. But I was more interested, I guess, in following the other side of that coin, and that is can we really get together as a community—not because of what's in it for me, but because of that old sense of value that has sustained all communities on earth throughout history. And to me, the element of love must play a large role in it.

Crawford: That brings me to a political question. You had clearly stated ten years ago that you didn't feel Chicano literature was strongest when it was narrowly addressed to political struggle and resistance. Ten years ago, the climate was very politically charged. What do you think about this now?

Anaya: What I have come to see is that there is even more need now for what we call a political stance, in our poetry and our novels. That seems to be a big change from where I was ten years ago. I guess I thought then that the literature we were writing would be very good for our community, one more place where we could reflect on our history and our identity and move on from there, and that we didn't have to overwhelm the reader with "message," so to speak; we didn't have to hit the reader over the head with ideology. I think that's principally the reason I wasn't in tune with the political writings of the Chicano movement at the time. I felt all too often that the ideology came up short—all too often it was only a Marxist ideology—and, too, I tended to see in writers whose main concern was message a lack of aesthetic attention to what they were practicing, what they were learning to be. They didn't really want to be writers, they wanted to be politicians, and I think there's two different animals there. Can you get those two together in the same work? Can a very good writer who has learned and paid attention and practiced his craft communicate his political feelings about the society? I think yes; I feel stronger about that now than I did then. I still think it's probably the hardest kind of writing to do, because you tend to put the reader off. The reader wants story and you're talking message; the reader may quickly leave you. But it is important in this country, especially when you speak of our community, the Southwest. We have not only the story to write, we also have to remind our people about their history and their traditions and their culture and their language, things that are under that threat that we talked about right now, and liable to disappear if we don't look closely at ourselves in a historical process—and part of analyzing that historical process is not only story and myth and legend and tradition, it's a political space we occupy. How have we occupied it? How have we been used in that political space?

Recently I've played around with an essay in which I talk about writing in colonial space, which is a political concept, right? How do we feel as a minority group, a clearly recognizable ethnic group, when we have to respond to colonial space—how do we carve out our own identity? This is what the Chicano movement was all about, trying to create within colonial space the space for our own community, our literature. And that process is tied into the political process.

So in a sense you're always tied into it—I think my three novels are. The fact that they don't clearly call for one specific ideology may be interpreted as a critical fault in a political novel, but I didn't set out to write political novels. Though I do see their importance.

I think probably the novel that I'm writing now, which is again set in Albuquerque, is my analysis of my contemporary world, the present, today: What role do the different cultures of New Mexico play vis-à-vis each other? how is the Southwest changing? what is the concept of the Sunbelt all about? who is coming here and why are tremendous investments being made across the Southwest? what do they mean to our communities that have been here a long time? I think probably the only way we respond to some of these questions, critical questions if we're going to exist as a culture, *is* in novels that carry that social-political impact and perhaps allow the public to think on those questions that are crucial. But I'm still of the opinion that you do that through a well-told story.

Crawford: I've noticed there seem to be affinities between the ideas you're expressing and the writings of magic realism in Central and South America—being political in the broadest sense, describing what is happening in the Americas, and doing it with art—not leaving it to rhetoric. Do you have any direct relationships with Marquez or Fuentes or. . . .

Anaya: No, I haven't. If I were more inclined to go around visiting with writers, I would have found ways, but I'm not. I have one short story called "B. Traven Is Alive and Well in Cuernavaca" which begins something like this: "I don't go to Mexico to meet writers; I go to write!"

Crawford: I want to go back to *Tortuga*. It seems to me it's the most political novel you've done because it's the most concentrated on this extended metaphor we've been talking about—because that hospital is also a prison. The Indian boy that gets out dies very soon. It's as if people have been cut off from the land so that in going back to it, it becomes dangerous.

Anaya: Yeah . . . the idyllic and pastoral llano and river valley of *Bless Me, Ultima!* becomes the cancerous desert, the blinding sandstorms that you have to cross to get back home, the frozen mountain in midwinter that the Indian boy has to cross and that kills him. So even the land has almost become an antagonist, whereas before it was the nurturing mother. We get the sense of the unnatural storms, radiation, death in the desert, grasses described as brittle, and that's all part of the extended metaphor, the reflection of what we are doing to ourselves, what we are doing to our earth.

Crawford: One thing you did in that book struck me in a very personal way, because I spent some time myself in children's hospitals. It's where you talk about pain. You say that for someone who's had a great deal of pain, it's very hard to avoid things like drugs and alcohol later, because pain is a high and you get used to it. That's a very clear insight. When I read that I thought, "This guy has been there." You must have known something about that experience to be able to write that way.

Anaya: Yeah, well, I spent a summer in one of those hospitals and that's where the germ of the novel comes from—the experience, some of the characters, and some of the things that he went through. Around that is the reflection of what we are doing to ourselves and to the earth. It does have the hope in it that my characters seem to keep looking around—there must be *somebody* out there who I can make contact with—like the persons I knew in childhood who were a little wiser and more solid because they were sharing themselves. And even though the rest of the landscape alternates between the dead desert with the sandstorms and the frozen mountains around the hospital on the west side, the springs of the mountain are still running, there is still hope, it's not too late, and you can go there and you can bathe and be made whole. But there's very little of that left, you know. And we've got to touch base with it pretty quick. Otherwise, living in this region that has so much potential to it, because it's a very special corridor in this country, the Rio Grande Valley and the cultures that have been here for thousands of years—it's a very special place—if we don't realize that, we're going to lose part of the hope that this region has to offer us and the people in it.

Crawford: We might end with one other question about that. It seems to me that some of the most responsible writers, as well as some of the best, from the three cultures here have written about this sense of place in one way or another— I'm thinking of Edward Abbey, who's really a westerner; Leslie Silko and Simon Ortiz; certainly yourself; and several others who have addressed it in a big way, in novels. What do you think the prospects are for this multicultural work becoming a national forum that people can begin to see as a model for such statements?

Anaya: I think that has already happened. I see any number of regions around the country that are in a sense turning inward and looking at themselves and producing wonderfully gifted writers. I'm not sure that we in the Southwest caused that forum; the times themselves are calling for a truly representative speaking to each other, letting down some of these false borders that we've had between us. I think that's a very positive thing. What's happening in this country—if we are part of it, much more power to us—is that if we are able to take our different perspectives of how the world ought to be—alerted to the fact that there are people out there who thrive on destroying—and share these perspectives, you know, communicate among groups, then we have something to offer the whole country and the world. The world *is* interested; that's one thing that is conveyed to me every time a visitor comes through here. They've locked into the Southwest as a place going through a very interesting experiment—it has to do with how people can live with each other, can share—and this is as important to the whites and the Maori of New Zealand as it may be to the Catalonians and the Basques, the Nicaraguans and the Misquitos, you know what I mean? It's important to us to realize that we are a center of focus—a lot of people are looking at us, and we can do something very positive with all the changes that are coming across this land, or we can blow it. And I tend to want to work more on the positive things that are going on here, so that we can learn from each other.

Photo by Rountry/Williams

chapter eight
Paula Gunn Allen
Interview by Annie O. Eysturoy

Paula Gunn Allen, of Laguna Pueblo/Sioux/Lebanese descent, was born in Cubero, New Mexico, in 1939. She is a member of the Laguna and Acoma Pueblo Indian communities from which a generation of writers has descended: Leslie Marmon Silko, Simon Ortiz, Carol Lee Sanchez, Harold Littlebird, to name a few. She has commented, "I never make the error of designating what is true in Cubero as universal, though I suppose I should because hardly anything of worth goes on anywhere that does not go on there." Allen holds a Ph.D. from the University of New Mexico and is currently Professor of Ethnic Studies and Native American Studies at the University of California at Berkeley. Since 1975 she has published seven books of poetry—two after this interview—and has written many critical essays, some of which are incorporated into a volume of course designs and essays, *Studies in American Indian Literature*, which she compiled for the Modern Language Association (1983). Her recent volume *The Sacred Hoop* (1986) is an important feminist revisioning of Native American history and literature. She is also the author of a major novel, *The Woman Who Owned the Shadows* (1983), and is working on a second, *Raven's Road*, of which portions have already been published. This interview with Annie Eysturoy of the University of New Mexico took place at Allen's parents' house in Albuquerque in March 1987, when the author was in town to give a poetry reading.

Selected Bibliography:

The Blind Lion, poetry (Berkeley: Thorp Springs Press, 1974).

A Cannon Between My Knees, poetry (New York: Strawberry Press, 1981).

Coyote's Daylight Trip, poetry (Albuquerque: La Confluencia, 1978).

Star Child, poetry (Marvin, S.D.: Blue Cloud Quarterly, 1981).

Shadow Country, poetry (Los Angeles: UCLA American Indian Studies Center, 1982).

Editor, *Studies in American Indian Literature: Critical Essays and Course Designs,* with essays (New York: Modern Language Association, 1983).

The Woman Who Owned the Shadows, novel (San Francisco: Spinsters Ink, 1983).

The Sacred Hoop: Recovering the Feminine in American Indian Traditions, essays (Boston: Beacon Press, 1986).

Wyrds, poetry (San Francisco: Taurean Horn Press, 1987).

Skins and Bones, poetry (Albuquerque: West End Press, 1988).

Editor, *Spider Woman's Granddaughters: Native American Women's Traditional and Short Stories* (Boston: Beacon Press, 1989).

Eysturoy: You were born and raised here. How has that influenced you and your work?

Allen: My work is all tangled up with landscape around here. But landscape for me does not mean "the landscape"; it does not mean something that great dramas are enacted upon. Maybe that's because so much of the drama in the Southwest *is* the land, not the people. We are, to me, the background against which the land enacts *her* drama, and by landscape I don't mean only the mountains and those vast plains, but the weather, the climatic conditions and rainstorms, the overpowering thunderstorms.

Eysturoy: So it is the power of the landscape, more than anything else, that has left an impression on you?

Allen: Right. It has given me an entirely different notion of how women are supposed to be. Other people in America keep thinking that women are supposed to be sort of helpless, cute, and that's femininity. But to me femininity means these great craggy mountains and these deep arroyos and tremendous storms, because mother nature after all is feminine, right? This is all mother nature happening, so I cannot think of her as something that is so terrifying that I have to control her, because storms are exciting, terribly exciting.

You see, you have to live with her, in her, and there is no escape from it. Maybe in England—I have never been there—everything is gentler, more controlled, so that creates the belief that people should be either weak and helpless or power mad, one or the other; maybe that's what creates all those truly bizarre images descending from the English literary tradition. Certainly all the rhetorical forms and especially the artistic forms, those that are about nature, tend to be about a tidy little gentle place.

Eysturoy: So this very powerful natural setting of the Southwest does not invite images of a conquering and controlling of nature?

Allen: Right, and those images we do have are going to have an effect. Certainly my own writing comes out of the consciousness of my own landscape, where I come from, the trees and mesas I climbed, my physical interaction with where I was. To me that is the real world. American writers tend to think of the real world as ugly, social stuff. They focus on reality as being the yucky things that people do. To me reality is the natural world, and the yucky social stuff, like ugly cities or dreadful political conditions, is the artificiality.

Eysturoy: You see this as a balance in nature?

Allen: That's right. She gives us our life, so she has a right to take it. What I notice the most when I look at my work is that the land is always there.

Eysturoy: The landscape, then, has been important in shaping your perception of the world?

Allen: Right. I look at the natural world to see what something in the human world means, because I have no other way of knowing. The natural world might mean inside my body, but even then I will check with the world out there, the planet, the climate, the seasons, how plants function, how the earthy people function. Then I know how I am functioning, because I am an earthy person.

Eysturoy: What about the people of the Southwest, your family and the people you grew up with?

Allen: My dad mentioned this morning that most of the poems I read last night were either about my family or they were somehow connected to it, and we talked about that. I think that Indian writers, Chicano writers and black and Asian American writers do a lot of family stuff, because we don't distinguish ourselves from the family base. We exist within the matrix of the people who are our relatives or family friends, or our tribe. I'm raised that way, and I can't write any other way. It may seem this is too peculiar, too local, too personal and not universal. But that's not true, because everybody has a human part that is about their connections, their blood-ties. To me, my work has to speak back to the people from whom it comes, if it comes through my voice, my mind, and my art.

Eysturoy: Does your spiritual view of life also originate in your family?

Allen: It was just something you knew, I guess we all knew. There were always the dances, those things going on at the pueblo. There was Mass, there was church, but this is something more than that. I knew about magic. My mother used to read me European fairytales, Greek mythology, Indian stories, and the Bible, and she did not make any distinction among them. They were all literature. So I grew up thinking that these were all analogues of one another, because she said they were. It must be where I got the whole thing about spirituality, the metaphysics.

I also think that nature herself is metaphysical. I think that if you are really connecting with the land then you are going to have to connect with the spirits. So probably as a consequence of being with the land, I developed a spiritual dimension, because there is no way not to. I think you have to get away from the land and think of it as something you take pictures of before you can lose your spiritual connections. But if you talk to the tree periodically, which I do, you cannot lose your spiritual connection, because the tree talks back and so you know that there is a person in there.

Eysturoy: How did you realize that you wanted to become a writer?

Allen: I think it was an accident! When I was younger I wanted to become an actress. My first two years in college I majored in drama, and I was pretty good at it; I liked it. I wrote some poems that looked like prose poems, but it wasn't what I focused on. Then I got married, and I wrote some essays just because I needed to say some things. I was reading Ayn Rand and wrote two or three essays in response to what she was saying.

Then I got divorced, moved to Albuquerque, and decided to sign up for something called "The Famous Writers School." At that point I thought I would be a fiction writer. At the time, I had two babies and a job making seventy-five cents an hour. I don't know how I lived through those years, I really don't. But I did. . . . Then I decided to go back to the university.

I had met a young man from Kenya, and as I was sitting in his house one day there was a book of poems by Robert Creeley on the table. Poetry was not going to be my thing, but I really liked that poetry, so I took the book home, read it from cover to cover, and took it back to my friend who said, "Well, you know, Creeley is teaching on campus. Why don't you see if you can get into his class?" So I went. It was sort of intentional and sort of not.

Meanwhile I had decided that I could not become an actress. For one thing I had two babies; I couldn't get on a bus and go to New York City and live on the streets. So to some extent I became a writer because I had these babies and couldn't just go and do anything I wanted.

In Creeley's class I got an A. He really liked my work, but every time he looked at me he could not believe I had done it, because I looked like a housewife from Grants. This was the early sixties when a person was supposed to look cool, you know. And in fiction I got A's, so it was sort of easy. So, to some extent it was a forced choice. I couldn't do what I wanted to do and there didn't seem to be any way out, so that must be fate. . . .

I don't like to write. I do once I get going, but it is difficult. I'll clean house, I'll do anything other than sit down and write; it is very difficult. In Oregon, once, I had to write a little thing about writing, and I remember writing that as far as I could see writing was a series of small suicides, some of which are fatal. And I still believe that; it is amazing how many delusions and illusions you have to blow to smithereens just to write a paragraph, a good paragraph.

In a way writing is more painful than birthing, and birthing hurts. That was also something I said I was never going to do again after the first time. I did it again, but very, very unhappily, because I knew what it was going to cost. I wanted the kids, but I did not want the anguish. It is the same thing with writing: I want the book, but, oh, I don't want the agony.

Eysturoy: How long did it take you to write *The Woman Who Owned the Shadows*?

Allen: Thirteen years! I wrote parts in Albuquerque, then I moved to California and wrote parts in San Francisco. I moved back to Albuquerque, wrote a little more, moved back to San Francisco and finished it there. Later I revised it in L. A. and added a number of new passages in El Cerrito.

Eysturoy: Is writing like a vision quest for you?

Allen: I like that question, because that's exactly right. That's what I am searching for, to pull the vision out of me, because it is here, I know it is. It is a path, a road, and it is *how* I am that molecule that does that dance that makes up her being. Our job is to be conscious of our dance, because that's the way we play for our mother. And that is what I do and, I think, that's what writers must do. That's why writers are important, as long as they are working toward consciousness.

I don't mean evolution. I mean noticing what we already know; we were born knowing it; maybe it is in our genes, or maybe it is in our soul. I don't know where it is, but I know that it is. So the trick is to get back to our origin, to know what it knows or what she knows.

That's what a vision quest is for, you know. You go out in the wilderness— or men do—and you find out who you are. Well, a writer goes into the wilderness and finds out who she is. And it is awful! But I love it once I get past the garbage, the fear, all the walls and resistance, and I finally am working; when the voice begins to come and the work starts doing me—because I am not doing it by then—then it is great rejoicing and I won't leave the word processor.

But it might take me four days of work to get to that point; in that sense it is sacred.

Eysturoy: Do you think the vision quest of women is different from that of men?

Allen: As far as I understand, it *was* different for women. A person with the female anatomy might go on a mountaintop vision quest; but by and large she stayed very near the village. There are reasons for that. For one thing, how far do you have to go when you have so much happening in your own body?

Certainly, the cultures that do vision quests also do menstrual huts, and that's a vision quest all by itself and very frightening.

It is not as though we are not allowed to do vision quests, but rather that the male impulse requires one set of circumstances and the female impulse requires another. Our anatomies are different and so we have to have different methods suited to our anatomies, to our hormonal system that will work for that entity.

The forms are different and their way of sharing is different, but the fact of sharing is always the same; you don't get to keep it. You have to put it to use in the community or you didn't do anything.

Eysturoy: Is your writing, then, an act of sharing with others what you are envisioning on your quest?

Allen: That's right. It's like cooking; you'll try to make something that will feed and nourish your guests.

Eysturoy: Is putting the past together, remembering, or as you say, re-membering the past a form of providing nourishment for others?

Allen: Right—re-membering the past, putting it back together, recovering; knowing who we are and who we have been. How are we going to know who we are going to be, if we don't know where we have been?

The Indian potters, the women, take old pottery and grind it up and put it into the clay-mix with the new pot. The reason why they do it that way is that the clay will bond more securely all around so it will not fall apart easily. If you don't do it right, the pot will blow up when you are cooking it; it doesn't have the right consistency. But if you don't do it at all, the pot will crumble; it won't hold up over time and you won't be able to put water in it.

Eysturoy: So you see yourself as creating a fabric that will strengthen and nurture others, and give them a sense of who they are and where they came from?

Allen: That's right.

Eysturoy: In *The Sacred Hoop* you talk about alienation as a predominant theme in American Indian fiction. . . . Most of those writers are male. Do you think that that in itself could have been a reason for the predominance of the alienation theme?

Allen: You know, I don't know yet; it very well might be. For one thing, there are not that many women writing novels yet, so it is hard to tell. But thinking of Anna Lee Walters's stories, for example, then she is certainly telling a different story entirely.

I wrote that essay, "Stranger in My Own Land," in 1977. At that time there were a lot of urban, marginal Indians writing, who really did not have any connections back to a homeland. But on the other hand, those same men writing in the eighties do write differently. There are a lot more people from the reservations or from intact communities who are in print now, you know, and we don't find the alienation theme, the degree of it, with nearly the kind of intensity that you did in the seventies.

I am thinking about James Welch. There is a real progression in his three novels to where his new novel, *Fools Crow*, explains the alienation. He goes back to the conquest of that particular band, the Blackfeet, to which tribe he belongs. In a way it is a healing process, because I am sure it has healed something, not only his consciousness, but also in the consciousness of his people. And I think that is true for Indians across the country. So the alienation of the seventies has moved to the spiritual, powerful voice of the eighties.

Eysturoy: Do you see it as a process of exorcising the alienation and then coming back to the original center?

Allen: Right. Now where are we? That's where *The Sacred Hoop* comes in, and that's right where *The Woman Who Owned the Shadow* ends. It stops where the healing process begins, and *The Sacred Hoop* is about recovery, recovery of our selves.

Eysturoy: A lot of people will probably say, after having read *The Sacred Hoop*, that the theories presented there of a gynocratic Indian past are mostly conjecture. If we can generalize, how gynocratic *were* the tribes in the past?

Allen: Well, we can generalize, in fact, I can make better generalizations as each year goes by. *The Sacred Hoop* was published in 1985, was at the press in '83, so almost everything in it was written by '82–'83, except for the introduction, so we are dealing with a time-lag here.

By '77 social anthropologists could say that if you drew a line from Maine through San Diego, everything south of that line would be gynocratic, and the way you could tell was that they were corn-based cultures. Where you found corn, squash, and beans, you found predominantly female deities and powerful female beings, and you would always have a matrilocality, matrifocality, and matrilineality. What is that if not a gynarchy? Some are still arguing about this, but if you descend from a woman, and if the culture is centered on female deities, I am willing to call that a gynarchy or a gynocentric civilization.

I have never found a patriarchal culture in Native America, North or South. Never. I have found cultures where women appeared to be under the dominance of clan head men, but I have never found a culture where that meant that the men told the women what to do. In a lot of these cultures the older women told the younger women what to do, and the older men told the younger men what to do. But if the young woman or the young man did not want to do it, there were not a lot of mechanisms of enforcement. So in the sense of a non-authoritarianism, in the sense of equal distribution of goods—or equal distribution of starvation—and in the sense of sharing of tasks and responsibilities between genders, I don't think you are going to find a Native American culture where that is not going on.

You are never going to find a patriarchy, is what I am saying. Absolutely never. There isn't any.

Eysturoy: Do they then fulfill the Jungian androgynous ideal of balance?

Allen: They might. . . . Certainly, that's why I used the term gynocratic or gynocentric, because I am not talking about matriarchy, and I won't use that word. It tends to mean that women dominate, because patriarchy means that the men dominate. So to avoid triggering that idea in people's minds, I use the term gynarchy or gynocentrism, meaning that femaleness or femininity is the central cultural value.

This is reflected in the female deities. The status of individual women ranges from abject dependency to complete and absolute autonomy, just as it does with men, and you can find anything in between, but you find significant female deities and you find significant female rituals that are necessary to the ongoing life of the tribe. You find women significantly present in one way or another in every ceremony, whether it be male or female. Now, that's saying something about all of Native America, and that is not really all that conjectural.

Eysturoy: You mention in *The Sacred Hoop* that deities who were perceived as only feminine in the past have recently emerged as male after having gone through an androgynous process. Is it your contention, then, that that process in itself says something about the social structures they must have reflected in the past?

Allen: Right, that's my point. The female deities reflected the social system and the understandings of the people within that system. Metaphysically I would argue that the people were reflecting the gods. But in a sociological, scholarly framework I am perfectly willing to argue in the other direction, that the gods reflected the people.

Eysturoy: It works both ways . . .

Allen: Yes, they go both ways; you cannot have one without the other.

Eysturoy: So when you are talking about the centrality of the role of women, you are talking about a value rather than a position of power or control?

Allen: Absolutely. That was never going on—not as far as I can tell—in any Native American system.

Eysturoy: It seems to me that in *The Woman Who Owned the Shadows*, Ephanie, the central character, is on a vision quest. On that quest she moves further and further into a female universe, while the male characters are basically negative characters. How do you achieve the balance there that—as we have talked about—is so important in American Indian philosophy, the balance of male and female? How does Ephanie reach that balance?

Allen: She reaches it because in a woman's life femininity is central; in a man's life masculinity is central. You don't get egalitarianism by women relating to men and you don't get it by men relating to women. What I am saying is that gender norms are for the gender to which they apply; they are not for the other gender. For Ephanie to locate who she is, she has to move from thinking of her reference group as male to thinking of her reference group as female. That says nothing about the men. Ephanie herself is pretty crazy—out of touch with herself—until she understands that she is female.

Eysturoy: So she has to move into a female universe in order to explore herself?

Allen: A truly female universe.

Eysturoy: . . . from which she can emerge and be her true self, and then unite with her male counterpart?

Allen: Or not. Uniting is one of the things white people do. There is a male and there is a female. There is not a "unite" in there anywhere, and there never is in the tribes. And why should they unite? They are different.

Eysturoy: So they should operate in their separate spheres with balance between those spheres?

Allen: That's right. Yes, and with mutual respect. You know, if you look at the plain we are on, you see the Sandias, which I have always thought of as male, and across, way across, is Mt. Taylor, whom I always have thought of as female. She stays there, and he stays here and they converse. They don't get mixed up in thinking that one has to be the other one, and they don't think they have to merge. If they ever do think that, we are in trouble, all of us who live in between. And that's why the mountains are that way, and that's how I see the appropriate balance of genders. I think that we live in separate spheres. We have different consciousnesses, because we have different bodies. We need each other; but only if we recognize the validity of our own way, and therefore the validity of the other person's way, are we ever going to be able to actually function together.

Eysturoy: We should accept the differences?

Allen: Absolutely, and use them; it is essential. You know, patriarchy is about monogamy, it is about monotony, it is about monotheism, it is about unity, and it is about uniformity. No Indian system is like that, in any sense. They never wanted other people to be like them. That's why they don't recruit members. They don't only respect difference and acknowledge it; they expect it, and they always have. That's why they got conquered, as a matter of fact. They did not understand that there were people who thought that there was only one way of doing things and that was their way, and if you did not do it their way they would kill you.

Ephanie, in *The Woman Who Owned the Shadows,* is not supposed to unite with the men. She keeps expecting men to do her life for her, because she got feminized in the western way instead of the tribal way. She made a terrible mistake and she paid for it until she understood that she had power in her own right.

Eysturoy: And the healing process is the recovering of her past?

Allen: Her past and her place in the world, yes; her past, her place, and therefore her identity.

Eysturoy: How has all this helped you resolve your own sense of who you are, your own sense of identity?

Allen: I had a lot of questions about that when I was quite a bit younger. It was really important in my twenties. By the time I was in my early thirties, I had pretty much resolved it for myself. I am Lebanese-American, I am Indian, I am a breed, and I am New Mexican and they have a lot to do with how I act and what I think and how I interpret things. I was raised in a family and in a world that was multicultural, multiethnic, multireligious, and multilinguistic, with a number of social classes involved. All of those people were my relatives, and all of those people were part of me, because they had an impact on me.

Eysturoy: You mention in *The Sacred Hoop* that there is an unconscious assumption that these identities must be in conflict, and a choice therfore has to be made, but that you don't see that this necessarily has to be.

Allen: No, it does not have to be. Though, certainly, there are times where the Lebanese Paula and the Indian Paula come into awful conflict, because they are different. So certainly, there is intra-psychic conflict and stress that arises. And then I have a kind of overlaying or underlaying American or Anglo culture that I mostly picked up in school. It is all me. It sometimes comes into conflict with itself, but it is all me.

Eysturoy: Does incorporating all parts of your origins, rather than making a choice, become a means of survival?

Allen: You have to incorporate them all. I think that's where you get into alienation, thinking that you cannot have the whole bulk, that you *have* to choose.

Eysturoy: Do you think the philosophy or ideology that you have to be either one or the other is part of the colonization process?

Allen: Yes, I do, absolutely. It is very clear in the case of the Native Americans. They have been propagandized for anywhere from one hundred to four hundred years—depending on the region of the country—that they have to choose. Then all the stories that were written about the Indian between two chairs—all of La Farge and Frank Waters—and of course the Indian between two chairs has to choose, cannot choose, and therefore dies. This tells all the youngsters growing up that they are going to die. It is a genocidal myth. I know all kinds of people, Indian people, full bloods, traditionals, half-bloods, whatever, who can manage to do both quite nicely. But they are not the ones that show up in literature, and there is a reason for that. If it is white writers, it is because they really want all the Indians dead. They are not going to admit that; they really think they pity the Indian. But why are they killing them all in their books, if they really want them to live? How come they are always dying? Good question!

Eysturoy: You see these writers creating a myth they would like to see realized?

Allen: That's right. What is it? The self-fulfilling tendency of expectation? And it works very insidiously, but it works. So I have been teaching for a long, long time that you must accept all your identities; they are yours, and nobody has the right to take them away from you. You have to be a lot smarter to manage two cultures or five cultures than you do to manage one. Americans—white Americans, I mean, because nobody else in America has this luxury but white Americans—think they are smarter because they have only one culture, and they don't understand that the more cultures you have, the greater your range; your personal range, your intellectual range, and your emotional range is much greater. It is like assuming that if you only eat potatoes, that somehow you are better than the people who eat rice, corn, wheat, potatoes, and pasta.

And I think that of the western nations the United States is very peculiar in that way. It tends to think that there is only the Anglo-Protestant capitalist way of doing things.

You know how white folks like to go out to the reservation to see Indians? Well, I love to watch TV and watch white folks; it's great fun. But I didn't know why I liked it so much. I used to get mad, because they said the dumbest things, until it finally dawned on me that they are talking to each other, and to them American means this very narrow group of middle- to upper-class Anglo-European people who go to Protestant church—not fundamentalist Protestant, but respectable Protestant—and they have homes and cars, and they all look the same way, eat the same food, and do the same things. They are only these people on TV, and that leaves out at least 40 percent of the people in the United States, a lot of whom are white, a lot of whom are European, but they don't happen to live in that little tiny culture box, so they don't show up on TV as being Americans.

I finally realized that that's because we are *not* Americans. Americans are a very specifically defined cultural entity to which a lot of citizens of the United States do not belong. We are citizens of the United States, but we are not Americans. And that's definitely very weird! It doesn't make me mad anymore; it strikes me as hilarious and stupid and short sighted, and possibly dangerous. But it is pretty funny. How can you live in Washington, DC, surrounded by black people and think that way?

Eysturoy: You say that you have incorporated your different ethnic backgrounds. How does Ephanie, in *The Woman Who Owned the Shadows*, incorporate the white world? She seems to go further and further into her Indianness.

Allen: And then she goes back to teach white people. So her resolution is that this is not about race; this is about vision. The people who live on this continent are Indians, that is to say, they live on the Indian continent, and what we must do is teach them how to live here. We tried and they kept killing us. That was then; but now maybe there are people here, lots of them, who are ready. . . . Ephanie goes back to the world as a teacher and she knows who she is.

Eysturoy: Is that why she says "I mix my metaphors with care"?

Allen: That's right. You have to do it, and she learns very carefully. She has to have that whole period of isolation and relearning herself before she is in any position to be able to do that. Then she is going as herself back into the white world; it is different from the way she originally did it. First she went into the white world to find herself, and that did not work; it made her crazy, literally crazy and suicidal. You can't do that, you can't borrow an identity, you have to go out from your own identity.

Eysturoy: Ephanie goes into the mythical past and recovers the myth. As a writer, do you see yourself as a recoverer of myths or as a creator of myths?

Allen: As a writer I am not a creator of myths. As a channel I am.

Eysturoy: How do you distinguish between being a writer and being a channel?

Allen: Well, writers invent and I do it, too. But there are passages where, frankly, somebody else takes over. It is not me, and the reason I know it is not me is because they say stuff I wouldn't have said, and in fact, some of it I disagree with.

There is a passage in *The Woman Who Owned the Shadows* about the Grandmothers, "And then for long eons they slept." I love that passage, and I wrote it in the physical sense of writing down the words, but, frankly, somebody took hold of my pencil and they wrote it. I was just the typewriter, so to speak. And it wasn't as though I was in a trance or unconscious; I don't mean that. It was conscious, but I would not have thought of writing that. So I am talking about another order. I think you touch into the mythstream that is always there; it is part of the world; it is part of the universe.

Eysturoy: Is that what you are getting at when you mention that rather than say "I wrote it," you say "I listened"?

Allen: Yes, and a writer's job is to be as accurate a receiver as you can be. It is hard work. For one thing you have to read a lot, talk a lot, and think a lot, and take a lot of time for yourself. You have to know a lot of people, and you have to have a good ear. Otherwise, when the stuff comes through, you are going to try to change it, because you are not going to recognize it. So you have to be a very knowledgeable, experimental instrument; you have to have a range of knowledge and adaptability and physical experience, because only then can you become a good instrument.

Eysturoy: And you have to learn how to listen.

Allen: That's it; you have to learn how, especially if you were raised in America. I don't mean rural America, though, because I was raised on those mesas, with a great deal of freedom to listen to myself. My mother was very verbal about it. She would complain about people who would not let their children just daydream. I spent weeks up on the mesa. I didn't talk a lot to people; I did not learn to talk to people until I was well into my twenties. I was an introverted person and I needed to be, so I would have the ability to listen.

Eysturoy: What new directions are you taking in your new novel, *Raven's Road?*

Allen: That's such a hard book, another thirteen-year book, and I really would like to get it done soon instead of thirteen years from now. But I have a cast of characters that is huge, and an outline that is seventeen pages long and I can't make head or tails of it. I started out to write a very simple lesbian novel just for fun. But I got involved. So I have a story about Indian people in Albuquerque, an urban group; some folks out in Isleta; a lesbian community in Albuquerque; the national lesbian community; alcoholism and battering; the bomb; and the antipornography movement, and I am trying to work this out over a time frame of about forty years, from '45 to '85. Meanwhile I want to write a thousand-page novel, and I don't want to write a trilogy; so I am stuck.

Eysturoy: The excerpt that was published in *The New Native American Novel*, where Allie and Raven watch a nuclear explosion at Yucca Flats, Nevada, seems to suggest that you are dealing with the geopolitical aspect of the nuclear bomb, and also that you see a deeper meaning behind nuclear power.

Allen: That excerpt is the sacred heart of the novel.

As I see it at this point, the bomb is seen because of the Grandmothers, and because Allie and Raven are both medicine-women, for lack of a better word. They are who they are because of what another Indian woman had said to Raven years before.

The bomb is about cleansing the planet; it is about the voice of another power. There are reasons why I see it that way, some of which are metaphysical. Well, for heaven's sake, all the Buddhists have always been praying for enlightenment, so why are they not thrilled about this bomb? It would be very enlightening. You get more light from those things than you could possibly get in any other way....

Uranium was first mined at Laguna, and the form it comes in is called yellowcake. The color of femaleness is yellow, and at Laguna a woman's face is painted yellow with some red spots when she dies, so that when she comes to Shipap, the Mother will know who she is and that she is respectful and respectable. So that is sitting in my head. Then the bomb is all of this light, and for me light means two things: it means colonization and genocide, and it also means "Turn on the light so I can see in the dark."

Since I think the planet is the Mother and the galaxy is the Grandmother, and since I think that nothing goes on here that She did not think of to begin with, then I am left with the question of why She would think of this. That's the question I am working on in those segments. I don't know what the answer is going to be, and neither do Allie and Raven. All they know is that they are supposed to be watching this thing. But certainly, one of the things I can see right now is that a bunch of complacent colonizers are threatened with the extinction that they have visited upon everyone else. And, I don't know—I have a tacky sense of humor—I enjoy it. I think it is very funny watching them racing around trying to stop their own ultimate extinction.

They haven't cared about ultimate extinction before. They have extinguished race after race after race, and all the species of animals who ever lived—right now 99 percent are extinct—and nobody cared. Now all of a sudden . . .

Eysturoy: But were they not created by the Mother, too?

Allen: Yes, they were created, and they have to leave. I mean, I figure that even privilege was created to create exactly *this* situation, but I am not really sure if we have to blow up. Sometimes I think, great, I can't think of a better way to get to Nirvana. I mean—think of it—instant vaporization; there couldn't be a more pleasant way to die. Fifteen minutes is all you've got; you don't have six months or three years, you know. Not only that, but you're instantly vaporized, turned into spirit. That's really something to think about. So maybe that's what She is doing; that's a neat way to do it . . .

Eysturoy: So you think there is a meaning behind it all, a pattern that we are just enacting?

Allen: We might find it very uncomfortable; I am sure that we don't want to go. But people don't like it too much when a mountain blows up and there is a volcano; they will have to get out of the way or perish. The Mother cares for us greatly, but not for us more than for herself. And the thing is, we don't know what time it is.

Eysturoy: You have talked a lot about the Mother, the Mother Earth, Grandmother Universe. What has being a mother meant to you?

Allen: I always thought that I would go on to the beach, become a beatnik and have a good time. But I had to feed the kids, and more importantly, I lived in a world that to my eyes was a real mess, and here I had brought these innocent people into it—it was my idea, after all, it wasn't their idea—so I was responsible. That meant I had to work, I had to write, and I had to teach, because I had to have some input into the situation that they would grow up in, and I think that their existence impelled me. They are also very bright and interesting people, so they themselves push me in all kinds of directions. And then there is the simple fact of knowing what being a mother means. Sometimes it means not being nice; sometimes it is not smelling sweet and baking cookies, and doing everything baby wants just because that's what baby wants.

It is like that in nature, and you have to think about the larger picture, the whole, and what's going on around you. It has allowed me to notice parts of Mother Earth that I didn't understand before, because I could just have said that mothers are terrible people, which people in America love to say, if-my-mother-hadn't-been-so-rotten-I-would-have-been-wonderful, you know. Some mothers really are dreadful, and that's part of it. Have you even seen birds function with babies? They are not nice. In a patriarchy, of course, we are supposed to think that we are better than the animals, but I don't think so; they seem to be pretty smart. But I had to notice all that, because I had to reconcile conflicts within myself; I wanted to be a good mother, but then I had to bring out what that means, had to think about it.

Eysturoy: So being a mother led you back to the earth and its mothering cycle?

Allen: Yes. And then, in fact, you become immortal; not because you have kids, but because you reclaim yourself for being. You close the circle.

Photo by Cynthia Farah

chapter nine
Mark Medoff
Interview by Nancy Gage

Mark Medoff was born in 1940 in Illinois. He obtained a B.A. degree from the University of Miami in 1962 and an M.A. from Stanford University in 1966. He has worked as a playwright, actor, and director. He was hired by New Mexico State University at Las Cruces in 1966 as an instructor, working his way to professor of English by 1979; he is also NMSU dramatist-in-residence and head of the drama department.

The Southwest provided a setting for his earliest plays, beginning with *Doing a Good One for the Red Man: A Red Farce* (1969), which was produced by the Dallas Theater Center. *The Wager* followed in 1972. His first national success, *When You Comin' Back, Red Ryder?* (1973), went Off-Off-Broadway where it was produced by the Circle Repertory Theater Company. Medoff renewed his relationship with the Dallas Theater Center with *Firekeeper*, another southwestern drama (1979). His most recognized play, *Children of a Lesser God*, the story of a love affair between a deaf woman and a hearing man, opened in Los Angeles in 1979 and went on to Broadway in 1980–81. It has been pointed out that the latter play is atypically optimistic for Medoff's works, which are often dark, satirical, and violent. *When You Comin' Back, Red Ryder?* and *Children of a Lesser God* have also been made into motion pictures. University of New Mexico teacher, playwright, and fiction writer Nancy Gage interviewed Medoff in Las Cruces in the spring of 1986.

Plays written and produced:

Doing a Good One for the Red Man, 1969.

The Wager, 1972.

When You Comin' Back, Red Ryder? 1973.

Firekeeper, 1979.

Children of a Lesser God, 1980.

The Heart Outright, 1985.

The Majestic Kid, 1986.

The Hands of Its Enemy, 1987.

The Homage that Follows, 1987.

Stumps, 1989.

Gage: How did you wind up in Las Cruces, New Mexico?

Medoff: I first came here by accident, when I accepted a teaching position here at New Mexico State. I actually thought I was going to what was—in the geographic morass of my mind—Utah. When I got here the first thing I saw were cows, and I was appalled. I spent the first few months after I graduated from Stanford University's graduate school looking for another job. I really didn't want to be here. I didn't want to be anywhere. Well, I wanted to be somewhere, but I didn't want to be teaching. I wanted to go to Europe and hang out and pretend to be Ernest Hemingway, I suppose. I came here because an old mentor of mine had taught here when he was a young man, and he said that the way to learn to be a writer is to go settle down somewhere where you can make a living and yet still have time to write, and the only way you're going to do that is to teach in a college. So I said, "Well, but it's too late in the year. There are no jobs. I'll wait for a year, and then I'll do it." And he said, "No, no, let me make a call." So I ended up here, but I went looking for other jobs during the summer, other than teaching jobs. Then my father pointed out to me that I had really made a verbal commitment to come here for at least a year, so I should honor it. So it's now twenty years later.

The first couple of years I was here, I was not at home, and though anybody who's ever read my work knows that I have a large hangup with the West and the mythology of the West, I still wanted to get out of here, yet each spring, when I would prepare my letter of resignation, I would retract it. It took me three years, literally, to decide that the reason that I was retracting it was because in my heart I really wanted to be here. I like it here. And I wanted to become a small-town Western type, though I had grown up in Miami Beach, Florida, and lived most of my life in cosmopolitan areas. But I yearned in some Jungian way for something out of the past I couldn't even define: another life, a part of the collective unconscious that has to do with areas like this.

Gage: Was it here that you started writing plays?

Medoff: Yes. Actually I started sort of by accident, when some of the first people I met were involved in the Las Cruces community theatre, and they also taught in the English Department. And they said to me *a la* Mickey Rooney and Judy Garland one day, "Why don't you write a play, and we'll do it?" At the time I was writing prose, and I happened to have a short story I was working on that was really nothing but dialogue, and I decided to turn it into a play, and that was the first play I wrote. It was a play called *The Wager,* which was then a long one-act play, and eight years later it would open in New York in three acts. And I've been writing plays since, so the area has had a great deal to do in terms of feeding me spiritually.

Gage: And that's the reason you continue to stay?

Medoff: The reason I stay here now has to do with the loyalty that I receive from the university and the support I receive from people in Las Cruces and El Paso for the work I do here in the theatre. I feel very at home here. I think it's a wonderful place to raise children. There's still a civility among people here that you don't find a lot of other places. So it's that combination of things that keeps me here.

People always ask me if I feel that I've suffered any by virtue of not being in New York or Los Angeles, and in certain ways living here is an inconvenience because of the traveling I have to do. If I were living in one or the other of the larger theatre centers, I would be aligned constantly with the theatre, and I would not have the hassles of always having to find some place to do my work every time out. But, on balance, I would much rather live here.

Gage: So Las Cruces is home.

Medoff: As I've said, one of the reasons I stay is because of the loyalty the university and the community have shown me. I'm a big believer in loyalty. It's one of the few things you can believe in. And I have to have some place to do my work the first time. So here I have an audience that is anxious to see my new work, that likes to see my new work done here first and to feel a part of it, and to feel like they own a piece of it. And I like that feeling from them in return.

Also, we're trying to develop an undergraduate theatre program. We have an enormous amount of support in the community, and we've been trying to develop a resident professional company to work with the undergraduate program for three or four years, and it's been very successful. We have a subscription base of 2,600. We generate a lot of our own money, including forty grants from local businesses. We have a big following, both in Las Cruces and El Paso. Our audience defines itself more and more each year and gets larger every year. We have grand designs for a professional theatre company that will serve these two communities, and I think they hope that we can succeed. And that's exciting.

Gage: So your support comes from El Paso as well as from Las Cruces.

Medoff: Oh, yeah. More and more support from El Paso. The west side of El Paso is forty minutes away, and most of the people who live on the west side are very willing to come up here, and a lot of them even say they like it. When I talk about doing the season up here and down there, they say—many of them—"don't bother. We'd just as soon drive up there." But if we're ever going to really reach the whole population of El Paso, we're going to have to start working down there for part of the season.

Gage: Speaking of the season, how do you choose which plays to do?

Medoff: We always do one new play by somebody of some repute. We do my stuff when it's ready. We try to do one classic play a year, a Christmas play of some sort, and usually three pieces that just turn us on. And we do a children's play, and I try always to make it a new play, a play that is brand new, sometimes written by someone who's here working. We do a new play festival of student plays. We do quite a bit of work with the students in our other theatre. We're very busy. We figured out once that for the last eight years we've been averaging sixteen productions a year. And every year we say we're going to do a little less, but we don't.

Gage: Do people send you tons of scripts?

Medoff: We get quite a few here. I've gotten so busy now that I can't even read them. I have a couple of other people, though, who do read anything we get and critique it, because I think it's important that they get that human response from somebody.

Gage: Do students come here from all over because you're here?

Medoff: Yes, but the biggest problem we have as a state university is that there's no out-of-state tuition waiver for scholarships, and it's a big, big problem. And we're never going to have a great big department, a great big deal, until we can do something about that. We still get most of our students from New Mexico, but we're getting better and better students. And we're getting more and more students and doing more and more with them.

Gage: Has your association with the professional theatre affected your work with the university theatre?

Medoff: We always have at least one resident professional person in every show, and I think most of the students agree that it's a terrific experience working with these people who have achieved to some degree what they aspire to. And though on the one hand people say, "Well, you're taking away a good role that a student could play," I tell them the students learn as much or more by working next to somebody. Also, just from an economic point of view, the truth of the matter is that if I did not attract professionals here and thereby attract a larger audience than most university programs generate, we wouldn't have three-fourths of the people on the staff we have now because we wouldn't have the money to hire them.

Gage: Your ability to attract students and professionals alike, plus your growing fame, must make you something of a celebrity. Is that a problem for you here in Las Cruces?

Medoff: Nah. People here are so nice. And I never think of myself as a celebrity. I think of myself as a very successful writer, and I know that as a playwright I'm well-known. But I don't think of myself as a celebrity. I've hung around with Robert Redford for a period of time, and *that's* celebrity, and that crazy-making, that's scary, that's a real lack of privacy. And what I am to the world is teeny-tiny compared to that kind of problem.

Gage: Well, the world doesn't appreciate writers as it does actors.

Medoff: That's definitely true, but I don't mind that so much. I don't know that I'd want to have the kind of visibility that someone like Hemingway had, or Truman Capote had, because then you've got to be two people. You have to be a facade that goes out in public, and then you have to be the person who stays home and does the work.

Gage: Do you associate with other playwrights?

Medoff: Not at all. I don't associate with any of the so-called show-biz crowd. My wife and I would much rather be with each other and with our kids than anybody else, and it's not at all a negative comment about people we know. It's just that we know that the kids will be gone soon, we enjoy each other's company, and just would prefer to be insulated inside the family. In fact, I'd say the greatest problem I have in running a theatre and being even a small public figure is I have a great deal of difficulty being around people as much as I have to.

Gage: Do you keep up with what other playwrights are doing?

Medoff: I don't really like going to see what other playwrights are doing, to tell you the truth. In a way I don't care. In another way, I don't really want to know because I just want to do what I need to do and write it the way I need to write it. If I'm in a realistic period, fine; it doesn't matter if everybody else is in their absurdist period. I'd much rather read a book or go to a movie, to tell you the truth.

Gage: What about your own plays? Do you enjoy going to productions of them by other theatres?

Medoff: I can for awhile after a play is released, and then I get to a point where I can't stand them anymore. And though I don't like seeing bad productions of my work, I will three or four times a year accept invitations to go places where they are working on my work and spend some time with them because I'm a teacher involved with university theatre. And though I often find the production is below what I would like it to be qualitatively, I still feel like there's an agreement that a playwright makes with the world that if the work is popular, you can't say who can do it and who can't do it.

Gage: Do you feel the same about reviewers?

Medoff: It would be nice if there were no critics, if there were a way to have the arts without critics of the arts. But that's also part of the game, and though I get upset when I get bad notices and I want to do physical damage to the people who write them, I know that's part of the game. And whereas it used to take me weeks to get over any kind of rejection of my work, I can do it inside twenty-four hours now.

Gage: But critics come after the fact. Let's go to the other end. How do you approach writing a play?

Medoff: It's like athletic competition. I've been an athlete all my life, and for many years I was a brutal competitor. I liked to get in a room or on a tennis court, whatever, with one person and just try to beat the crap out of him. But I realized not too many years ago that throughout life I also played team sports, and that I also loved them, and that the thing I loved about them was that collaborative, familial business. And that's what I like about the theatre, which combines those two things.

I like competition. There's practically nothing I like better than someone challenging me to do something and to do it in a time frame. I like to be up against the clock. I like to be under pressure. It just seems to be a natural part of the process. I rewrite constantly. I rewrite on my feet in rehearsal. I take everyone's suggestions with me, think about them, pick out the good ones, go home and make them my own, and come back the next day with new material. I will do that right through the opening of a play, and I usually do two or three productions of a play—sometimes more—before I let it go. And it's always a different script. It's never the same script. I'm always working on them.

Gage: When you are working on a play, are you single-minded, or do you ever work on several things at once?

Medoff: I always work on several things at once. I'm working on *The Heart Outright* now; I'm working on a movie for Goldie Hawn based on Betty Rollins's book *Last Wish*; just finished an adaptation of a film based on a book called *Clara's Heart*, and a movie called *Off Beat* that's in the theaters right now. I have one called *Apology* that'll be an HBO premiere this summer. *Children of a Lesser God* will be out in October, and another one called *Man on Fire*, on which I share screen credit, is getting ready to shoot.

Gage: Have you found that the awards that you've won over your career have helped your work or your confidence?

Medoff: They're good for my ego. I think the most important thing that happened really was the success of *Red Ryder* because that was really the *imprimatur* of success. So when *Children* was a ten-times bigger success commercially and critically, that really didn't make a whole lot of difference to my ego because I felt very good about myself from the time that *Red Ryder* was successful and very confident about my work. But it's always nice to be stroked. I would much rather be stroked than pummeled. But I think that by the time you get any such judgment of your work, you're on to something else.

Gage: And what you're on to right now is *The Heart Outright*, in which you bring back several characters from *When You Comin' Back, Red Ryder?* What made you decide to do this?

Medoff: I was in Africa a couple of years ago. My wife and I were trying to escape telephones and the bustle of our very nice lives; but still to get away from it all, we went to Kenya on a photo safari and hung out with the animals for a couple of weeks. And I found myself thinking about Stephen and Angel. They just took up residence in my head again and wanted me to write about what happened to them afterward, so I did. And at that time it was actually ten years after I had done the play in New York. I thought it was a nice time space, a decade. People change so much from their late teens to their late twenties. And I started thinking about it, and I started writing notes, and things just started happening as they always do. It started to gestate, and over a two-year period, I wrote these two pieces as an evening.

The first part of the play is a monologue that is Stephen on stage by himself at age twenty-seven, eight years later. And the second part of the play is a four-character play with Stephen, Angel, Stephen's stepfather, who is referred to in *When You Comin' Back, Red Ryder?* but does not appear, and then a fourth character who ties it all together. We talk about Teddy, and if people happen to know *Red Ryder*, then they'll know him in one way, and if they don't, I don't think it matters. It still has to do with a traumatic moment in life. We all have traumatic moments that we carry with us like heavy baggage, and at some point we try to deal with it, or at some time we have the opportunity to deal with it. And in this case they have this one opportunity to deal with it, and he doesn't want to, and she does, although the play is about a lot more than that particular moment. But it is that moment that haunts them, as moments that we share with people do haunt us, and especially if we thought our behavior was bad, that we could have behaved differently or better.

Gage: Do you find that you have other characters that stay with you and want to come back on-stage?

Medoff: I think in different ways all writers recreate characters that they like or are obsessed with. There are very specific characters I have in my head. There is a character in *The Wager* whose brother is the main male character in *Children of a Lesser God*, and in my head there's a whole family cycle of plays that I will probably get around to at some point.

Gage: How have your characters changed over the years?

Medoff: For the first seven, eight years that I was writing successfully as a playwright, I was repeating the same kind of male protagonist. But when I was writing *Children of a Lesser God*, Gordon Davidson, who was directing out at the Mark Taper, kept urging me to work on the woman, make her bigger, make her fuller, make her equal. And I felt that it was time and that I should just have to guts to do that, and I did, and my life changed both as a human being and as a writer. And now I'm in a period where I think I'm writing very good women's roles. In fact, one of my staff paid me the great compliment some weeks ago of saying she thought I now wrote better women than I wrote men, which I thought was quite remarkable.

Gage: What do you do when you run into trouble with a character or a play? Do you ever just quit?

Medoff: I had a play in New York—third play I had in New York—ran sixteen days, something like that, and it had a ferocious power about it. I think it was maybe the most powerful thing I ever wrote, and yet I could not make it accessible to an audience. And I tried it over and over, and in fact just this last year I did a long intermissionless version of it. And I went to see that, and I realized that I was never going to make it work. And then, rather than releasing it, I said no. And I'll never release it probably. No one will ever see it. And I did a play at the Dallas Theater Center some years ago that I thought had some real interesting possibilities, a real classical kind of "well-made play" about the tri-cultures of this area that I really wanted to deal with. And I went back to it again and realized I did it just about as well as I was going to do it in 1978 or '79, whatever it was, and I just kind of forgot it, but I won't release it. So it's another play that will never see the light of day. A lot of people must let go of anything; when they're finished, they go out into the world. I just decided that at this point I don't want to do that. If I'm not really comfortable with them, if I don't feel like I've completed them, however imperfectly, I'll just let them die.

Gage: Have you been doing a lot of screenwriting?

Medoff: Yup. Doing more and more screenwriting.

Gage: Adapting your own plays? Or original screenplays?

Medoff: Well, I adapted *Red Ryder.* I'm having to share screen credit on the movie of *Children of a Lesser God* because they took it away from me and cut out a whole hunk of what I wanted it to be about, what the play was about. They cut all the politics out of it. And so they threw me in a closet and stopped speaking. So anyway, I'm sharing screen credit on that, but those are the only two plays I've been involved in adapting. The rest are original screenplays or based on books.

Gage: Losing your autonomy with *Children of a Lesser God* must have been a frustrating experience.

Medoff: Yeah. That's the major difference between writing for the theatre and writing for a film. In the theatre a writer has ultimate control of his destiny, and nobody can do anything without his permission. In film, you're a hired hand, and you're very well paid, so you have to look at yourself as a high-class hooker. Maybe not high-class, just high-priced. And in selling yourself to these people, you do the work, and they have the right then to do to the product whatever they want to. On many movies you'll notice that the screenplay is by so-and-so *and* so-and-so. You can be sure that almost inevitably so-and-so and so-and-so have never met and certainly did not work together. And that doesn't mean that there weren't two or three other writers who were brought in to work a little bit on this section or polish that section or maybe look at it with a fresh eye and do some editing. And in that sense it's a very, very ugly and demeaning business. For me to be sharing screen credit on *Children of a Lesser God* is about the most embarrassing thing that's happened to me in many, many years. Because they took my baby away from me. It's preposterous, but they paid me enormously well to do so. And then someone came in and hacked a limb off the baby. So it's sort a two-legged, one-armed baby to my mind, however good it may appear to be as a movie.

Gage: Do you still write fiction?

Medoff: Not really. Actually I would like to write a book. I have a couple of books in my head. I have a book that I started years ago, and in fact just yesterday pulled it out again. I suddenly got the urge to do it again, work on it again. I usually want to write fiction as soon as I'm through doing a new play because I'm so sick of being around other people that I can't stand it. And I think that I can never go through that again, and then, of course, within a matter of a month or two I've forgotten what the agony was like, and I'm ready to go and do another play. But I really would like to unencumber myself of almost everything for a couple of years and go write a book, all by myself, not talk to anybody, except my wife and children, and go to the gym. I think I could do that.

Gage: How has your approach to playwriting changed over the years?

Medoff: The big change in my work from the time I wrote *Red Ryder*, say, to what I'm writing today is that when I was in my thirties, I was very cynical, very cynical, and feeling very nihilistic about the world, and felt that what I really wanted to do was bring the audiences into the theatre and punish them—for their humanness. And what happened with *Children of a Lesser God* is that I not only got in touch with the female side of myself and started writing good women, but I began to realize through life with my children and my wife that, though the world is very inhospitable and I want to continue to write the most dramatic material I can conceive, within the realm of that inhospitable world, I want to find something positive to say for my children's sake. And so the work I'm doing now is quite different in its tone than the work I was doing then. And though I put people through hell in everything I write—I try to—I have much greater affection for their humanness and therefore try to come with them to a more positive end. And I know I'm doing that for my children.

Photo by Cynthia Farah

chapter ten
John Nichols
Interview by Phyllis Thompson

Born in 1940 in New York state, John Nichols graduated from Hamilton College in 1962. He wrote a highly successful first novel, *The Sterile Cuckoo*, in 1965, followed with another, *The Wizard of Loneliness*, in 1966, and left the East soon afterward. After a period of rambling and working at odd jobs, which included blues singer in Greenwich Village, firefighter in the Chiricahua Mountains of Arizona, and dishwasher in Hartford, Connecticut, he settled in Taos, New Mexico, where he has lived the last eighteen years. His political and personal concerns seem to have fused there, "For Taos," he says, "is locked in a life and death struggle to survive in some kind of healthy and balanced manner." Not only has he worked relentlessly for progressive causes in his adopted state, he has chronicled the political and social development of Taos in three artistically lush and beautiful New Mexico novels: *The Milagro Beanfield War* (1974), *The Magic Journey* (1978), and *The Nirvana Blues* (1981). He has also written several nonfiction works about the land and the struggle to save it. Two of his novels have been made into movies: *The Sterile Cuckoo* (1969) and *The Milagro Beanfield War* (1987). Recently he completed a Vietnam era novel that again breaks with conventional expectation, *American Blood* (1987). That is the work Nichols is most concerned with in this interview. With him is his wife Juanita, whom he married in 1985. The interviewer, poet and teacher Phyllis Thompson, credits Juanita Nichols, then Juanita Dow, with first having brought her to New Mexico.

Selected Bibliography:

The Sterile Cuckoo, novel (New York: McKay, 1965).

The Wizard of Loneliness, novel (New York: Putnam, 1966).

The Milagro Beanfield War, novel (New York: Holt Rinhehart, 1974).

The Magic Journey, novel (New York: Holt Rinehart, 1978).

If Mountains Die, long essay (New York: Knopf, 1979).

The Nirvana Blues, novel (New York: Holt Rinehart, 1981).

The Last Beautiful Days of Autumn, nonfiction (New York: Holt Rinehart, 1982).

American Blood, novel (New York: Henry Holt, 1987).

Thompson: Well, I want to get you to talk about your novel *American Blood.* I was really moved by it.

John Nichols: Oh, a woman who used to work for the newspaper came up to me today and handed me this little sheet they're calling "The Chamisaville Times," pulling it out of *Milagro* and *Magic Journey.* Here's a quote from it: "Was it William Blake or John Nichols who said, 'Desire fuels the Universe?'" Then they have a review of *American Blood.* And it's the most insulting review of the book that I've ever read.

Thompson: Insulting?

John Nichols: Yeah. Listen to this:

> *I hate January. What gets me through it is working shorter hours, drinking warm Ovaltine, hiding under an electric blanket, and eating buttered popcorn. Sometimes shock therapy is the only thing that will get me moving.*
> *That must be why I picked up* American Blood *by John Nichols. Have you read it? My guess is you have not. Most people have been putting it off. Perhaps they're waiting for a warm sunny day because they reason they'll be better able to cope. If they're like me they'll pick it up on the coldest, darkest day, adding insult to injury, daring Nichols to move them toward the light.*
> *Ostensibly the plot centers around a real subhero type who returns from Vietnam and proceeds to inflict or fantasize inflicting the horrors and atrocities of the war on the women he meets. Nichols' premise is that war is somebody's orgasm on a cosmic scale, so it follows that atrocities in war lead to atrocities in sexual behavior. These don't end when the war does. In the hands of a less exuberant writer, this story could plumb the subtle regions of profound human experience. But Nichols is not concerned with depth and subtlety. He wants redemption. The reader wants rhetoric relief, but that's another issue. This is why the madonna prostitute rears her pretty li'l head. It's like, if you pummel a few breasts you can fondle them later and make*

up for everything. In fact, see, women absorb hate and anger through their vaginas as the earth absorbs oil spills and leaks from toxic dump sites. Then after a suitable period of shock or mourning or whatever, women will forgive and forget, kiss and make up. Where is Medusa when we need her? It's because, see, women and the earth want it all along. In a world without God, this is the best hope we've got.

Well, I don't buy Nichols' jism-speak. Let him swallow it. He just ain't convincin'. Funk for the saucy wench behind the soda fountain, her halo crooked but her nipples hard.

[People] dumped all over me when I did an ecology thing. I gave a speech on ecology and how we were destroying the earth. I read from Barry Commoner, *The Closing Circle*. . . . Anyway, they got all upset because I read political stuff instead of being humorous. So there's *The Chamisaville Times* review of *American Blood*.

Thompson: Well, I really like it best of your books so far. It's got truth. It's what happens to men when they go to war. They come back screwed up in a serious way.

John Nichols: To a large degree the book has been cast in the mold of a Vietnam veteran novel, which is real distressing to me. Theoretically the premise of the novel is that the war is not in Vietnam, the war is at home. That it's within the culture, that those defects, those emotional, sado-sexual, cruel, discompassionate, confused, chauvinistic, mad, violence-oriented genes are basically forged in the crucible of U.S. culture, society and history, and I chose Vietnam as the handiest, largest, and most easily recognized metaphor for a society that bases not only its foreign policy but its opulence, its greed, on the foundation of this kind of anger, frustration, violence. Basically, to live like we do, you gotta commit genocide on somebody. We not only do it to people in the third world, but in our own country—we do it to minorities, we do it to women. Chauvinism is simply racism against women. Chauvinism and racism are tools of a class society to maintain class divisions for economic reasons.

Thompson: It's in the character of America, and it's inside your hero's character. I was moved by how he coped with all of it. In persisting in the love of that woman, he chose something completely other than himself or his earlier values. He learned that the only way to get that love he wanted was to let it be, let it go free. He changed. At the end of the book, the resolution you gave is the only possible answer. It made me weep.

John Nichols: I think of it as a hopeful book. But people who read it think of it as real gory.

Thompson: When your hero was sitting out in the car waiting, and he didn't go in—that thoughtful time, like a necessary meditation—he needed that before going in and finding out what had happened. I thought that ultimately what he did was to forgive. Not just shrug his shoulders. It was a positive act.

John Nichols: It's a real positive political act simply to choose to survive, to choose not to wreak the kind of revenge that will destroy your world forever. To somehow work your way through all the horrors and all the struggles and decide to have hope and compassion and to try and be loving.

Thompson: Has anybody said about that last moment, that last day that it's like Hardy? Fated?

John Nichols: No. First of all, 80 percent of the reviews of the book were fairly negative, what you call "mixed." It triggered an awful lot of hostility. But I like to think that one reason it did is that there's nothing very romantic or palatable about the violence.

I once had a little book of portraits of people who had been maimed in World War I—just head shots of people who had their faces blown apart but had lived. So you were looking at these faces with huge caverns. You could see into the skull, with eye sockets that were empty, with noses that were gone, with mouths that had no bottom jaw. You could only look at two or three of those portraits before you were nauseous and had to put the book away. There was nothing artistic about it. It was just straight-on shots. After looking at that I could never imagine anybody ever going to war. Or considering that it could be in any way glamorous or heroic. I hope that *American Blood* is awful in that way, that it makes violence unpalatable. Which also means people can't stomach it, if the book works, right?

Twenty or thirty years from now I may look back and say, "Boy, I really blew that"—But that really doesn't worry me. All I can do from this perspective is to make a guess as to what works and what doesn't. It's like *Moby Dick*, this totally unreadable book. I believe Herman Melville sold only 100 copies in his lifetime and thought he was a total failure. Then it develops into one of the classics of English literature. People really had to work to get to the point where they could consider it a special thing. They also gotta work for *Finnegan's Wake*.

Thompson: So, Juanita, what did you think of *American Blood?*

Juanita Nichols: I found it very upsetting. I read an earlier version, not the published one. And this is when we're first married, so that we're making love every five minutes, romping in the yard, and suddenly he'll go, "Excuse me, I'm going to go and do horror now." He'll go into his little office. Later, I'm sitting on the edge of the tub and he gives me the book and the water's coming up and I'm reading this horrible thing. And he comes in, opens the door, and he goes, "Oh, dear. I'll leave you alone," and backs out.

Often I think there's something so abstract about the way we live. So when we deal with something like *American Blood,* or when somebody talks about environment in ways that are real direct, we're just not used to dealing with it, even when we think we are. It's so hard to incorporate desperate truths. We want them filtered in some way that's easier. As John and I were walking on the road just now, we were talking about distancing everything. You know, how we make fashion out of war. You can go to Banana Republic, and wear something quite fashionable that looks like battle fatigues.

So when you deal with anyone who, instead of entertaining you in a book or a lecture, switches it into something directly relevant, there's no place to move. I think that's why *American Blood* is so uncomfortable. I just sit there and squirm when I read it. There's no place to shift.

Thompson: Yes, so how do people read the book then?

John Nichols: A problem with real life and the conscience of art is that it's hard to merge the two. It's hard to walk into the ghetto and see these kids living in bombed-out houses, or go into Latin America and take a look at twenty-eight out of every thousand kids who are dying of diarrhea—it's hard to artistically transcribe the horrors that exist on the globe. Who causes them? Well, the United States is one of the biggest causal agents in the world, because we demand so much. A lot of the energy we consume is human lives, our own and other people's.

But when you try and transpose that outrage through an artistic medium, it's difficult to figure out how to do it. The instinct is just to say "Up against the wall," and rub people's faces in it. But if you rub too deeply, they're going to rebel or just walk away from it, when you want and need them to sympathize with your perceptions.

There are rules to drama, to emotional proselytizing. It's been a long time since I've written anything I didn't consider to be propaganda. I feel that all art is propaganda, and that's an unpopular idea in a capitalist nation when the shibboleth is that art and politics don't mix. But the fact is that everything artistic is political.

On the one hand I admire people where every sentence seems crafted—Scott Fitzgerald—in this exquisite sort of aesthetic crucible, you know. And I admire William Burroughs and John Rechy where it's just insane, undisciplined, raw, brutal.

I worked with Costa-Gavras for four or five years trying to put together a couple of films about nuclear war and human survival in the nuclear age. The problem of making a film about nuclear physics in the twentieth century, about the arms race and about waiting for the nuclear holocaust, is how to get the human imagination to imagine something that is basically so horrible it's unimaginable. To imagine it in a vivid enough way that people will be moved and will put energy into trying to avoid it. If you make it too palatable or too diverting, too "artistic," people can ignore it. If you make it too horrible, they can't watch it.

Sitting in these little screening rooms just looking at hour after hour of documentary footage of the aftermath of Hiroshima and Nagasaki, you can't watch it, but you *have* to watch it. Doctors with forceps going to pick a little scab off the face of a kid, and they pluck the scab and half their body flesh comes off with their cheek all the way down to their ankle. Now, anybody in the United States who is in favor of Ronald Reagan's nuclear policies ought to have to sit in little screening rooms—240 million people once a week—and watch the documentary footage of Hiroshima, a little teeny weeny atomic bomb that didn't hurt very many people, and be forced to watch this before they have a fucking debate about whether or not to build this missile or the Pershing 2's or whatnot. One problem with art is you gotta get it into the theatre. But you can't get real life Hiroshima to play in a theatre.

And that's the problem with *American Blood*. I've got so much anger. I want to write something that will move people, that will trouble their conscience, that will make them feel guilty, and at the same time that will move in all those realms that become another spark of energy pushing the world to turn out this good way instead of that bad way. It's always an educational process.

Of course, we all like entertainment. I like Steve Martin being stupid on Saturday Night Live. We all oughta laugh, right? But he's not trying to teach us how the world should be run.

Thompson: Oh, yes he is. That's exactly what he does try to do. That's why I respect him so much. He's saying something which matters. Did you see "Pennies from Heaven?"

John Nichols: I'm always quoting this from Nelson Algren's *Chicago: City on the Make*. When Jean Paul Sartre asked "What is literature?" Algren answered him: "I submit that literature is made upon any occasion that a challenge is put to the ruling apparatus by a conscience in touch with humanity." Or how about Heinrich Heine? Here's another quote I'm always giving people: "A poet should have on his casket not a wreath but a pistol to show that he was a faithful private in the liberation struggles of humanity." I like that. I think the definition of the artist is basically as a political person. That's why in many countries, if you're a poet, you spend half of your life an exile. Because your art puts a challenge to your country, against the inequities.

Juanita Nichols: But we don't see poets as leaders. Yet in other countries . . .

John Nichols: In other countries of the world, somebody gets to be president, it turns out they're a fine poet. Whether they're Ho Chi Minh, Mao Tse'tung or . . .

Thompson: Gene McCarthy.

Juanita Nichols: Zip, zip.

Thompson: What you just said reminds me of a question I asked Henry Roth last week about James Joyce and his influence. I asked Henry why he said, "Joyce is my master," and Henry answered in political terms, not literary. That Joyce had turned his back on what had brought him into being, in leaving Ireland and in choosing exile. Henry said, "That's what I did also. I turned my back on Judaism. I chose something quite different." I tried to get him back to the question about *literary* influence, but he talked about choosing exile as Joyce had done. That's a *political* answer. That's interesting to me. I don't think that way. I think in what I loosely call religious terms, not political, though I do engage in political action.

John Nichols: How can you separate it?

Thompson: I guess I can't.

John Nichols: To me political means everything that happens on the earth.

Thompson: To me, that's religious.

John Nichols: Religion is extraordinarily political, whether it's liberation theology, or the reactionary philosophy of the Vatican, or whether it's simply looking upon all living things as sacred.

Thompson: To me, the practical problem is not so much aesthetic distance as simply time-lapse between what the artist creates and what gets out there to work in the world. So many years intervene. I used to demonstrate with Maxine Kingston on the Pali Highway, all alone out there with signs against the draft or the war. And long after the war was over, her book came out, and there was a chapter on the brother who went to Vietnam. It was art, but the only so-called immediate action we could take, we had taken out there on the highway.

John Nichols: That was the point of *American Blood*. That Vietnam started when the first pilgrim landed at Plymouth Rock, not in 1954 or 1965. And we're not out of it yet. We're never out of it. Every day you wake up and you pick up your newspaper and there's four Linda Lee Daniels that got raped and murdered here in Albuquerque. There's fifteen people that got killed in auto accidents. The United States is funding contras, and funding people in El Salvador. Phyllis, the reason that your daughter in South Korea is looking at another dictator being elected over there is that the United States has maintained dictatorships in Korea ever since the end of World War II as part of our world-wide economic imperialism.

The tragedy of the Vietnamese War is that a lot of people looked at it as an aberration of an otherwise benevolent democratic foreign policy. But there have been hundreds of Vietnams before . . . and after.

This is not to say that history all over the globe hasn't been a pretty brutal experience. But the fact is we in the United States have been more successful at it than anyone else, so that we bear the most enormous responsibility. We only have 6 percent of the world's population, and yet we consume 50 percent of the world's resources, and we create 70 percent of the world's solid waste. So whether or not the planet survives, including most of the exploited people in three-quarters of the countries on earth, depends basically on how the United States goes. When the last U.S. soldier left Vietnam in 1973, we still had a million and a half troops in our army, mainly stationed in foreign countries, from Chile to West Germany. We've got thirty thousand troops in South Korea since 1953 keeping the dictators in power. They're there because of us, *our* economic desires.

Thompson: But what happens with the artist, when you know you've got a gift, you have some kind of power in your hands to do something, and yet, what is so hard to recognize is that what you can do is no more than anybody else can do. Even if you can write it, and get it published, and people can read it, it's gonna go slow. I'm saying there's a distance between the history and the work of art which comes out of that history.

John Nichols: A lot of people panic because change doesn't happen fast enough. We're in a culture that is into instant gratification, including its revolutionaries and its artists, who want to have an effect *now*, who want to be recognized *now*. But history is long. Things don't happen overnight. If you consider yourself a serious artist and/or a serious revolutionary, you don't worry. The world has been in real trouble before. Things have been horrible. You just keep working at it. . . .

We live in a very racist, reactionary country and culture. But always keep in your mind it's a real cop-out to get cynical, because we live in a country that encourages that. In fact, some of the most venerated art is the art of despair, the art of the antihero, the art of cynicism: "It's impossible to make it better so let's all eat, drink, and be merry, for tomorrow we die."

Juanita Nichols: As Freeman Dyson said, "Anger is creative; depression is useless."

John Nichols: I always quote Marge Piercy, "Despair is the worst betrayal. . . . To believe at last that the enemy will prevail."

Juanita Nichols: Colin [her son] is going through this now. He's a psychology major. He's trying to find a little route to life, something beyond what he's getting in the classroom, to find those intelligent conversations, even to become a psychologist . . .

John Nichols: Colin has got a problem if he's got a conscience. If he starts to understand the nature of the exploitations within the culture, he's going to have a hard time reconciling his education with actually getting a job. A professional psychologist in this country is trained to help people resolve their problems so they can function within this society. Very rarely will a shrink sit there with you and say, "You know, this *society* is nuts." No. Most often they simply try to teach people how to function as lunatics in a lunatic society.

Thompson: My son John was going through the same thing when he was trying to get into medical school. The question was, considering all of this, do I really *want* to be a doctor? It's hard.

John Nichols: It's hard to be an ethical doctor. It's hard to be a good, ethical lawyer. It's hard for somebody who gets a law degree and ends up working as the public defender or in legal aid for the rest of their lives. They think, "I'm entitled to forty thousand dollars a year." But to get that they get out there and propagate total injustice. George Jackson gets one year to life for a seventy-two dollar gas station holdup, but Richard Nixon's friend C. Arnholt Smith only gets his hand slapped for embezzling ninety-two million dollars.

Thompson: This is America. What did you expect?

John Nichols: "Love it or leave it," Phyllis.

Thompson: Well, the fact is I really do love it.

John Nichols: So do I. When you're born, bred, and raised here. . . . But it's not how much you love it that counts. Sometimes, it's how much you hate it.

Juanita Nichols: You mean, how much you care.

John Nichols: Yes.

Thompson: It's so beautiful. Driving up today . . .

Juanita Nichols: Every day it's like this. Talk about a microcosm. Yet it's also like a crazy script. For example, John called me at the gallery the other day. I was talking about that to four people who were totally suicidal, and he says, "Well, my friend Isabel called just now and I had to run over to her little ranch and be a midwife . . ."

John Nichols: She'd had a goat that had had two kids, but a third one was dead inside, with the legs sticking out, and she had to take it to the vet, and her truck was stuck in the snow . . .

So I go over to her house, and it takes forty-five minutes to get the truck unstuck, pulling it with my truck, just about ruining my clutch. I keep telling her, "Isabel! Put it in first."

Juanita Nichols: This is a woman in her seventies.

John Nichols: And her boyfriend, Carl, is in his seventies or eighties, he's limping around, ragged jacket, and sneakers on in the snow. And I go back to check— this is a woman who's been driving for twenty-nine years—and I say, "Isabel, you're putting it in second." But she says, "No, that's where Mr. Vigil [her former husband] always put it." And I say, "Well, let me try it. See, it says right here on the handle, first is way up here." And I go Baroom! Baroom! and the shifting stick goes up and hits the dashboard almost. It's probably the first time that gear's been used in twenty-nine years! And then the truck goes right out of the snow. So next I'm dealing with the goat, and it's enormous. I can't lift it by myself, I do it with Carl, and we get it on the slab, and we dump the goat into a wheelbarrow, and I push the wheelbarrow while Carl tries to hold it on the wheelbarrow, and we get it on the truck. Carl tries to pull up the front legs, and I try to lift the whole rear end, and I step into the wheelbarrow to get better leverage, and as soon as I get the goat out, the wheelbarrow slips, and I fall with the goat on top of me, and Carl almost gets yanked out of the truck! So I jump up and *fling* this goat into the bed of the truck finally, a superhuman effort.

Then Isabel has to take off and go to the vet, who has just been attacked by a German Shepherd and had his thumb crushed, and he'll be in a cast for six weeks.

So the vet can barely walk, and he'll take anybody who'll come in, because as soon as people hear a vet can't perform operations or do stuff like that, man, they go elsewhere. And the vet's broke inside of two weeks. So that's the difference between Albuquerque and Taos. Albuquerque is a city. You're much more anonymous—not so intimately involved in the lives of your neighbors . . .

How hard it is when you get typecast. I know that years ago I got so mad that when anybody said "John Nichols is the author of *The Sterile Cuckoo*," I wanted to hit them. I got thoroughly sick of being identified by that book. *Now* I'm so sick of being the author of *Milagro*. I finished that in 1973. You move on.

Thompson: Well, there's a world out there expecting one kind of success. But probably there are other people out there you're picking up that would have liked *The Sterile Cuckoo*.

John Nichols: Well, maybe. But it's hard in the arts. You know, you work thirty years and finally do something that gets a bit of approbation, but then you seek to move on and it turns out that nobody's interested again. Well, tough beans! When I published *American Blood*, I realized I was in for a lickin', but so what. If you get affected by what society wants, then you're weak in an area where you need to be strong. An awful lot of good or great work is often at odds with the society that spawned it.

Photo by Cynthia Farah

chapter eleven
Pat Mora
Interview by Tey Diana Rebolledo

Pat Mora was born on January 19, 1942 in El Paso, Texas. She has a B.A. and an M.A. in English from the University of Texas, El Paso and has served as assistant to the president and director of the El Paso Centennial Museum at the University of Texas, El Paso. She is the author of two books of poetry, *Chants* (1984) and *Borders* (1986), is finishing a new manuscript, *Journeys*, and is also working on a children's book on Tomás Rivera. She was interviewed by Tey Diana Rebolledo of the University of New Mexico in El Paso, Texas, in the fall of 1987.

Selected Bibliography:

Chants, poetry (Houston: Arte Publico Press, 1984).

Borders, poetry (Houston: Arte Publico Press, 1986).

Rebolledo: Tell me a little about yourself and your family.

Mora: I'm from El Paso, where my mother was also born. My dad was born in Chihuahua, and moved here when he was two years old, so he really doesn't have very many memories of that. Both my parents grew up in homes where no one spoke English, and my mother loves to tell the story that her mother said the only reason my mother learned it was so she could fight with the kids at school.

Rebolledo: Were they teaching English in school?

Mora: They learned it the hard way. My mom always says, "I learned English in self-defense." She says she doesn't really know how she did it (she went on to be very active in speech tournaments in high school), because no one in her family could have really given her any assistance or even understood what she was saying.

Rebolledo: Tell me about your mother's family.

Mora: My mother's maiden name was Delgado. Her dad had been a circuit judge in Mexico, had married and moved to Juárez and was a lawyer there. At the time of the revolution he was told he'd better get his three daughters out of town, and so the aunt I write about so much, my beloved Lobo, was in this flat bed truck that came across the river. My friend Oscar Martínez has her description of that in his book about the border.

Rebolledo: So Lobo was your mother's sister?

Mora: She was my mother's half-sister. When my grandfather moved here, he married a woman who was considerably younger and had three more children. So my mother grew up with this set of half-sisters with very strong traditions. But Lobo never married and lived with us. She is the one who became almost like a grandmother to me.

So while my mother accepted the fact that we loved her so much, in part she remembered her almost like a witch, this person who could be obsessed on Sunday with cleaning. To the end of her life, my beloved aunt, would, on her hands and knees, clean the room in her boarding house.

My dad came from a very different kind of family. I think they had less of a tradition of education. My father's father was a tailor, who had worked at the time of the war doing tailoring for Fort Bliss. My father is one of those amazing people who has worked as far back as he can remember and always manages to be positive. He has trouble understanding how anybody could be unhappy in their work, because he believes you do the best job you can.

Rebolledo: Did you know your grandparents on your father's side?

Mora: I have a vague recollection of my grandfather and I've got one tiny little poem, the only poem in Spanish about him. I have this memory of putting my hands up and dancing with him, you know. I did know my dad's mother, whom I would characterize as a classic weeper. She wept on every occasion possible. We were closer to my mother's side of the family. My mother's mother lived with us, so I really lived with two older women who were very much a part of my life.

Rebolledo: What did your dad do?

Mora: My dad was in the optical business and started his own optical company when we were little. It supported us very well. Through a lot of work and sacrifice he put us through Catholic school, which you know wasn't easy. He would leave for work at seven in the morning and sometimes get back at ten or eleven at night. Then when a lot of the big optical conglomerates began to take over, about the time I was in college, he lost his business and went to work for American Optical. About twenty years ago they moved to Santa Monica where he worked for an opthalmologist and a couple of years ago, in his seventies, he opened his own business because he still didn't want to retire.

Rebolledo: Are your parents still together?

Mora: They are still together, probably to the amazement of their children and to each other, as they could not be more different.

Rebolledo: What do you remember about your growing up years? What things do you think were important to you as a child?

Mora: Well, it's very important for me to please. I really have to fight against that, usually unsuccessfully . . . I just finished Denise Levertov's second book of essays. She has been a political activist her whole life as well as a poet, and she refers to the fact that when she has to make a choice of going to a meeting or giving a reading, she realizes that the real issue is, "Am I willing to displease people?" I think that is a pressure for me. I dislike displeasing people. My favorite role is being a facilitator: that's my day-to-day work.

Rebolledo: A lot of Chicano poets and writers say they feel they are translating all the time. You have a lot of poems that deal with shifting back and forth from one culture to another. Are you constantly in your life translating, shifting?

Mora: I would have to think about that. My first reaction to the question is that I am not convinced that it is bad.

Rebolledo: No, no. I think it's a positive thing myself.

Mora: Those of us who have had certain opportunities through flukes of fate, the opportunity to spend time reading, to spend more time looking, to spend more time traveling—why shouldn't we feel a sense of responsibility and a sense of pleasure if we can translate certain things for people who have not had those opportunities? One of my opportunities is being Chicana or Mexican American, you know, and I feel that it's a wonderful thing to be.

Rebolledo: The reason I ask this question is because I am writing about myth. Of course one of our big myths is Malinche, which is really seen as a negative stereotype. I wonder why we focus on that myth in particular, when we have so many examples of people who translate and are seen as psychics or as people of great knowledge; people who are able to capture, as you do with your *curandera*, all the secrets of nature. So I wonder why we are always looking toward Malinche as betrayer, rather than the *curandera* as the person who has that wisdom.

Mora: I think that a lot of what we are as a group is a result of the sixties movement; you know, the tremors are still being felt. Many times the translator or facilitator can be viewed as a sellout. That's where I think the negative comes in. But I just finished reading a book about Pima ethnobotany and I was really, really struck by the idea of healing with all kinds of desert plants, or cactus, and then applying it to the part of the body that was sick. You know, they would boil the nopal and place it on the woman's breast to encourage the milk to flow. Well, to me that is incredible, and some of us have the chance to maybe listen a little bit closer to the ground, and then if you come back up, why wouldn't you share it?

Rebolledo: Many of my students who read your poems say, "Wow is this woman strong! She knows exactly where she is and she is so secure in herself. She knows who she is and is not afraid to state it."

Mora: Well, I do think my previous description was of my daytime self. During the day I very much like to do people work. But I see that as a very different side of me than the person who sits alone to write. I think people who always expect you to be always the same person are just being naive.

Rebolledo: That is pretty much what they used to say about the Mexican writer Rosario Castellanos, because she was always *la mujer mexicana bien vestida,* you know, with her make-up on perfectly, very well dressed and she would appear in public like this, a woman who was immaculately groomed, very prim and proper; yet she wrote poetry that was so discordant with her public image, because it was coming from an interior part of herself, that people would say, "This woman couldn't have written that poem."

Mora: I am far more private than people think. When my first book came out, I showed it to a friend I work with and he glanced at the book, looked at me and said, "You didn't write this."

Rebolledo: I remember you told me that story. But generally men respond to your writing almost as much as women do. I have had students weep over your poems; I have had students say, "She is really striking a chord." How do you manage to do that? What is it about your writing, do you think, that has penetrated so deeply into our own sense of ourselves as Chicanos?

Mora: I am totally surprised by your comments! I don't know, I try to listen, you know. I would say my overall reaction to most of what I do, usually, is dissatisfaction . . .

Rebolledo: You're unhappy about the poems you have written?

Mora: There is so much more I wish I could do. I don't know whether this is an excuse or not. I always blame time as a factor. I think writing is like anything else. If you have time to really polish and improve, you gain the courage to experiment. I think it's very hard to have the courage to experiment, but I think that you always can be more inventive. Now poetry is not going to affect some people, but what I really love to do is to have people sort of gasp a little bit; poets who can do that are the ones I love. I can be reading them on a plane and I just go back in my seat . . .

Rebolledo: You do that quite often in your poems as well . . .

Mora: I think you're a little biased.

Rebolledo: Do you think you're a regional writer? I am not using the word *regional* in a pejorative sense. Do you feel you are able to capture a certain segment of the region in your writing?

Mora: I would like to think so. The whole sense of audience is always a difficult one and I have argued that minority writers have more trouble with it than nonminority writers. When I talk to nonminority writers they will say, "Well, you really shouldn't be thinking about any other audience than yourself, you know, write for the inner voices." While I understand that, on the other hand

I think if you look at minority writers in this country, they *do* have a clear sense of audience. Yet I realize that one of the myths is to think that there is such a thing as *a* Chicano audience, or *a* Chicano community. One of the things that I have to have the courage to do is to write the best I can at a particular time. There are going to be some people who like it and some people who may say, "Well, she is stuck with writing about the desert; she is stuck writing about the Southwest." It's a tension . . .

Rebolledo: A lot of your poems come from stories that you've heard, right? I know once you told me that you get stories from people who come from the country in Mexico, women who come in from the villages, and you are fascinated by all that . . . and obviously in those stories if you are not capturing necessarily the idea of region, still something of that comes across just in the tale, in the content of the tale.

Mora: Right, but I do think that for the third collection, if it goes the way I would like, there are going to be big sections that deal with other countries, because I have done some traveling I would not have expected to do, and I see it as important that our perspective not be limited. In other words, how we might view women in Pakistan or wherever should be of interest.

Rebolledo: And yet the Southwest has been so strong in your two previous collections *Chants* and *Borders* . . .

Mora: Well, I don't think that I would probably ever have a collection where it wouldn't be, because I've spent forty-five years of my life here, but I think it's good for me to record what I see or what I hear, wherever I go.

Rebolledo: When did you start writing? Have you been writing all your life; were you a child prodigy at age four?

Mora: No, I'd say I've always loved words. I was always a reader.

Rebolledo: What did you read when you were a kid? Nancy Drew?

Mora: I read Nancy Drew, the entire Pollyanna series, the entire *Little House on the Prairie* series, before it was famous. I loved libraries, although I did not see a Chicano or Chicana working in our library until I was a parent; it was very much an Anglo world. I loved writing in school; it came pretty easily to me. In Catholic school, when you graduated from eighth grade they had this special graduation ceremony and a mass and all. My parents gave me a typewriter and some really pretty stationery—I can remember the stationery to this day—and I came home and went through a long serious religious phase in my life. I spent my whole youth planning to be a nun.

Rebolledo: I did too.

Mora: Did you?

Rebolledo: Yes, I thought we all did. (Laughter)

Mora: So I came home and typed up all these very religious poems on my new typewriter, and they rhymed and all. Later when I went back to try writing I got very interested in children's books.

Rebolledo: How old were you then?

Mora: About twenty-four. In fact the first money I ever got for writing was from Hallmark Cards. They sent me a hundred dollars for a children's book I did.

Rebolledo: Was it ever published?

Mora: No . . . and again it was all rhyming. I was very intrigued by repetition then . . . I would say that was one thing. Again it was very private, nobody knew about it and it just stopped completely. Then, when I went through my divorce and I realized I was edging toward forty, I said to myself, it's now or never. If you're not going to be serious about writing it's never going to happen.

Rebolledo: But you'd been writing all this time?

Mora: No, I really had not, I was a good letter writer!

Rebolledo: You started writing again as a result of your divorce and you put feelings from that . . .

Mora: So a lot of it was the stuff that most people have to go through, you know.

Rebolledo: What a great title for a book.

Mora: What?

Rebolledo: Edging toward forty. It could be the title of your autobiography, right?

Mora: That's a good one, Diana . . . you get the credit. It was hard at the beginning. I have had many more rejections than people would ever think.

Rebolledo: Why poetry? It seems to be a trend with many Chicana writers that they begin writing poems and then go to short stories and then to a novel. Are you going to do that?

Mora: I would say poetry is pure pleasure, and I love playing with language, but I am aware that there are a lot of people who are discouraged by poetry itself, so I am exploring other genres—in part because of that, in part because I think it's good for me. I have a children's manuscript I have been working on about Tomás Rivera. I am working on a collection of essays as a way for me to describe trips that I take, and am trying to combine that with speeches I have given. I would like to have a book of personal essays. *Life* magazine used to have a woman who did personal essays and that was one of my dreams. I wanted to grow up and be able to do that. Now I really have much less interest in the slick magazine world, maybe because I think we are bombarded by information.

Rebolledo: When Gary Soto was at the University of New Mexico recently, somebody asked him, "Why poetry and why narrative?" He said it was easier to write short stories; for him writing poetry was the really hard thing to do, because words had to be carefully chosen; and that he felt that he could write a novel or a short story and it didn't have to be perfect . . . do you feel that?

Mora: I think the difference for me is that many times I think prose is cumbersome, there's so much of it, so heavy, to me there's so much to manipulate. I might start out with an idea and I find myself drawn back to poetry. I don't know if that's because of the time factor. I have ideas for short stories I would like to explore because I don't think they would work in a poem. There is particular pleasure for me in poetry, there's just no doubt about that, but I see children's books as very close to that. I have very strong feelings that Chicano kids need good children's books, well illustrated, from big publishing houses, and that is something I would really like to work at.

Rebolledo: Pat, in your poetry you've created a lot of strong women who become "mythic." You have Doña Luz and you have the *curandera*, you have this kind of woman who is enjoying her own sense of sexuality, and the really strong women connected to the landscape. Where is that coming from?

Mora: I am almost startled by the strong women I meet. In other words I see it as reality. I think that we just do not take the time to look at the strength of the women around us. Yesterday for example I happened to be getting a hair cut. The woman who was doing my hair has raised four children, works all day on her feet, goes home and fixes dinner. She had one daughter who is getting married, so she's involved with repainting the house and all and she says, "You know, we're thinking of adopting a baby." Well I just about fell off the seat, because I am thinking that finally another one is moving out of the house. I said, "You're thinking of adopting a baby?" And she says, "Yes, why give the money to the government when we could give it to some little child?" I think we are surrounded by that kind of bravery, that we're just too busy in this country to really savor that at all.

Rebolledo: What does your family think about your writing?

Mora: My children find it a great source of amusement, and if there's anything that keeps me humble . . . I'll say, "Well, here's an article that came out about Mom, do you want to glance at it?" and they will immediately do a full parody of the article, throw themselves on the bed just howling in laughter, or they will say, "I can write one of my mom's poems, I can write one," and they will take a cadence that they may have heard. Now I think that the oldest one, because he is older, takes it more seriously; I think he's pleased about it. But I think that since one of the things that poetry does is to reveal a lot, children have very mixed feelings about their parents revealing that much; so I think most of their lives they will view my writing out of the corner of their eyes, because they won't want to know too much about that more personal side of me.

Rebolledo: What about your mother? What does she feel about your writing?

Mora: I think she's proud of it. My parents are very supportive and if it makes me happy then they think it's good. If I wrote and said "My writing is driving me crazy and I am not going to do it any more," they would say, "Well, that's fine dear, you don't have to do it any more. . . ." I consider myself an advocate rather than an activist, but in my family I'm at the left, way at the left.

Rebolledo: *I* thought you were pretty radical. (Laughter) If you were doing this interview as the interviewer, what questions would you like to have explored?

Mora: Well, I've never been asked many questions about revision. I think that's an aspect of writing that may seem dull, but I agree with the notion that the process is a big part of the pleasure. If you're talking about craft, if you're talking about tightening and tightening and getting every word to do a job, that's where revision comes in.

I have a good time when I do a first draft of a poem. I am a mutterer, so I will read it out loud. Then I put it aside for awhile and I might come back in an hour or two and begin to cross out a word, or a slew of words. Maybe by the next day I may reorder; maybe the first part goes and the whole poem begins to move up. I think that the whole process is a very interesting one to the writer, though maybe not exactly what you call headline material. If we are thinking about students, if they're serious about being writers, whatever job they are going into, they should test themselves by seeing if they enjoy the revision process. It's just like being a cook: if you like the dessert when it's finished but you really didn't enjoy putting it together very much, you're not going to be one of those people who says, "I just love to cook."

Rebolledo: What is your favorite poem?

Mora: I tend to judge my poetry a lot. I love poetry readings because I really love the response of the audiences, so what I think of right away are the poems I know audiences like . . .

Rebolledo: Yes, but that's not the question I am asking you. I know which of your poems the audiences like, too, and, of course, being a teacher I use that. I want to know which poems *you* like.

Mora: Well, some I like are probably a bit otherworldly, like "Bride" or "Luna, Luna." It's very hard for an audience in a group setting to be able to fly away with you a bit, which is what it takes.

Rebolledo: One of my favorite poems, as you know, is "1910." Of course I like that poem because it shows that we were not good Catholic girls all the time, that we have a little vengeance in our hearts, and perhaps that's necessary for our survival. I am very admiring of that character who has a capacity not to be a victim, not to be passive.

Mora: Well, I read that at almost every reading.

Rebolledo: I know, I do too. (Laughter)

Mora: OK, I do think audiences like that one. You never know why you write one better than another one.

One of the big arguments I am having with myself right now is the last poem in *Chants,* a poem the audiences like a lot, "Illegal Alien." Some of my critical friends have said to me, "Well, you know, Pat, I am not convinced that's a poem." That's where you get into that fine line; I try not to have a message, when I start out, I really do. If I have a message then I say to myself "That's great, but that's not a poem." I like to begin with an idea, a line, an image and see where it goes. But I am stubborn enough that a lot of my deep feelings are obviously going to come in, because of the way I see the world.

I think one of my big reasons for writing poetry is to help people feel less lonely; that's what poetry did for me. You know, I was able to read women writers and feel less lonely, and so any time my poetry does that for somebody, that is probably my definition of success. But I think a real interesting question is why poetry doesn't communicate as much today.

Rebolledo: I think we have lost the knack of working at things we want. We want to be able to understand everything instantly; we want the computer to run a million megaseconds and spit out all the calculations to us. I really feel we don't take the time to sit down and think about better language as we should.

Mora: And I think our goal is entertainment, you know. Well, I would say it's visual entertainment that we are about. We are about very concrete images, while poetry does require work. I think you are exactly right that the whole notion of poetry really goes against what our society points to.

Rebolledo: But if we are going to survive as a society, we really need to maintain the ability to work our brains in that way; otherwise we might as well sell out to computers, and computers will never be able to write poetry.

Mora: What I respect in Denise Levertov is not only her craft as a poet and her very steady commitment to poetry throughout her life; I also respect her very strong stand, as evidenced by her first book of essays *The Poet and the World*. Contemporary American poets often are removed from the bulk of the population. I think Denise has always argued for the role of the poet as taking what she would call an *appropriate* place—just because you happen to write poetry doesn't mean that you shouldn't have a conscience and shouldn't participate in the world you live in. It doesn't mean you are some kind of special creature. You know, Pablo Neruda has a poem about the fisherman singing and he has his place, it's his work.

Rebolledo: Are there any male writers who have influenced you?

Mora: I derive a special solace, there is no doubt about it, from women writers. And so, when I sit with their books, it is a different kind of psychological experience for me. However, I am, for example, trying to work through a book by William Carlos Williams again. I think it's important to try to learn where you can. But I know when I'm looking at what books to buy I am drawn to books written by women.

Rebolledo: If I were to use the word "space" or "spaces" to you, what would you respond? What's the image that comes to your mind?

Mora: Well, first it's positive. That probably has to do with the fact that I've grown up where there's tremendous space—the desert to me has a lot of space. Another thing is that I have been economically fortunate; I have never lived in small cramped quarters. To me it implies room, usually quiet because if you have space you can get away from people. So it implies both the room and the quiet—to be alone. And another thought that comes to my mind is internal space.

Rebolledo: Then how would you speak about public spaces versus private?

Mora: Private space is going to include internal space and the home.

Rebolledo: Is that Spanish or English? Not necessarily in language but . . .

Mora: I don't know. I walk around with this image of this internal space, and in fact I've got a poem that will be in the new book called "The Old Crone," about the old crone that lived inside this space and I'm trying to change her. (Laughter)

Rebolledo: Gabriela Mistral was always trying to change her old crones too, and kill them off, and she never could.

Mora: Never could?

Rebolledo: You know why? Because the old crones were her more creative aspect. She's got some terrible poems in which she says, "I killed this one off"—and she talks about all the things in this one way, this one . . .

Mora: Voice?

Rebolledo: And you realize that when she kills it off, she kills off the stuff that was nonconformist. It's really sad.

Mora: But see, my old crone is the conformist. My old crone is the voice that says "Why aren't you home with your kids?" And I'm trying to encourage this nice motherly, all-accepting mother to move into that space. What do you mean by public space?

Rebolledo: Areas like schools, outside space. I don't know. I was hoping you would define it.

Mora: I am trying to get away from male military imagery. OK? I have been trying to find a good substitute for terms like battlegrounds, and I think as women we should probably do that. Public spaces to me involve conflict; that's because I live on the border. For those of us who are in policy making rooms at certain times, we're involved in certain decisions that affect a community; we're talking about a veiled conflict, about strategies. One of my real quarrels with the confrontational mode is that I think often people who are labeled moderates are people who realize that to win at this kind of conflict we have to have many strategies. I think we need all that. I'm very supportive of the confrontational mode; it's just not mine. I think you need all kinds of styles in order to produce change. Some people bring tension, other people resolve tension. But to me public space, almost all public space, is an area for conflict, it's just very carefully veiled. There's that tension and that jockeying that's taking place all the time.

Rebolledo: So then Doña Luz's burning down of Upton's Five and Ten is just one response to the conflict?

Mora: That's right.

Rebolledo: In your poems what would be the optimum resolution? Your poems are full of conflict, you know.

Mora: Um hum.

Rebolledo: Actually the poems are about borders and frontiers shifting back and forth, trying to find accommodation.

Mora: Probably there is no resolution. I don't know that we even want resolution. We could talk about occasional joy. I think occasional joy is related to having the courage to continue the search.

Rebolledo: Your poems often end with questions. If they are not explicit questions, they are implied questions, like what? or why? or when? Isn't that true?

Mora: Yes and I was going to say, maybe you can have momentary resolution in private. For example, a poem like "Spring," where you have a personal experience with the desert or with a person, and you achieve momentary peace. I don't think the border is that different from any other place, though I think conflict can be magnified; that's the interesting thing about borders. Once you return to the real world, then you are going to face conflict. And so I guess that's why I don't see resolution as even believable.

Rebolledo: You know the poem that spooks my students the most? It's the poem in which you talk about doing the spell on the lover. (Laughter) And it works so well you can't stand it and you are just trying to escape. And the students say, "That's what it would be like if you ever really achieved what it was you intensely desired and then you are stuck with it."

Mora: I have almost a fear of intensely desiring things. There is that kind of awareness deep down that although we like to wish, we are also afraid. Maybe we know that when we wish, we may be wrong. Maybe we wished for this and it limited us.

Photo by Rick Powers

chapter twelve
Linda Hogan
Interview by Patricia Clark Smith

Linda Hogan, Chickasaw poet, playwright, fiction and essay writer, was born in Denver, Colorado, in 1947 and spent most of her childhood in Colorado and southern Oklahoma. She received an M.A. in creative writing from the University of Colorado in 1978. In recent years she has taught at the University of Minnesota and is currently at the University of Colorado. She is widely published. A recent volume of poems, *Seeing through the Sun* (1985), won an American Book Award from the Before Columbus Foundation. She has published several other collections of poems and short fiction. She is also coeditor of *The Stories We Hold Secret*, a fiction anthology, and has a novel, *Mean Spirit*, forthcoming from Knopf. At the time of this interview, in June 1986, she was on leave from her teaching responsibilities, with grants from the National Endowment for the Arts (fiction) and the Minnesota State Arts Board. She spoke over the telephone from Minneapolis with Patricia Clark Smith.

Selected Bibliography:

Calling Myself Home, poetry (Greenfield Center: Greenfield Review Press, 1979).

Daughters, I Love You, poetry (Loretto Heights College: Research Center on Women, 1981).

Eclipse, poetry (Los Angeles: UCLA American Indian Studies Center, 1983).

Seeing through the Sun, poetry (Amherst: Massachusetts University Press, 1985).

That Horse, fiction (Acoma Pueblo: Pueblo of Acoma Press, 1985).

Coeditor, with Carol Bruchac and Judith McDaniel, *The Stories We Hold Secret* (Greenfield Center: Greenfield Review Press, 1985).

Savings, poetry (Minneapolis: Coffee House Press, 1988).

Smith: Linda, I know you were on the move a lot as a kid. What kind of a relationship did you have to Oklahoma, all that time?

Hogan: Well, most of my family is from Oklahoma; so when I was a girl, my grandparents lived there, and we went back and forth between there and Colorado.

Smith: But when your folks talked about going home, that meant Oklahoma?

Hogan: That's my father's family's home, um-hum.

Smith: So you had grandparents there, and you mention an uncle in the poem "Heritage," I guess—the one who carves?

Hogan: Yeah, that's my Uncle Wesley—he's the oldest brother of my father's generation. He went to Denver to work for the railroad and was one of the organizers of the White Buffalo Council, which was an Indian organization in Denver. It's interesting, because when I came here to Minneapolis, I was in touch with a woman from the Denver area, an Indian woman, whose mother worked with my uncle organizing that. Small world . . .

Smith: Was that an Indian rights group, or . . .

Hogan: No, it was to help people coming in on relocation from other parts of the country to be cared for, taken care of. Later, when I was young, my uncle would take me to powwows and things, and it sort of became a group that sponsored powwows and continued to help with housing issues. This was before Denver Native American United was formed and there were no help groups for native people coming into the Denver area except for the White Buffalo Council and the BIA.

Smith: So you were pretty close to him.

Hogan: Yeah.

Smith: And he did carve, like the person in the novel that's coming out, *The Grace of Wooden Birds?*

Hogan: Um-hum, that's a woman, Roberta, the main character, who carves birds. She has an uncle and he's a wood carver. I don't really—well, when I write, I sort of transform people. My characters are composites of many people. In "Amen," for instance, the main character is a combination of my grandfather and one of his brothers; and, after he read it, my father told me I had made a mistake anyway, because the reason my relative turned his head to one side was not really because he had trouble with his eye, but because he was deaf in one ear.

Smith: Oh, so he was just trying to get the good ear kind of pointed toward the sound?

Hogan: Yeah, but I liked the story the way it was; so I just left it that way, even with my misinformation. My dad loves me to stick to the facts, but I always think there are *other* facts involved, too . . .

Smith: Yeah, well, my folks are like that too; if it's not absolutely literal, and you've transposed characters, they get real upset. Were Wesley or any of those others on that side of the family storytellers—would you say you grew up in a storytelling tradition?

Hogan: Yeah, I did. My father's a storyteller, my Uncle Wesley was a storyteller, and my grandmother. My grandfather was not a storyteller. He was a very quiet man. What can I say? It's all part of that way of living, I think.

Smith: Um-hum. You know, you were saying the other day about your not particularly growing up as a reader, but it's probably so much more important that you were hearing stories.

Hogan: Yeah. Let me see, I've got something written down here about that—is it OK if I just read this? (Reads)

> As I grew up, education wasn't valued. We had different values from the dominant society, and I'm now seeing that the values of mid-America are difficult and painful ones—and are the source of dislocation and stress for people. I didn't read when I was young. I wasn't interested in literature, but I did listen to stories, and I still do. I listened carefully and acutely, and I heard what was behind words, and voices, as well as that which was spoken. Now I love to read poetry, phone books, playing cards, novels, newspapers, bathroom walls—there's a story in all of it. And I love poets who bring together poetry and life in all its motion—Neruda, Forche, Cardenal, Dugan, Bishop. Louise Edrich's book Love Medicine gave me a new way of understanding how fiction could work with values and commercial values—I think her book is really important in that respect, because it's a new direction for Indian writers. I think also how radical writers have tried very hard to do what she did—intending, for herself, just to write fiction—that is, telling the plain stories of people and their lives without pity, judgment, opinion, or romanticization. Jamaica Kinkaid's writing gave me a faster music for my own work. Audre Lorde has great strength, and I admire that. Paula Allen has uncanny perception and intellect. Joy Harjo has mystery. Meridel LeSueur has a sense of history and political commitment I admire. Tillie Olsen is incredible in those ways also, and I'm overwhelmed by her innate sense of form. I could list hundreds of people whose work has influenced me. I don't want to omit anyone because I learn from all of what I read and hear. And as Lame Deer said, we're surrounded by books. The stones are books, and we may read their stories. The trees are books with a story written in them. The water and land and each animal is a book, with a poem and story and song.

Smith: When I think about things that meant a lot to me very early on, there were particular trees, particular rocks, particular corners of the farm where I grew up that were—transcendent. Did your early landscapes work for you like that?

Hogan: Yeah, I think Oklahoma landscape is the most important for me. It still is. I really think that home is in the blood. I've been thinking a lot about Scott Momaday and genetic memory, and I'm not sure, but I do think there is such a thing.

When you look at the studies showing how people have gestures like a grandfather they never saw, because they were adopted out—how could it *not* happen? Because learning actually is a genetic, biochemical thing itself. Ever since we started talking about home, I've thought—what is home for a tree, for instance? Is it its mother tree? Or the place where it first began taking root, or the place where the tree is finally transplanted? I just think that *all* soil is home, maybe. And I just started to think, trees don't bother themselves with these silly questions we humans ask of ourselves. But my human history is Oklahoma.

My mother is from Nebraska, and I care very much for my mother, but I've never felt that home was Nebraska. Even though my mother's body was at one time my homeland, Nebraska is just not where I, in my own individuation, became defined in my own living and being. I think my connection to Oklahoma is maybe not even a birth connection; that doesn't seem to make sense. But my identity with family is there, with Chickasaw people and land, and maybe my idea of what a home is, is *there*, in south-central Oklahoma. I think also, this is where I was *loved*. I felt *loved* there, cared for, wanted. I kissed my cousins in the hay, and played spin-the-bottle. That's where I first got attacked by a tarantula, and fell apart, where I caught a blue racer snake, and a turtle. It was where I heard my own history, and stories, and gossip about other Chickasaw people. And I think Oklahoma was where magic lived for me, and still does, in the fireflies, and in the breezy motion of trees, and the stillness. And even though I've been so many places in my life, it still feels like home. I know, in my mind, that the air and earth and my body are all really home, but my *heart* home is there, in Chickasaw country.

Smith: You're reminding me of Joy Harjo's poem, "The Last Song," that "wet grass womb" . . .

Hogan: Yeah, that's true, she's located there, too.

Smith: And you know, the most amazing fireflies I ever saw were in Oklahoma.

Hogan: Yeah, I love fireflies. You should have seen them in Louisiana last month, they were great.

Smith: Mmmm. I think they like it wet and warm best of all. I miss them here; it's one of the things we don't have.

Hogan: I know. Wouldn't it be nice to just have everything in one place?

Smith: Yup.

Hogan: Minnesota in some ways would be ideal for me, if I could just bring all these things here, have a mountain outside, instead of an apartment building . . .

Smith: I would settle for an ocean and fireflies.

Hogan: Yeah, an ocean would be real nice too—I want all of those!

Smith: Was there a particular family place in Oklahoma you'd go back to, then?

Hogan: Yeah, it's called Gene Autry, Oklahoma.

Smith: Yes! What's that town like?

Hogan: It's not really a town. It's outside of Ardmore, and Gene Autry is kind of a post office. My Aunt Patsy used to be the postmistress in Gene Autry. You know, when I first heard Eudora Welty's story, "Why I Live at the PO," I just sort of flipped out, because I used to think my Aunt Patsy lived at the post office. I was a student at the University of Colorado when I first heard that story on a tape, and I got really excited and interrupted the whole class to talk about my Aunt Patsy, which I realize now is *not* the thing to do in an academic environment.

Smith: Did Gene Autry actually live there?

Hogan: Well, it used to be called Lou. I had a great aunt, and the town was originally named after her. Later it was called Burwyn. It had been a boom town at one time.

Smith: For oil?

Hogan: I think it was the railroad that created a lot of business. I've seen pictures of it back in the old days, when there were a lot of people, a lot of streets. But now there's nothing much there. Then Gene Autry bought a ranch outside the town, and so they changed the name to Gene Autry, and it remains that now.

Smith: And yet this is a heavily Indian community, right?

Hogan: Well, Tishomingo, the Chickasaw capitol, is near there, and Mannsville is a large Chickasaw Indian community. The Burwyn High School is still there, and that's where all my relatives on my father's side went to school.

Smith: Did you grow up listening to the Gene Autry radio program or going to western movies when you were a kid?

Hogan: There wasn't any electricity.

Smith: Which kept you from that particular irony. Were you conscious of who Autry was?

Hogan: No. I never heard of Gene Autry until I was older. I never even really knew that was the name of the town. My grandparents lived outside of Gene Autry, and that was just where my grandfather would have to go to get water for drinking and cooking and bathing and things. So I didn't recall hearing it actually called by name; that was just where you'd go to get water.

Smith: Did your grandfather ranch, or farm?

Hogan: He did, before he lost his allotment land.

Smith: What's the story about losing that?

Hogan: Well, my family was one of the Chickasaw families that were foreclosed upon during the thirties by the government, by the banks, and who lost everything else in bank closings; they were taken advantage of by loans, just as is happening now, and has also been happening in this part of the country [the Upper Midwest] for some time. For Indian people, you could almost say it was another death, another destruction of Indian people, or a step toward that—the people being hungry, and having the banks come out and offer to loan them money—and, at that time, people were desperate. And they would of course take the money, because you had to survive for the *now,* and they were all unable to pay back, and they lost their land, and that's the history of land loss among that particular Chickasaw and Choctaw people. That's why it is a landless tribe. There is no reservation, and I really know of no one who still has their original allotment.

Smith: When you were growing up, were you conscious of the land your family had lost, and where it is?

Hogan: Yes, I sure was. The Ardmore airport, in Ardmore, Oklahoma—that was my family's ranch land.

Smith: Wow . . .

Hogan: I know what it looked like. It had hills, and it had ponds, and there was a little lake, and a lot of trees. And now it's just paved-over airport, but now the airport's closed down, and they're drilling oil.

Smith: So now it's kind of at the third stage of removal . . .

Hogan: My family even showed me where the pastures were.

Smith: Astonishing. You did some time on a Tribal Historical fellowship?

Hogan: Yeah.

Smith: Did you work with some of that allotment history?

Hogan: No, I didn't do that then. I was just looking at oral history, oral literature, looking at materials that had to do with healing tradition, although I didn't know that originally, but that's what I ended up doing.

Smith: And the healing tradition has stayed real important to you, I guess.

Hogan: Yes.

Smith: How were people making their living in your family after they lost the land?

Hogan: My grandmother sold eggs in town, and my grandfather worked as a janitor at the church.

Smith: Your poem "Heritage" ends: "From my family I have learned the secrets/ of never having a home." You don't go into a lot of detail in that one, certainly, about the history of deprivation and guilt, but . . .

Hogan: Well, you know, it's a very difficult subject; one of the problems of coming out of a poverty situation in this country—and this is true for a lot of non-Indian people as well—is that we live under a dominant culture that blames victims. The real truth is that to come from that kind of a background means you have no self-esteem, and you think it's your own fault that you're living hungry and in poverty. It's very difficult for people to talk about that. When I talk about how my own family lived, it is seen, even by my own family, as an insult. These things should not be spoken because it is telling a story of pain that makes the people feel that they themselves look bad. That's not the *truth*, but it's hard to let that be understood. You know I've thought a lot about radical writers in this country, like Meridel LeSueur and Tillie Olsen, who are educated either through universities, or their own reading, and whose lives teach us that ability to have access to books, to people. In some ways, city working class is really different from the rural poor, who have no access, no options, and are not going to be, very often, the energy of a movement. It's a great difference, a real split. If any of those radical writers had appeared in *those* communities, they would probably just have been shot.

Smith: It's always struck me about your work and yourself that whatever place you're writing about, or out of, the connection with natural life is strong. There isn't always a particular rooted landscape in your work, but life is always manifesting itself, in a cat lost by a highway, or a particular stalk of yarrow, some wild plant. Not just in the work, but in the ways you actually spend your time, you've stayed very much in connection with wildlife. You're working now in a wildlife rescue clinic. Can you talk a little about that?

Hogan: Oh my goodness, if you get me started, you'll just have to listen to this! Yeah, it's a wildlife rescue clinic here at the vet school on the St. Paul campus. There's a separate raptor clinic for eagles, owls—birds of prey—that's very well funded, but the clinic where I work has very little funding. Even the food's often donated by those of us who work there. We get all the nonraptor wildlife—sometimes unusual animals. We had a beaver with a head injury, who'd fallen down a twelve-foot embankment. And very plain animals, too, like ducks and geese and snowy egrets, cormorants and blue herons. In the springtime there's a lot of orphans, baby rabbits and such, who need a lot of care. It's very important for me to do this work; I consider caretaking the basic work of living on earth. I've often thought about how one of the things that was probably necessary for the woman's movement—the dominant culture woman's movement—was to break free of the duty of being a caretaker. . . . But then, for women to *return* to being caretakers, because it's important to offer service to the living, and to the planet. I find many women now who are returning to the idea of being a caretaker, of nourishing as one of the primary roles of *both* men and women. I see a direct relation between how we care for the animal-people and the plants and insects and land and water, and how we care for each other, and for ourselves. Part of our work here is to care for life.

Smith: And what you're saying, I guess, is you can't *limit* that care to just your family and friends, to just the human creatures you love who come your way—you have to widen that.

Hogan: Yeah, it has to be widened. If you look at the book *Call to Consciousness* for instance, a community is not just us—our nuclear family, or the Indian community, or a "University community," as they say here—but the community of all living creatures.

Smith: Sometimes it strikes me as ironic that when people come up with images for the need to extend the caretaking, it comes in space-alien movies like E.T.

Hogan: Yes. And yet *he* becomes the caretaker there. What I loved about that movie is that it's strictly a religious movie. The being comes from up above and is injured in the descent, and then becomes the superior being who teaches the people, and who is persecuted, much as Jesus was persecuted, and has healing abilities. You know, how his finger lights up and he can touch the wound and make it well? And people on earth are not ready for that. I think it was such a successful movie because it fulfilled people's needs for spirituality, and—I'm just gonna go off on my spiel now; you've had it! I think a lot about "the American way"—you know, we, all American peoples, believe in hierarchies. Even the colonized peoples often believe more in the American Dream than middle class white Americans.

Smith: Oh, God, yes.

Hogan: And there's a hierarchy of respect, according to title. Often I hear people from working-class backgrounds talk about how somebody should be a good person because they went to college. There's no direct correlation, but there's a *sense* that people have certain superior traits if they've gone up the ladder.

Smith: Or that they acquire them in the climb.

Hogan: And we have a hierarchy of politics, of economics, and even of the spirit, of religion. And animal-people—well, animals are considered to be a lower class, with humans at the top of the hierarchy, and *disembodied* humans—spirits—they're even higher, higher than those who have matter as their chief substance. The more a sense of *wildness* things have, the more lower-class they are.

Smith: Yeah. All those bad words that are associated with animals, like "He's a pig," or "She's a real dog" . . .

Hogan: That's right! And women! That's another interesting thing, that women and Indians are often equated with animals, in ways that have negative connotations for all three. Animal words evoke stereotypes, often erotic stereotypes, for all three, and allow for the perpetuation of violence on all three.

Smith: And underline the horror people seem to have of the physical . . .

Hogan: . . . and of the body, of all matter. Matter is *not* our primary concern in this country, or in Western thinking.

Smith: There's that whole split, people being unable to conceive of matter as spiritual, or invested with spirit. I just taught a whole American Lit survey around those themes, using just the classics . . .

Hogan: Great. I'd love to see your notes.

Smith: Well, the kids got really excited. I used a lot of books that deal with women or people of color and connect them with that lower hierarchy, and wilderness. They're all closer to the devil, and to things like sex that frighten those writers terribly. There's this one Hawthorne story, "The Birthmark" . . .

Hogan: Right, I remember that.

Smith: The scientist guy is trying to get rid of the birthmark on his wife's face, which I swear to God is a menstrual thing—it's red, and it comes and goes . . .

Hogan: . . . and it comes every three weeks, and she gets cramps when it arrives?

Smith: Well, it comes when she gets emotional. And the scientist has this black servant, Aminadab, whom he calls "Thou thing of earth," and he *needs* him, but he clearly sees him as far below himself, and the things that are going on there, linking wife and servant and earth, are just amazing. I think Hawthorne knew pretty well what he was doing there.

Hogan: You know, one other thing about the way animals are seen—I want to talk about coinage, American coins, and how the means of exchange has to do with death, and extinction, that at times when there's genocide being perpetrated against Native American people, the face of the Indian appears on the coin . . .

Smith: Yeah, and the buffalo.

Hogan: And the eagle. I mentioned this to a friend last night, and *she* said, yeah, and John F. Kennedy too. It's like what is gone becomes the means of exchange. Which is literally true, because people have exchanged valuable land for this abstraction called money . . .

Smith: Which is dirty.

Hogan: Well, not so much that it's dirty, as that it's not what it means; what the money stands for is no longer there.

Smith: Yeah. I didn't mean *I* thought it was dirty, but I remember that from very early, your parents saying don't put that in your mouth, it's *dirty* . . .

Hogan: Oh, because people touched it with their physical hands, and *germs* get transmitted that way . . . One of the things I find really interesting about the Midwest is the concept of cleanliness people have out here, and how women will *not* sit down on toilet seats, so in all the bathrooms I go in, the seats are covered with urine . . .

Smith: Because people stand up . . .

Hogan: Yeah, and it's not *true* that you can pass on germs that way, but what you are transmitting is a lot of urine to other people's backsides . . .

Smith: Is this the first time you've lived in the Midwest, this job at the University of Minnesota?

Hogan: Yes, um-hum. And it's just been shocking.

Smith: Is that partly just being in a city, as well as being in the Midwest?

Hogan: Yeah, it probably is. Just a combination of things. I find I don't really know a lot about this place, because I haven't had time. You lose time in the city; you do not have time any longer. Interesting, when you think how this is a place where time is so marked by seasons. But, living here, time changes. It's just like Einstein's Theory of Relativity. Time *does* different things here than in the Southwest. People don't seem to develop friendly relationships here as easily, because there's no leisurely time for being together, as human beings. And I don't know the history of the Dakotah, Ojibway, Chippewah people here as well as I know the history of other tribes . . . I haven't had *time*.

And there's other things. The racism here—it's kind of like Gallup, in some ways. The divisions between the color of people are very sharp. And the racism here seems primarily focused toward the Indian people. At the same time that Minneapolis prides itself on being liberal, radical, progressive, it romanticizes Indian people, as Jimmie Durham says, "to death." It's hard to teach here, in Indian Studies, because of the combination of spiritual, romantic, destructive stereotypes. From my experiences living in different American Indian communities around the country, what happens is that our living out the crises of America, as we have had to do, does not always leave us with an especially strong identity. It's very easy to get caught up in the stereotypes projected on us by non-Indian people, and to get so caught up is to lose totally. But it's very difficult *not* to be. This is not a gentle place; this is a hard place for Indian people. The people here are not tender people, as people have more of an opportunity to be in other regions of the country.

Smith: So, partly, for you it's been a matter of expending extra energy fighting off the stereotype, and that's hard—like fighting off the guilt of the victim . . .

Hogan: Yeah. And, even as an educator, I don't want to spend all my time educating other people about *everything*. I've realized that I have many choices I must make, as a person who is now having health problems. I have had to consider—do I really want to educate people about the fact that I'm an Indian woman? A person, now, with a chronic illness? And have *that* be my living, my work, too?

I was thinking about a short story today. You know, many people here will come up to me and tell me how they are reincarnated Indians . . .

Smith: Oh, yes. Princesses, usually, no?

Hogan: Yeah, and they always come from big tribes with a lot of stereotypes attached to them—Navajo, or Sioux, but never *Hunkpapa* Sioux—and I wanted to make a short story about this young white woman who comes up to this old Indian woman, who's the narrator's mother, and tells her she's a reincarnated member of this certain tribe, and the old woman looks her in the eye and says, "Yes, and I'm Yassir Arafat." So the title to the story would be, "My Mother Is Yassir Arafat."

Smith: Great! When Paula Allen was still living out here, and the Don Juan books and the whole concept of the Wise Old Indian Man who's the possessor of many secrets sitting out there some place in the desert started to get real popular, we always talked about writing a series of books about a Wise Old Anglo Man.

Hogan: Yeah. Another thing I find interesting is the rejection of Anglo old people, and the *total* romantic acceptance of Indian old people. The rejection of white culture by white people. White religions aren't "good," you know? In my classes, Indian spirituality is *where it's at,* as they say.

Smith: Um-hum. What made me feel comfortable when I lived in the Midwest, I think, was *where* we lived—this little town, Decorah, Iowa, where there was so much consciousness of Norwegian heritage and pride in it, and paradoxically that made it easier for an outsider, because people really did accept and value themselves, valued Lutheranism and Norwegian immigrant culture.

Hogan: Yeah. They *need* to do that.

Smith: But you know, it's not just American Indian stuff that gets popular. It's OK to be *India* Indian too.

Hogan: Or anything.

Smith: Yeah, any culture that was colonized and taken over, including the Celtic. There's a big thing now for Marion Zimmer Bradley's *The Mists of Avalon* and the religion and values of the Celtic people, who were themselves colonized and taken over. That's OK too, that's fancy. But Irish Catholicism, no.

Hogan: Yeah. It's fascinating, all the psychological and spiritual projections the dominant culture puts on colonized people, things they won't believe in their own culture, and yet those projections are really coming from them—We're getting off on a tangent.

Smith: There are no tangents. Just talking . . . hey, you said you were going to read me a story about a porcupine.

Hogan: You know what? I don't have it here.

Smith: Is it the same porcupine as the one that gets run over in the poem in the new book, what is it, "Porcupine on the Road to the River"?

Hogan: No, uh-uh, there are too many of them to go over the same one twice. (Groans, laughter) That's just my humor.

Smith: I hear you. Want to talk about the wolf project?

Hogan: Yeah, OK. After I realized how important it was to be doing wildlife rescue work, I heard about a world research project "up North," as they say in Minnesota, in Ely. The Department of the Interior, the Division of Natural Resources was funding a research project on wolf-deer relationships, and how many wolves could live in a certain amount of territory, and I signed up to go as a student. Coming away from that I realized, as Barry Lopez points out in *Of Wolves and Men,* wolves really are the projection of people's inner fears or desires, and what I also realized was how difficult it is for people to see difference—between one human being and another, between species. What people look for is either similarities—*or* shadow—the shadow-self, as Jung says, so you can look for evil on the outside and not have to acknowledge your inner evil. People will never know what wolves are, because—no wolf has spoken. But I felt very unhappy with the way the research is being conducted. For instance, in order to put radio-tracking collars on wolves, they're actually using leg traps and they've lost many wolves in the course of the research.

Smith: God, people are clumsy, aren't they?

Hogan: People are clumsy. And they've interfered with the habits of the wolves by using the radio collars some of which have tranquilizing darts in them, that can be activated with small planes. Wolves may be survivors, but they're not good at taking the stress humans impose. And the community in Ely, and towns thereabouts, does not like, quote, "The Wolf." They think wolves are evil, and so they're not happy with the wildlife biologists, whom *they* perceive as people who are trying to save wolves. What I want to work on now is what I know about wolves from other situations I've been in—including having lived around my sister's dog, who's half wolf—and what I think about these kinds of interbreedings.

Smith: And what that does to the animal. What's the dog like?

Hogan: Well, he just wants to run, and he doesn't behave like a regular dog—he doesn't know how. But he's not wild; he's actually more gentle than any domestic dog.

Smith: You wonder what it's like for an animal to be a breed, and what his consciousness must be.

Hogan: Yeah, dog-wolf consciousness.

Smith: I was just thinking about that poem where you describe yourself as having a Chickasaw hand in one pocket, and a white hand in the other . . .

Hogan: Um-hum!

Smith: And sleeping in twin beds . . .

Hogan: I know! And I've been living in the Twin Cities! This is *it*; this psychic split has gone too far! Time to get things together; I need to live in some place called Unity.

Smith: There must be seven or eight towns named that, I betcha.

Hogan: I betcha I could find one, get some Minnesota astrologer to help me.

Smith: Unity, Pennsylvania.

Hogan: You know, one of the things I have to say about living in Minnesota is that it's changed me. I'm a much harder thinker than I was before. I've had to be. I assimilate more here in one single day of my life than I used to have to assimilate in a month. I have this new poem . . . I told you how Minneapolis is a very racist place? Well, about two years ago here an Indian man was accused of stealing a bottle of Lysol from a store, and white merchants hung him up on a meathook and beat him. The only reason this came out was that they'd recently insisted on hiring several Indian police, and one of the people who investigated the incident was Indian. Anyway, this is called "The New Apartment, Minneapolis":

> The floorboards creak,
> the moon is on the wrong side of the building,
> and burns remain on the floor.
>
> The house wants to fall down the universe
> when the earth turns. It still holds
> the coughs of old men, and their canes
> tapping on the floor.

I think of Indian people here before me,
and how last spring
white merchants hung an elder on a meathook and beat him
and he was one of The People.

I remember this war, and all the wars,
and relocation,
like putting the moon in prison with no food,
and that moon was a crescent already.

But be warned:
the moon grows full again,
and the roofs of this town are all red
and we are looking through the walls of houses
at people suspended in air.
Some are baking
with flour on their hands;
or sweeping on Floor Three,
or getting drunk.
I see the businessmen who hit their wives,
and the men who are tender fathers.
There are women crying or making jokes.
Children are laughing under beds.
Girls in navy blue robes
talk on the phone all night,
and some Pawnee is singing '49's,
strumming the table.

Inside the walls, world changes are planned,
bosses overthrown.

If we had no coffee, cigarettes, or liquor,
says the woman in room twelve,
they'd have a revolution on their hands.

Beyond walls are lakes and plains,
canyons, and the universe.
The stars are the key
turning in the lock of night.
Turn the deadbolt,
and I am home.

I have walked the dark earth,
opened a door to night where there are no apartments,
just drumming and singing
the duck song
the snake song
the drunk song.

No one here remembers the city,
or has ever lost the will to go on.

Hello, aunt.
Hello, brother.
Hello, trees,
and deer walking quietly on the soft red earth.

(Laughter)

Hogan: You like that, huh?

Smith: Oh, *yeah.* You know, it's not like it's not recognizably Linda Hogan . . .

Hogan: But it's different, I know. I think I'm getting better.

Smith: Yeah! Listen, it's funny, but I have this pet bull snake, he lives right here by the phone, and he's *very* interested. He kind of woke up about halfway through this phone call.

Hogan: Yeah, they know.

Smith: The poem makes me think—American Indian writing often gets tagged as kind of regional, local-color writing, but it seems to me that the contemporary writers, especially the women, like you and Joy Harjo, Paula Gunn Allen, Leslie Silko, and now Louise Erdrich—you really are expressing more global concerns in your work than a lot of other writers do.

Hogan: Well, in our human development we begin with ourselves and move outward toward relationship, and in writing work, it seems to be the same, that most writers begin with their own identity, with autobiography, and then move out toward family, friends, environment, country, world. I have noticed there's a return for many writers as they age—James Wright, for instance, in *Two Citizens,* went straight back to family and aunts, and the precise and honest pain of a white man growing up inside the dominant culture, and what that does to people. And I've noticed that for others the world expands outward more and more, never returning to self. Meridel LeSueur, for instance—she's gone larger into the world and into history, but has left her own life untouched, *not* telling us about aging. What a wonderful thing she could give us, about that process! And almost no one has done that. It's one of our areas of silence. Instead, she's chosen to radiate outward, and that's been valuable, too—though I wish we had both. I like writers that do both. I think of Audre Lorde, in *Cancer Journals,* a book that talks about disease, poetry, language, facing death, facing life, *and* it talks about the political and economic context of cancer in the U.S.—the cancer "business," the A.M.A. We need for writers to do both. We need the personal in its global context.

Smith: And yourself, your work?

Hogan: In my own work, I work best if I allow the process to take place. That doesn't mean I *don't* think, take measurements of what is just, feel out what is valuable to life, to self, to earth, where to take, where to return, what is the responsibility of my own work—you know, response-ability. I ask myself how best to let my words serve. I know that part of that is to take a global perspective, because I see what's happening in the world, and others see, and our combined voices are a chorus, a movement toward life. They are a protest against human-imposed suffering. They are vital energy going out into the world. We feed each other with that energy when we read each other's work.

My other responsibility, I think, is to be honest about my life. That doesn't mean I won't write fiction, or that I'll "tell all"—like, what I did last Saturday night—nothing! (Laughter) But it means this: that I, as an Indian woman, from a non middle-class background, on the margin, not a member of the dominant culture—I need to speak what my struggle has been, and offer the strength of that survival to keep us all moving together, to offer back my own words. This means to speak about what it's like to be of mixed blood, to have suffered losses, to have not been educated, to have worked primarily at working-class jobs until fairly recently—*and* to have worked as a writer. Not that I think my own life is so significant—although sometimes I think it's pretty incredible, I'll tell ya!

Smith: I think it's pretty damn significant . . .

Hogan: Well, it's part of a historical process. It's a woman's experience, and an Indian woman's experience. And I've been given this gift of words, and I need to speak this life, and the political dimensions of it. I need to make the interpretation of my own place and the places of others in the American context. But I don't want to get too serious here. These responsibilities shouldn't be taken so seriously by writers, by women, as to take away passion, and joy, and play. Because we've got to keep energy moving. We must take in and out, like breathing. I've always thought there's nothing less peaceful than a somber peace movement, you know what I mean? You know those T shirts with Emma Goldman, saying, "If I can't dance, I don't want to be part of your revolution?" That's what peace and equality must mean to us all—that we can have joy in living, and no more cold war of the inner self. Listen, is this being an OK interview?

Smith: Oh, *lady!*

Photo by Cynthia Farah

chapter thirteen
Denise Chávez
Interview by Annie O. Eysturoy

Denise Chávez is a recently acclaimed Chicana writer of fiction, drama, and oral history, with a strong interest in community arts programs. Born in Las Cruces, New Mexico, in 1948 of a *mexicano* family, she worked at a variety of jobs, in a hospital, in an art gallery, and as a corporate public relations representative, before pursuing a career as a writer, actor, and teacher. She graduated with an M.A. from the Creative Writing program at the University of New Mexico in 1984. She has taught in several artist-in-residence programs, taught and facilitated at the Radium Springs Center for Women in New Mexico, given many writers' workshops and readings from her work, presented plays and performance pieces, and seen her play *Plaza* tour New Mexico and win a place in festivals in New York and Edinburgh. Altogether she has written twenty-two plays, having produced seventeen of these. Her story collection *The Last of the Menu Girls* was published in 1986; she is finishing a novel, *Face of an Angel*, and a history of her family. Currently she teaches at the University of Texas, Houston campus. She was interviewed in March 1988 by Annie Eysturoy when on a visit to Albuquerque.

Plays written and produced:

Novitiates (1971, 1971).

Hecho en Mexico (1982, 1983).

The Green Madonna (1982, 1982).

Novena Narrativas (1986).

Other literature:

The Last of the Menu Girls, fiction (Houston: Arte Publico Press, 1986).

Eysturoy: Where were you born?

Chávez: I was born in Las Cruces in 1948, in what later was to become my bedroom; I think I was the last child born at home. My mother was a teacher and had moved from West Texas. She was a widow and met my father in Las Cruces. His family was originally from Socorro and around there; they were farmers. I was the first child of that union. My mother had an older child, my half-sister. I have two sisters. My parents divorced when I was ten years old, so I basically grew up in a house of women, and I think that has probably affected my writing quite a bit.

I never felt that I was really connected to the United States; I never knew what it was to me. Las Cruces was a world unto itself, and to me that world included the Organ Mountains, which I could see directly from the street, and the world of the ditches. At that time in Las Cruces they had a very large ditch system and we played there and hung out in the trees. They had to spray the ditches for the mosquitos that would spread encephalitis—I haven't really written about that—but it was a magical time in a way, because people would come by wearing this futuristic head gear and would spray, and all the little kids would run inside the house and the whole street would be filled with this spray. Now I think that was probably not very healthy, to spray it out just like that.

My mother's family comes from the Big Bend area in West Texas. They were Mexicans who had originally come from Chihuahua, so we are *mexicanos*. They had come up through the Rio Grande and settled in a town called El Polvo, the dust; so that is where my mother's family originated, in the dust. They came into the area in the late eighteen hundreds. Settlers were wanted, so people were given money to come over and settle this place that nobody wanted to live in. After my parents were divorced, we spent a lot of time in Texas with my mother's relatives. My grandfather and my grandmother were alive then, and there were a lot of elderly relatives, male and female; so I was around a lot of old people from a very early age, and I think that has been a blessing. I remember taking my grandmother to the bathroom, cleaning her, and attending to a lot of older men and women, and that is good, because I don't think a lot of young people do that any more; just ship them off to the nursing home.

So I grew up with a lot of people of different ages and different environments, and I think all those images of dust and rain and heat and wild flowers and wild land and mountains and sky certainly affected my writing.

Eysturoy: Is there any particular part of your cultural background that has most strongly influenced your writing?

Chávez: Well, my mother was a great influence. She was such a strong woman. Her family were the first Hispanic graduates of Sul Ross College in Texas. All of them were voracious readers, and they forged ahead in a time and a place where, I tell you, it was not done. One of my aunts was Texas Mother of the Year for several years. My grandmother's English was impeccable, and that naturally gave her an advantage; so when she got older she became the postmistress of the small town.

There was always a yearning for education and improvement in the family, so my mother instilled this into us. She taught Spanish for many years. She was always challenging us to look up words or to read and she instilled a love of the culture and the traditions. She was also a very devout Catholic. I went to Catholic school for twelve years, so I grew up with *los pastores*, the traditional folkplays, *las posadas*. I can remember going with my mother to *las posadas*, and on Good Friday going to Church and doing *las velorios,* waiting at night and praying, and all the other customs; later on I was in that miracle play myself. We also always put out *luminarias* for Christmas. My mother was an influence, and so were all the people I happened to be around. My father's relatives were very artistic; I come from a family of artists on both sides. On my father's side I have many cousins, male particularly, who are painters. Some of my father's cousins have enormous farms, and it is a sense of loss, I think, for me to know that that land at one point was my grandfather's land; now the Reyes and Chavez farms have all the chile. But I buy chile from my cousins, and I am very proud of them; maybe that was not the path for our family.

My mother passed away five years ago, and as I went through her things I found many poems; she did write and I am finding a lot of her material. It is very interesting to me that after a person dies you know them. Now I feel that I really didn't know her before.

I was, like I said, in Catholic elementary and high school. One of my stories is based on a May Day procession. All of the children in the neighborhood had to collect flowers, and they would spread out this white satin sheet and the kids would bring the flowers. Laying flowers at an altar made a beautiful scene. That was the time when Latin was spoken and there was a magic and mystery to those cultural things that we experienced.

Eysturoy: Many of your stories, and particularly your plays, seem to take a point of departure in religion. Has religion been a major influence, maybe inspiration as well?

Chávez: Like in the novel? Yes, absolutely so. The novel I am working on now has a chapter called "Saints" where I talk about all the different saints; I felt very connected to the patron saint of the mentally ill and to Saint Martin de Porres, a saint who is beloved by Hispanics even though they would never allow their daughters to marry a black man. That was, I think, a starting point in this particular chapter, my exploration of what did sainthood involve. This was instilled in us; what can you do to evolve and become fully yourself spiritually? What is your purpose in life? I think those things had a fundamental influence on me.

But at the same time I was also skeptical. Even as a young child I scrawled my initials out in the wooden pews during Mass; I did that like all the other kids did, drawing hearts and things. In high school I took another form of rebellion. I remember reading *Lady Chatterley's Lover* in Mass. The thing was to get by the nuns and get away with as much as you could. One of the biggest pranks that year was when two of the seniors switched the statues on the altar around when the nuns were not looking. I have written a play about elementary school and one about high school; they are all hilarious, wonderful experiences that give me great joy, and I laugh at them now and I see how crazy it was. There were twelve girls in this graduating class of Madonna High School, and we referred to ourselves as the apostolettes. I still see some of those women. We had a reunion last year, and we still get together. We are now very different, but there is that part of us that we still know.

I started doing a lot of creative work in high school; I started acting, took drama courses, and was always writing little skits and plays. It was such a small school you could do anything you wanted; if you had any creative bent you were free to do that.

Eysturoy: It was there you started your writing?

Chávez: Well, I probably started while I was in elementary school, in my diary at that time; I started early and was just writing all the time.

Eysturoy: So your diary writing developed into writing the skits, et cetera?

Chávez: Yes, and then I would act and perform the skits. I majored in drama in high school and won a drama scholarship for a role I did in a high school play. I took a playwriting class when I was a senior in college, and the first play I ever wrote won a prize in a New Mexico State literary contest. It was the first money I had ever earned in my life with my writing—fifteen dollars—and I kept that receipt for a long time.

I wrote it in the winter, in the room where I was born, and I remember it was so cold back there that I had a blanket over me. I didn't know how to type—I eventually taught myself how, but at that time I was still picking out the letters—and in that freezing back room I wrote this play. It was originally called "The Waiting" and it is interesting now, because I was doing a play on waitressing, and I had not thought about that connection. Later on when I was in graduate school somebody produced the play and I changed the name to "Novitiates," which is the period of time that one has to go through, like a trial period, on your road to priesthood, or the sisterhood. So the play is about characters in some kind of transitional period, going from one thing to another. There is a brother and a sister, a mother and grandmother; it is a very interesting play, it ambles all over the place. No one has seen this play, but I did send a copy of it to the UNM library, so it is there in the files. I just recently sent a massive amount of things to the library, and that play is in there. It was my first, and I was very proud of it.

Eysturoy: Do you ever go back and use diary writing for your creative writing?

Chávez: I do that all the time. I have a lot of characterizations and many poems there. I have a shelf of journals, and sometimes I go back there if I am working on something I want to remember. If I want to do something on the sixties, I might go back and reread some of the sixties stuff. I should go back and clean it up, because there is a lot of work there I am sure I could use and poems I probably should type up that have never seen the light of day.

Eysturoy: In *The Last of the Menu Girls* you say somewhere that going back is going forward. Is that what you are doing when you go back . . . or how would you explain it?

Chávez: Well, I do explain it that way. I think it is very true. You never understand a situation or experience or relationship when you are in the midst of it; you have to step back from it and look again, and that may be a matter of going back in time, or analyzing what that experience did to you. I will use an example: I mentioned my parents were divorced, and recently I found a diary. There is a book coming out of Smith College in which I have written a chapter about my origins as a writer, and that chapter has some excerpts from this diary. It wasn't until I worked on that chapter last year that I realized I was able to see myself as that ten-year-old going through a major life change. So you go back and you go forward.

Eysturoy: Do you think that is true culturally as well?

Chávez: Yes, to use the traditions and cultures and language; I pay great homage to that.

Eysturoy: Particularly in New Mexico, maybe?

Chávez: Yes, and in the Southwest and in other cultures, too, the South and the cultures that have a sense of family and connections to the land, that give a reverence to the cultural traditions, songs and music; I like to use those elements. I will sometimes use some of the old songs, the forms, the dances.

Eysturoy: What about the oral tradition?

Chávez: Oh, very much so; yes, I like that.

Eysturoy: Did you grow up with a lot of storytelling?

Chávez: Oh, my God, yes. My mother was a great storyteller, and we were around a lot of people who were great storytellers. Everybody old and young had their stories, especially when we went to Texas; it was a small town of under fifty people, and we would sleep outside because it was so hot. There was nothing to do there, so everybody was outside, mind you, on their cots and sweating out there; and we just started talking to each other, so there was always a lot of conversation going back and forth. My mother would take us to these places and there would be a lot of people telling their stories.

She was a humanitarian and she would collect rummage. We could never get anything into the trunk of her car because it was jam-packed full of stuff for other people; all the neighborhood would bring her their used clothing, and she would even take things to people in Juárez.

I grew up with maids because my mother was a teacher, and I have paid homage to them in a work called "Hecho en Mexico" where I talk about all those wonderful women who brought me up and taught me language and everything. So I now find myself driving around, and my husband gets upset with me; I always have something for the Goodwill or I will call the Vietnam Veterans, or I will take something over to the senior citizens. Like I said, I have been cleaning out my mother's house and I just gave away twelve enormous boxes of clothing material. I feel that if you have something you should give it to people, so I guess I am a bag lady like my mother was, too.

Eysturoy: Talking about influence—what about the southwestern landscape? Has it been an important influence on your creativity? How do you relate to it?

Chávez: Oh, very intimately; to me it has been a lover, mother, sister, any sort of relationship that you might have with a human being and even with God Himself, perhaps. I remember just sitting on the front porch, talking to the trees out there, sitting in the darkness and watching the darkness grow and just seeing the trees come to life; or hiking in the mountains, collecting wild flowers like I talk about in one of the stories—or waiting for the rain, a sign of release. We waited for the rains in the summer. We loved to go out there and play around; the irrigation ditch behind us would be really high and we children would play out in that water.

I am still very connected. When I am tired and have been writing, I go out and look at the landscape and it soothes me, particularly the mountains. I have written a lot about this in my poetry; I talk about the stone breath of horizons moving, and I think in a lot of my work I talk about the rain, the dust, the heat; I mean it was hot and it is still hot during the summer in Las Cruces, 110 degrees. You have to pay respect to that weather, because if not it just is too much for you.

There have been times when I have had a garden, but I have not been able to the last few years. I like going out there and puttering around, watching things grow, talking to my trees. I love nature and it has fed me in so many ways.

Eysturoy: Are you a religious person?

Chávez: Yes, I am. I did grow up as a Catholic, and I still go to church, probably not on a regular basis but I have a great spiritual nature, and I am a seeker, too. I am always searching out my heart, and I have gone through a lot of different experiences in the Church; I have gone on many retreats and gone through healing experiences and participated in charismatic work, I guess you might say, interdenominational to me. I don't feel it is necessary to have one particular religion. But I am a spiritual person and am drawn to people who have that; it makes all the difference in the world. For example, this weekend I am staying with a Native American healer. The altar is there and every day I go and I say my prayers. When you are in an environment of people like that you celebrate eating, celebrate everything you do; there is a sense of joy then which I think certainly makes life a lot fuller. But that is not to say that I don't have my personal demons or struggles.

Eysturoy: You grew up in Las Cruces, which is on the border of Mexico, and "Hecho en Mexico" deals with relationships between Mexico and the U.S. Is that relationship a central concern of yours?

Chávez: Yes, and I want to write more about it. Like I said, we grew up with women who came *como criadas;* they were servants. No, not servants, they were never servants; they were like an extended part of the family, so we knew their lives, we took them back to Mexico, we shared with them, we ate dinner with them; we knew their families, we went back and forth, and there was an exchange between us. It was very common for us to go to the *mercado,* buy our food, go shopping for the feastdays and do things; to have our hair done. I went to my first beauty salon in Juárez. I was going to a dance so I had my hair done with all these little curls.

We traveled in Mexico sometimes. My mother had studied at the university and traveled for thirteen summers in Mexico. She instilled in us a love for the country and the people and the literature, so when I go back to Mexico I feel that I am truly home. I love Nuevo Mexico, but I always do feel that is where I really came from. As opposed to some people who say they are Spanish, I say that I am a *mexicana,* although it is true that Chávez is a name which has Spanish roots.

I have been talking to a very good friend, the bishop in Las Cruces—he is a *mexicano*—and I asked him what themes can be explored now. So we started talking about these laborers who go to a certain destination, a spot, to be picked up at two and three o'clock in the morning and are taken over state lines to work all day on the farms and then taken back home about six o'clock. They catch whatever sleep they can get, or food, or rest, and then are back out on the streets again about two o'clock. And, you know, I think a lot of things can be said about the *maquiladores* and what is happening now with the Immigration Bill. In Houston, where I am now, I am connected with a group called La Resistencia which is demonstrating against this bill.

So I would like to pursue some of these other things in my work. But of course, I also do realize that you have to go around political themes with a certain sense of humor. I am not a didactic person, and hopefully not in my writing; whatever theories or philosophies I have to expound would be done in a different sort of way. "Hecho en Mexico" was about women who work as maids, but I was more focused on the characters of the women, on the suffering they had. We did show *la migra* and the aliens lined up, but you have this one alien—this was at the time of *E.T.*—the only alien who can get by is this E.T. with his greencard; he is the only one who has a greencard. You have to make statements, especially in theater, with a certain perspective that does not cut you off from the people you want to reach. I try to show the characters as they are, even one character who is a horrific woman, who although she has had a hysterectomy destroys her daughter's relationship with this teacher. Even if she is an awful woman, she suffers great, great pain; so I try to balance out the evil in that character with the great suffering she has had to endure.

Eysturoy: Is the Chicano relationship to the dominant culture something that you find you want to explore?

Chávez: I think so. Now when I teach, the students say to me that they want to hear about contemporary people, and it is the middle class they want to hear about now, you know. I have made a statement to the effect that we have written the *curanderas* out. We have those people who still work in that world, and healing is certainly a part of our lives—my mother was a *curandera* in many ways and other women I have known—but people now have a need to address some of the contemporary situations, divorce for example, and what is happening to the family. I have never seen adequate treatment of the high incidence of alcoholism in Hispanic families. I know that every male in my family was an alcoholic, and now the younger generation is into drugs. What character traits or circumstances cause these men to do this?

This has been an oppressed culture and so the oppressed have to oppress as well, and it has usually fallen on women, or those who have dark skin, or the people who are laborers and so on and so forth. This cycle of oppression continues, and I am exploring a lot of those themes in my current novel.

Eysturoy: In your new novel do you focus on the issues that are relevant to the contemporary Chicano community?

Chávez: Yes, I am enjoying that. There are themes of interest to myself as well, for instance the changing relationship between men and women as women are coming into their own. Our grandmothers did not have voices. My mother's voice was a cry, perhaps, a moan; it was a sad voice. Our voices are hopefully stronger, and we can sing our stories and other women's stories as well.

Eysturoy: You have taught a lot of different groups in New Mexico. Do the voices you hear in those workshops and classes become a source of inspiration to you? Are they the contemporary Chicano community, perhaps, that you relate to?

Chávez: Well, yes, but not only Chicanas and Chicanos. Like this woman who had murdered her two children and would only play a cat character . . . but in a writing class she wrote a poem called "Sea Child." She was from Washington, she had grown up in that wild environment, and she saw herself as the sea child. I want to write a play about that woman. And then there are some of my experiences working with the women prisoners at the Radium Springs Center for Women. There were a lot of gay women there, and I myself would be gay if I were there—and even if not there I certainly might be gay anyway—but many of the women were gay, and there were two women who wanted to get married. One of them was a really rough type. She was a younger version of one of my characters, Corine, la Cory Delgado. La Cory had shaved her eyebrows, completely erased them, but the stubs were coming out while about the middle of her forehead to the side she had painted eyebrows very high up there; so you had these low eyebrows and high eyebrows, and then her hair was dyed blond. She had been married, had kids, and gone through that whole scenario, you know. She had had everything, but it just wouldn't work for her, and here she was in prison and her play was going to be a wedding play; she was working on a play about a wedding between herself and this other woman. The concept in her work was really fascinating. She was an amazing woman, very resilient and powerful, and I admired her; she had a great sense of humor, but she was a tough cookie.

Eysturoy: You have mentioned women several times. Do you gain a lot of your inspiration from women? Are you trying to create an authentic female voice?

Chávez: I think so, yes. I am a transmitter of the woman's voice, a voice that may or may not have been heard; in the greater, larger world it has not been heard. And so I feel particularly close to many of my characters who are women, but I also have many men characters, too. In "Plaza," the little *viejito* on the park bench, Benito Sieta, watches the world as it comes and goes, and he philosophizes. But I do think that my focus has probably been on female characters.

Eysturoy: You mentioned your grandmother, and your great grandmother, and your mother; is that something you are very conscious of, that you are trying to channel their voices through yourself?

Chávez: I am. I have been working on a book called *Rio Grande Family* in which I go back to the past. I have tried to enter the voice of my various relatives, to actually become the voice of my grandmother—I have certain facts and I do talk about those things—or the voice of my mother, or my uncle, or my grandfather, and it has been very interesting because it is a family history, but from a different point of view; I try to get inside those people.

Eysturoy: You have mentioned that relationships were very important to you.

Chávez: Oh, yes, like I am writing in this novel now. The character is a woman, a forty-five-year-old waitress. She works for a living, but she has somebody that comes in and cleans her house; that is her luxury. She gets in there and works just as hard as the cleaning woman, but she won't deal with that horrible substance you use to clean stoves. She comes to the realization that it is all right for the other person to do it, or it has been up till now, but she won't touch it; it is like it is all right if *she* does the toilet, but *I* cannot do that. She realizes that she is not totally being equal, feeling that way.

When I go to Mexico, I cannot understand *los mexicanos* in that way; they just throw the garbage out in the street. It is the concept that it is not our land, it is somebody else's. That is the theme in my new novel. I am exploring this woman's relationship to garbage; not the relationship between men and women, which you can go on with forever, but the relationship to a stove. This woman realizes she cannot do that to the other person.

Eysturoy: The relationship among women is clearly a theme in *The Last of the Menu Girls*.

Chávez: Yes, and the relationship to our spirit, to our dreams, to our alter ego, to ourselves; the relationship to ourselves when we are young. It is like there are all these different personalities and we have all these relationships to the me of this time and the me of that time.

Eysturoy: The protagonist of the novel says at one point, "What does it mean to be a woman?" Is that something in your unconscious mind when you are writing?

Chávez: Right. In that short story, "Shooting Star," she talks about all her models and her disillusionment with them. It is a naive disillusionment, in a way, because it has been a naive world of imagining.

In my latest book I am also questioning what it means to serve. Women have traditionally been in service, so I think it is about time that we question it. I have one chapter called "Mothers Teach Your Sons," because I think it is very important. Unless mothers and women take the opportunity to teach male children what it is to clean house, to cook, to take responsibility, the cycle will go on as before.

My own husband is very sensitive, but he will say, "We did not do anything today except clean house," and I say "We didn't do anything? This is work." Cleaning house is a balance to the writing world and the creative world. I am the one who does the dishes and the laundry; he cooks, and we are working on that balance of what each of us does, that I do certain things and you do certain things. For the most part, women don't have that balance, and it has been unfortunate, but I blame the women equally, or even more than the men. So I am challenging women in this book, and it should be interesting how it comes out; I am sure I am going to get a lot of reaction.

Eysturoy: So you explore what it means to serve, both for the recipient and the giver, and what kind of relationship that creates?

Chávez: You can take that into the metaphysical or the spiritual, whatever. What is a life of service? Then what is work? Is it not in a way service, too? And what is meaningful work? I mean, here is a woman who is working as a waitress; most people don't find that to be a meaningful profession. An older waitress whom I worked with happened to be one of the strongest women that I have ever known, and she was a therapist. She may not have seen herself as a therapist, but she helped many people.

Eysturoy: We talked about the question of what it means to be a woman; that is also a search for identity. Rocio in *The Last of the Menu Girls* goes off to become a writer. How closely do you think the search for identity is connected to the urge toward creativity, the urge toward writing? Is it the same kind of search?

Chávez: Oh, I think so. Whatever your life's work is, if you are a plumber, if you design flower baskets, there is always that search for order and clarity in whatever you do; even if you make a salad it can be creative. It is the sense of love and devotion and commitment that you put into your work that I celebrate. Like this handyman in *The Last of the Menu Girls*; his work is slipshod, but he gets such delight out of this fountain—it does bring delight to him and to the mother; to her it is the beauty of the fountain, of being able to sit out in the early evening when the birds are there and look at that beauty. So I try to show those people, the nurses or whoever, who have a commitment to work, because it is a creative life and it should be, or else you have no business doing it. Too many people, I think, are in the wrong profession, doing something that is uncreative to them. I am lucky because I have almost always been able to do what is meaningful to me. Not always; I have had a lot of uncreative jobs, too, but you see that there is an end to it, you see that it has a purpose and even if it is painful or whatever, you can use it; nothing is ever lost, really.

Eysturoy: So in that search for clarity, in that process, you also clarify yourself?

Chávez: I think so. Definitely. Writing is a healing process. A writer told me she was working her way toward mental health. Not that one has to be crazy, or that you have to be schizophrenic or anything, but it is a healing process.

Eysturoy: A large bulk of your work has been drama. Was the transition to fiction difficult or did you find drama a useful background for writing fiction?

Chávez: There has really never been too much separation, because I use the monologue in the dialogue form. I can literally lift up scenes from my book and read them as theatrical pieces. I can cut out a few "she saids" or "she retorteds" and then I have the whole bulk of the scene there. I look at my characters as actors in the sense that I go in and I know them. I study their lives, do biographical sketches on my characters and know about their past. In this book I have been working on, I have this genealogical chart that has gone on forever, and the nicknames of the people, and the grandparents and where they came from; it is so involved and complex, this novel. What does the father do for a living? He wanted to be a plumber, his dream was to become a plumber, but he is a janitor. I mean, people might not think that dreaming to become a plumber is a big deal, but to him it was.

To me, the pieces in *The Last of the Menu Girls* are scenes; I don't know if they are short stories, I don't know if it is a novel. You have to come up with some kind of term that deals with what these pieces are. They are scenes in some way. But it has that dramatic element. I won't say that I rehearse my lines as an actor does, but I move toward my characters with the same kind of intensity. I have so many different worlds; I have the world of the restaurant, I have the family world, which is very extended, and I have the world of the character and her people and friends.

Eysturoy: Do you feel that you're taking a new direction in your new book?

Chávez: Yes, and it is scary. I have jumped from one chapter to another, and I sometimes don't know if I am connecting, or the linkages are seamless enough. I have three stories going on at the same time; I have broken it down into eight different phases so I have all those different environments, and then I am trying to remember who the people are, remember their names and how old they are and everything. It is just this enormous tapestry of things that I have to spread out on the wall, and I sometimes have to literally go up there and look at who a person is.

Eysturoy: You are obviously moving into a new direction technically, but do you feel that you are moving into new areas thematically as well?

Chávez: Yes, I think so. I think that *The Last of the Menu Girls* was in a sense a book that all writers have to write, a coming-of-age book. Perhaps my concern is a woman of thirty-nine because number one, I am growing older. I feel comfortable with myself, I feel I am becoming the person I am; sexuality is a very important theme to me, relationships between men and women, women and women, men and men. Just looking at some of the myths of sex, and I don't mean just the act of making love, but like I said, the face of an angel; women are to be this, we are to harness ourselves. We wear angel face powder, and we are angels. One of the voices in the book is the brother of the main character, Hector; he is the manager of a car park and he has got three women pregnant at the same time, the one he is to marry, the maid of one of the relatives, and a girlfriend on the side. His sister overhears him saying that—this is where the title of the book comes from—she has the face of an angel, but she likes to fuck. And his sister is so shocked, she doesn't know which woman he is talking about; in a way she understands too well what he means, but in a way she cannot understand what he means. The fact is that if one enjoys any kind of sexuality, intimacy, for women it is immediately put into a certain category and we have this myth to deal with and these lies, really, these lies that we have lived with for so long. Just basic things: my mother wore girdles for years, and when I started wearing pantyhose, I was skinny and I had to wear a girdle, too, and that was torture. The whole girdle mentality crippled many women; my mother had a very large bust and she had indentations from carrying around this load of her sex. People used to tease her all the time; she was like Dolly Parton and had a very good sense of humor about it. But she was harnessed; her yoke was her breasts and her girdle. She had very bad legs, and I am sure that the girdle contributed to that, but it got to the point where she could not take it off because her body was so stuck into this mold, and we as women have been stuck in this mentality. Fortunately women are not that way so much any more, but many women still are; we are stuck with this image and perception of how we should be and how our children should be.

Eysturoy: You mean that the physical girdle has been removed, but the psychological girdle is still there?

Chávez: Yes, right, and so we teach our children that way, our male and our female children, and perpetuate the cycle.

Eysturoy: So you see yourself as moving into areas that are central to you as a woman of thirty-nine?

Chávez: Yes.

Eysturoy: To someone who doesn't know your work in its totality, how would you describe its unifying theme? Is there such a theme?

Chávez: I think that there might be. I don't know, it is hard to say. One of the themes would be to impart a sense of acceptance and merciful love for characters. I try to portray people with problems and failings; they could be the handyman, or the nurses' aid or whoever, but each character has an existence that is sacred and I try to show that. I think I have a commitment to show characters who are strong, who endure. A central theme might be that one must endure and to do that we have to love and be merciful because we are human beings and are not perfect.

Eysturoy: Do you have any particular Chicana perspective in your writing?

Chávez: Yes, I try to bring that in the use of language, the situation. Talking about *compadrazco, comadrazco,* dealing with themes of that nature that maybe other people might understand, what *that* relationship is; talking in this new book about feast days and saints' days and all of those things that are cultural givens; the land, the wedding where they use the *lazo* and they pin the money on the bride's veil; just cultural traditions. As a Chicana I think I am very alert to what is, but I also have a very great respect for what was and what will be. Perhaps I am just a transmitter. I see myself as somebody who has been given a gift, something I never asked for. I am here to have this stuff move through me, and it is a responsibility and a commitment; I feel that I just need to do that. I think I try to demystify happiness as well, because what is happiness? We should not expect to be happy; we should expect to do our work, and I think that whatever happiness or state of contentment or peace one finally comes to—my characters are always looking for peace—it is a lonely, sad peace. But a strong peace. I think all human beings have to go through this because eventually, inevitably we are alone and there is that peace that no one can give you, really, other than you coming to grips with and confronting your own life and your own destiny, what work you have done and what you need to do.

Photo by Cynthia Farah

chapter fourteen
Joy Harjo
Interview by John Crawford and Patricia Clark Smith

Since Joy Harjo resists simplicities, such as the simplicities of headnotes, it is best to begin by letting her speak for herself, as she did a few years ago: "I am from Oklahoma. But that isn't my only name. I am Creek and other Oklahoma/Arkansas people. I am a woman, many women. The namings can go on and on and it is frustrating to name someone or something when in the *real* world all is in motion, in a state of change." Born in Tulsa in 1951, Joy Harjo lived as a young wife and mother in Albuquerque, where she acquired her B.A. from the University of New Mexico in 1976. She received an M.F.A. from the Iowa Writing School in 1978, and taught for a year at the Institute of American Indian Arts in Santa Fe in 1978–79. She has subsequently taught at several institutions, including Arizona State University in Tempe and the University of Colorado at Boulder, and after this interview was appointed to a tenured position at the University of Arizona at Tucson. Frequently anthologized, she has produced three books of poems, the most famous of which is *She Had Some Horses* (1983), as well as several reading cassettes in collaboration with other writers and performers. There is a new book of poems on the way. Always interested in a variety of art forms, she first went to college as a painter, has worked subsequently as a film writer and is currently performing in a jazz band. This interview was conducted in Albuquerque with John Crawford and Patricia Clark Smith in August 1987.

Selected Bibliography:

The Last Song, poetry (Las Cruces: Puerto del Sol Press, 1975).

What Moon Drove Me to This? poetry (New York: I. Reed Books, 1980).

She Had Some Horses, poetry (New York: Thunders Mouth Press, 1983).

Cassette tapes

Joy Harjo and Barney Bush, New Letters Magazine, 1983.

Furious Light, Watershed Foundation, 1985.

Crawford: Where did your work in film begin?

Harjo: I've done a lot of film writing. In 1982 I took the program in film making at the Anthropology Film Center in Santa Fe, and since then have written several scripts. The first one I wrote with a wonderful screenwriter, Henry Greenberg. It was a story for the White Mountain Apache tribe, the story of the Crown Dance. I did it within a contemporary frame, of a young Apache boy having bad dreams, needing to get something settled within himself. He's at the Phoenix Indian School, he runs away, goes home, it shows how that story is transformative in that child's life and all Apache peoples' lives. Since then I've done scripts for Nebraska Educational TV, Native American Public Broadcasting for which I'm also on the Board of Directors, and other jobs are pending. But I would like to do some of my own stories, and one project I've had in mind is Simon Ortiz's story "Kaiser and the War." It's always been such a visual story for me. I know what all those characters look like, sound like. I've met Kaiser.

Crawford: What were you doing in Tucson this summer?

Harjo: I participated in an NEH Seminar with Larry Evers on American Indian Verbal Art and Literature which focused on the oral art: poetry such as contemporary Hopi poetry, Kachina songs and so on. It gave me wonderful resources, background, discussion. . . . Scott Momaday was there, Vine DeLoria, Ophelia Zapata, Danny Lopez, Leslie Silko of course.

Smith: Is she in good shape?

Harjo: You know, she's running along the edge because she's still writing her novel, and you can tell . . . She reminds me of one of those actors who when they're playing a part stay in their part the whole time. Well, Leslie is still in her novel. And I'll be glad—it's a difficult part for her—and I'll be glad when she gets it done. I'm sure she will be too.

Smith: Did she have to teach this past year?

Harjo: Well, they made her quite a lucrative offer, but she said that she wouldn't teach there again—there were two stories—she would rather dance naked in the middle of Speedway, or she would rather dance topless in the El Rancho Bar than to teach at the University of Arizona. (Laughs) So that's where that stands. She's wonderful. I realize more and more how much I owe her in the whole process and business and place of writing poetry. She was there for me from the beginning. The first time I met her, she came to visit—she was living in Ketchikan, Alaska—Simon introduced her to me—and she and I kept in touch till she moved back to New Mexico. She was always there—she listened and she wrote to me—on a lot of levels she was there for me.

Smith: For you and a lot of people. We've finally just replaced the position she held at the University of New Mexico with Luci Tapahonso. But it was very hard to convince people that the loss of Leslie was more than just the loss of someone who could teach that material. To be there in the way Leslie was there for those students was something special.

Harjo: I have a general insecurity about teaching within an institution, because I'm not an academic, I'm not a scholar; I'm a poet, I'm a writer, my background is mostly art. At the University of New Mexico, I'd been working toward a B.F.A. in studio art (painting); my English Department B.A. in creative writing took all my art hours. I was in the first graduating class that got the B.A. for creative writing. Even in graduate school, in Iowa, where the program was fairly good, it was an M.F.A., not an M.A. program. I've always been more focused on being an artist. So I go through this nearly every time I get up in front of a class, in some form or other—sometimes it's just fleeting, sometimes it's very heavy, very hard to get through with these feelings that I don't know what I'm doing. But once I let that go and realize that I've got my experience and I do quite a bit of reading and talking and I've been right at the heart of things that are going on, and once I forget about how I feel I am supposed to think, and just move into who I am and what I understand of it and don't worry about it, it goes great. But first I have to throw fear off. It seems like it's always there.

Smith: I think it's a really common thing for women, not everybody but a lot of us. I always get diarrhea at the beginning of the semester, and I'm always thinking "My God, what if they find out I'm a fake?"

Harjo: And it does happen more to women.

Smith: And thinking "But I really only have a degree in creative writing and besides they accepted all my art hours."

Harjo: (Laughs) Right.

Crawford: How does it work the other way? Does teaching cut into your energies as an artist?

Harjo: It does, but it adds to them also. I wouldn't stay in it forever; there are other things I could do. But I realize how important it is; I've realized I am there for particular people, I mean I am there for everyone, and I can look across the classroom and I know that certain people are in the school because of skiing, it's the place for that; but I also recognize that there is that place, that heart within everyone, that remains, and that's what—that's who I talk to. I have a very strong sense that I am supposed to be there. And it's very important that I'm there, because no one else is teaching what I'm teaching, and it has to be done. And that keeps me going. But yes, it does [drain my energies]. Because I agonize over each class. I know I probably shouldn't do that. And I know not everybody does. They go in and wing it.

Smith: Or people for whom it isn't very emotional. It is very emotional for me—more so as I get older. There are so many classes where I'm just right on the edge of tears sometimes. What's happening in that room is so important; I can't take it lightly at all. I'm not just teaching English.

Harjo: Right. What I'm dealing with, I figure, are human beings, and talking about, you know, our connection, and who we are and who we become. In the poetry workshops, which are my favorite, I've had less of that apprehension—but I don't know all the "terms."

Crawford: You were talking to me before about some of the books that you've actually taken into classes. I was interested in that, because it seems like some of those would be natural choices, but so few people are doing them yet. Could you run down some of the things you've been most interested in doing?

Harjo: I figure I'm there to educate people to the diversity within themselves and the diversity in America. Because the canon remains. In the canon—I mean, if you were to come right down to what are considered the great books, very few of them would be American. There's still that Old Fart Tendency—look back to England—to the true English literature.

Crawford: Or American imitations of that.

Harjo: Yeah. And there's this real deep-rooted place within me that was taught to believe that writing that is not of that place and sensibility is not as important. I don't agree with it, of course—I think it's crap; but I was educated in this system—and it's an attitude I have to fight too, within myself. Thinking that what I do as a poet, because I'm a woman, and I'm Indian and so on, I'm an artist over all that; but somehow thinking—it's not even thinking—but on a deep emotional level feeling that it's not as important, because it's not given attention, or place, that formal place in terms of "Well, we recognize you." So what I want to give them—and this is what I've said in the last few classes when I've taught Native American Literature—"Realize if you realize nothing else in this class that this literature is part of who you are and part of you. This is not some foreign exotic literature, this is not something that is separate from you, but if you are living in this country, or even world, if you were born here, this *is* American literature, this is part of who you are." So approach it that way, rather than distancing it. Because there is so much distancing and separation that goes on, and that's how we were taught. . . .

Crawford: The other thing is that it's hard to step back and see what a tremendous development has taken place in the last twenty years due to the work of people like you and Leslie [Silko] and Audre [Lorde] and Sonia [Sanchez] and the many other people who are really making a statement now.

Harjo: I can smell that something really important has been going on. (Laughs) That's how I work. Not through books of literary criticism, but what is that smell? Am I close? And I have felt that. But often I don't have the perspective to put everything together and see how it works.

Smith: But you've got something a lot of writers don't have, I think, which is that sense of past and future, that things are transmitted beyond even someone's knowing.

Harjo: That's exciting to me, because the world is so much more fluid and alive and that's how it really works; it doesn't end, you know, just because one carrier dies.

Smith: Those two stories in your manuscript, the one about your daughter Rainy waking up at night when you're driving across Oklahoma and saying "I just dreamed someone. I wonder who was dreaming us," and the other one about the woman in the initiation ceremony who was given a power while she was fasting and the song turned out to be one of her grandmother's songs that she had never heard, but all the old women at the ceremony knew it was her grandmother's song. How old was Rainy at that time?

Harjo: Rainy was probably three. That child always said amazing things. It was interesting that she said it at that place. We were going back up to Iowa City; we'd been down here in the sun, and were slowly going back up to winter. It was at a midway point between the sun I loved and the winter that was so difficult. When she said that, I thought "I don't have to send this kid to school. She knows what she needs to know." I think real education would foster that: that memory, and these kinds of visions. Then people could see through the bullshit. You wouldn't have to have anyone uncovering Reagan's lies. They would be so upfront. I think maybe people do know, but it's just very subdued. People don't want to—people are frightened.

Crawford: I sense a sharper division, two senses of America, in the last four or five years. I think the Reagan people are really trying to faithfully reproduce Buffalo Bill and General Sherman and the entire history of the country as a kind of conquest.

Harjo: And those myths are real—they're very viable myths. I hear John Wayne in Reagan, like he's taken on that personality, that stance, like he stands behind that myth.

Crawford: Maybe it clarifies it for the rest of us that there is that level of reality.

Harjo: I think there's genuine evil going on too. I don't like to acknowledge it, because it's a terrible, terrible thing; this whole business—maybe it is a business—of separating people from themselves—from their souls—for their money. Maybe he doesn't even know quite his part in this—that he's got a part to play too. That it really smells like something very evil.

Crawford: And somewhere it has to be stopped.

Smith: This summer I was truly surprised by people's reaction to the Oliver North hearings. I watched the first few sessions and I said to myself, Oh, at last! Now people can just *see*. But then, of course—(Laughter).

Harjo: That's probably one of the most frightening events of this year—and there've been many, many of them. But that one—to see how people again want that John Wayne thing—perhaps John Wayne fulfills some role that people who think like that really need: a savior, and it could be Jesus Christ, not the incredible humanitarian but that image that the Organized Church has promulgated—if I look like John Wayne and I act like John Wayne then I don't have to think for myself because "myself" is frightened.

Crawford: I just had a letter from Don West. He was an organizer in the South in the thirties. He had gone to Germany in 1932, I think on a Fulbright. He just wrote to say, "Don't people understand that he"—Hitler—"looked just like this"—North—"he was young, personable . . ."—These things are not so different.

Harjo: No, he's slick.

Crawford: With your work—I know you've got a new manuscript—I've seen one poem, which I love—how do you see it developing, changing?

Harjo: Well, when I first started writing poems, you know, the place I entered the poems and the place I left the poems were very close. And what I notice happens is that the process of writing poems gets more and more intense. And the place that I enter the poems often can be years away from the place I come out. I think that's the major difference overall. There are poems that are more immediate and shorter, but that's the major difference. And I suppose that can parallel with some inner opening, or perception—and it could come with age. You know. I'm thirty-six now, which isn't old in some ways, though it's in the olden days with the kids (laughs). You start learning to perceive the world with a lot more sense of dimension. Every day, every year, the world kaleidoscopes, the perception of it just is huge. Sometimes it gets very overwhelming.

Smith: Thirty-six was an important age for me, because I can remember my own mother being thirty-six, and having a clear vision of her, not as "Mom" but as a woman. That was very significant for me somehow.

Harjo: Yeah, there's something about it, about not being self-conscious. And

I'm going to stop intellectualizing. (Laughs) It's a time when certain things are moving in and starting to make themselves at home. I'm still not explaining. But there's something about age—so when Rainy's grandmother was talking to me the other day, I was really listening to how she told the story, and trying to understand just from this new viewpoint of being a little older what she had to back her up; and I was trying to explain to Rainy, who's fourteen and knows everything, in the truck on the way back to Albuquerque, "You know your grandmother, she's seen a lot. And she knows a lot. And you should listen to her." But it's funny, maybe now that means I'm old. Because I can see that. (Laughs) You know, when we're young somehow we all feel we have this new important grand vision, but really it's all here, we all participate, it's always been here.

Smith: I know it wasn't just this year, your being thirty-six, but wasn't it pretty recently that you started the saxophone and the tap dancing . . .

Harjo: Tap dancing! (Laughs) Where did you hear that, I don't tap dance!

Smith: Somebody is tap dancing. Lookit, I didn't make that up.

Harjo: That got added onto the story.

Smith: Somebody somewhere in the world is tap dancing.

Harjo: No, the saxophone . . .

Smith: I'll be content with that. (Laughs)

Harjo: In September it'll be three years since I picked one up and started playing. I have a friend who's a musician and I always wanted to play. I always liked saxophone. To me, you can do magic things with the saxophone, like some people with a flute. And I'm not getting into it to try to make people fall in love with me. (Laughs) Let's get that clear, you know. It's such a sensual, incredible voice. It's real close to the human voice. When I was a kid I played clarinet for a few years, and I remember in band the teacher said, "We have an alto saxophone; who would like to play it? I raised my hand, along with several boys, but I had my hand up first, it was real obvious, and he said, "Well, you can't play it, you're a girl." So that was disappointing—I quit band shortly after that, for that reason and others. It's been years and years. But when I found I was sharing a house with Laura, who's an incredible player, she had an extra tenor, so she just started showing me how to play, giving me some scales, worked with me somewhat, and I just kept going. Played in a big band for a couple of years, that's how I've learned to play really, you know, jumping into deep water.

Smith: And they just kind of let you hang out?

Harjo: I'm just learning how to improvise, and you know, I love the music. I love jazz, blues. One thing I want to do at some point is to show that the Creeks, that somehow we were there somewhere at the beginning of jazz. That there is a connection.

Smith: Well, you guys were in the right place.

Harjo: Uh huh. Well . . . and I play flute too. I'm sure it makes a change in my work, the music. Whatever. I find that my poems are often collages of whatever events, dreams, things I hear come in my way. Used to be I would work on a poem till I had it done; if it didn't work, it didn't work. But now I give it more time often, you know, and say there's something here I need, and

I'll kind of go out looking. Not even always consciously. And it would come up, either through some piece of music, or a story I'd hear, or something, but you know it always comes to me.

Crawford: It's the way a songwriter would work; getting a snatch of something.

Harjo: I suppose. I think I work a lot like that—starting with rhythms, sounds. . . .

Crawford: On this trip I just made, the thing that really has amazed me was how the people I've talked to, quite a few writers I'm working with, are terribly afraid of the dangers in the world but at the same time have an enormous sense of the future. There was some phrase in the essay you just showed me about looking to the future, thinking how it may be possible. But it seems to be—it's strange to call it optimism, because it's so guarded . . .

Harjo: Right, I suppose it's the only kind of weapon you have. What else are you going to—I don't like to think in terms of fighting them, either, because then that pulls you right in there with them, that sets up a confrontation immediately when you say "fight"—a situation of conflict—I mean, you have to recognize what's going on, but maybe what you do is set up another structure better than the old structure and work within that, in which case the other one loses any kind of viability. . . .

Smith: Paula Gunn Allen was talking about stuff like that when she was here. She didn't use the word "fight." She said, "Well, I think there's got to be a lot of work" (laughter)—but she was trying to avoid that metaphor of "fight."

Harjo: I mean, what else do we know—we keep falling into these same patterns. This pattern has been going on since, to use a phrase, "time immemorial," and people have used the same excuses, the same stories, the weapons, versions of versions, you know, people have talked themselves crazy. You know, I think AIDS is a product of germ warfare . . . and I think there are some very ugly, ugly things going on now that people couldn't even imagine.

Crawford: So much of the best writing now is being produced by people who are very close to points of crisis. Some of Sonia [Sanchez's] most recent poems are about Philadelphia and the Operation Move shoot-out.

Harjo: Maybe that's how human beings work. I mean it sounds really sick, but maybe if things are easy, we won't accept the vision. We've grown to believe that you have to work hard for anything—that in order to accept any kind of gift you have to earn it—that it's not a normal human being's stance to have beauty around you. It frightens me to think that while we're moving among this incredible beauty we have to recognize the other side, and how do you do that without being sucked in? I've noticed that the last few years of my life I'll get to places or plateaus where one day I can understand this amazing creation, the amazing beauty and the intricacies and so on, and the next day it seems like I'm just at the other end of it, and everything is so blank and not clear. And *then* I see it all, then I understand. It gives me understanding; but sometimes it's hard for me to accept that in myself.

Crawford: It's painful.

Harjo: It's very painful, and still it's understandable. It's just like we were saying before about ———, and the way he acts. He's one of the tenderest people, but there's still another side. But still I don't think it has to be so cut and dried; there's no sharp edge. Or there doesn't have to be. And that's where I blame Catholicism, for example, because some of those organized religions, you know, just sharpen the edges.

Crawford: And it's something about men. In *She Had Some Horses,* you have some brilliant poems about the agony of the choice men seem to make that turns them toward violence and defeat.

Smith: There's a lot of things about edges in the book, about that line right between.

Harjo: That's why I get real frustrated both as a poet and human being, because I somehow have a sense of another world in which that just isn't so. I have a theory of communication: We're moving farther and farther away from true communication—media, you know, images, video, constant images is really where it's at right now—where you're not a participant. You watch these things happen. The next step backwards is the written language; but there's still room to lie there. Here I'm a poet, and of course I believe that incredible things can be done with the written language and that it's useful, but I also think that in developing that, we lost more than we gained. You don't have to look the person in the eyes, you don't have a voice, you don't have the atmosphere; and even though someone can read your work and participate, it's not on the level of someone being next to you. And before that, there's the oral. And there you have the eyes, you have the participation, and so on. But even then, there's a place before that in which you don't have to speak, and there is a total understanding, and no one can lie. And that's what we're going to go back to. And so that's when I think of those edges, and I know that something in me knows that place of no lies where we all understood each other. When the destruction started up, I think guilt was the first wedge, the first parting—some kind of guilt. And maybe that's what that old Adam and Eve story is about, is a version of that . . .

Crawford: And the fruit of the tree is a polarity of the knowledge of good and evil, and separation . . .

Smith: The edge. In that culture.

Harjo: But that story has parallels, and different interpretations. I'm sure that's not the Christian interpretation of it.

Crawford, Smith: No it's not—(Laughter).

Photo by Miguel Gandert

chapter fifteen
Jimmy Santiago Baca
Interview by John Crawford and Annie O. Eysturoy

Chicano writer Jimmy Santiago Baca was born in Santa Fe in 1952. He grew up on the llano southeast of Albuquerque and spent most of his teens in Albuquerque. He started writing in prison in 1973, and his first book of poems, entitled *Immigrants in Our Own Land*, was published by Louisiana State University Press in 1978. In 1986 he won the National Endowment for the Arts Award in Poetry. In 1987 he had two books of poetry, *Martín* and *Meditations on the South Valley*, published as a single volume by New Directions. He received the Vogelstein Foundation Award in 1988 and received an American Book Award from the Before Columbus Foundation. In November 1989 New Directions published his *Black Mesa Poems*, which won the Wallace Stevens' Poetry Award. He is currently finishing his first novel and a play entitled *Los Tres Hijos de Julia*, to be staged by the Los Angeles Theater Center. He is also writing a movie scheduled for release worldwide in 1990 and working on a documentary scheduled for release in 1991. He was nominated the Berkeley Fellow Lecturer for 1989. He lives on a farm in Albuquerque.

Selected Bibliography:

Immigrants in Our Own Land, poetry (Baton Rouge: Louisiana State University Press, 1979).

Swords of Darkness, poetry (San Jose: Mango Publications, 1981).

What's Happening, poetry (Willimantic: Curbstone Press, 1982).

Poems Taken from My Yard, poetry (Fulton, Mo.: Timberline Press, 1986).

Martín and Meditations on the South Valley, poetry (New York: New Directions Press, 1987).

Black Mesa Poems (New York: New Directions Press, 1989).

Crawford: How do you feel about the Southwest?

Baca: Our history was so fragmented by colonialism that I have felt mythology was needed, a putting together of everything in a modern sense. If you have a mythology then you have a place; if you don't have a mythology, you ain't got nothing. When I came back from prison, I decided to start writing about things I thought were as old as the earth; and so I started writing *Martín*, keeping in mind that I wanted to describe my existence in New Mexico. Whether those things are "true" or not is another question. A lot of them are not, but they are true in the sense that I needed something to explain my existence, and I did it best by going through the land and asking it its secrets.

Crawford: At that time in your work it was important?

Baca: It was important because my values are not money or strength; I am not trying to be the strongest person around. My values are pretty much trying to find meaning, why I do something and why I am here. So I started looking into the land and the experience of the people, and trying to write in such a way that it didn't deny the humanity of Martín. I wanted Martín to be a real human being and let him live in this world and have a mythology that was his as well as the people's. I was trying to take images and, without compromising their mythology, bring them into contemporaneity.

Crawford: But it seems to me you never lost contact with your own origins. They are still here, and you are still here.

Baca: I believe there was a violent, violent attempt by the authorities to bleed the Chicanos and the Indios and the Mestizos of any identity, any cultural remnants. There was a really strong effort at that, a most sophisticated effort. It was not outright "Let's go out and shoot them"; it was, "Let's do it through education, let's do it through religion, let's bleed these people so they haven't got nothing left, so their only alternative is to become who we want them to become," right? And they accomplished that to a certain degree.

Crawford: Did you have this in mind when you started to write about Martín?

Baca: I didn't know anything about Martín at all. I didn't have any premeditated thinking about how it was all to come out, or what the metaphors meant, even really simple metaphors like bell-ropes, for example.

As a child one of the big images you got was bell-ropes swinging all the time in the wind; the pueblos were so lonely that growing up you noticed bell-ropes swinging by themselves. Now, thirty-some years old, I write something and the image comes of the bell-rope swinging in the wind searching for a hand, and it is the searching for a hand that brings the whole mythology together. I find out later that the Pueblo Indians used to have games where they would swing ropes, and it would constitute the image of a song, and whoever grabbed the rope had to sing the song. I learned that only after I had written all this out.

These things are buried in the subconscious; as I was writing a book about a place, I realized that the more you go into your subconscious, the more these things are alive, and all you have to do is bring them forward and have the faith that what you are saying makes sense. My self is a recipient of the Mestizo culture, and that culture is so much embedded in the earth, and the earth is so much embedded in the subconscious, that you can't pull them apart; we are part of the earth, it is part of us.

Eysturoy: So you see the physical landscape and the mythology as very closely connected in the subconscious?

Baca: I think there is an intermarriage such that if it is ever broken then you will be broken. You can have all the mythology you want to learn in your English classes and not have the earth. You have got to find the beating heart of that which is you, and if you are able to find that then you are in business.

Eysturoy: What has sustained the people of the Southwest, do you think?

Baca: Visions . . . I think that Chicano or Mestizo literature from the Southwest is going to become very powerful in the next decade, and it is because there are certain Chicanos and Chicanas who are going through the dark area where those things have been lost; and they ask, "What is Chicano culture?" because they don't know. The challenge is that they have to jump into the abyss, and once they jump, then they become the creators, they become the people who receive what has always been there, what has been lost.

It is not a static thing; you cannot lose something so that it is gone forever. It comes to you in dreams, and that's why I say visions. Visions are probably the biggest impetus toward leaping into the darkness to retrieve the mythology that has been buried by violence and injustice.

Crawford: Has everything been damaged by this other culture that has come in?

Baca: Yes. You know, when universities and foundations fund organizations to go out and accumulate sayings and folklore, you have a folklore that is really superficial and thin. You have fairytales, and if you ask the old people, the majority will say that there is nothing to tell other than "I came from there and nothing was happening." In fact, the destruction was right before their eyes, but they weren't able to see it as destruction. All they were concerned about was having their sons speak English, so they could go to the city and go to school.

Now with this generation, we see a huge empty space that has got to have something in it. It is those people who go into that massive empty space that come back with something. Each writer is doing that in his or her own way, putting the whole thing together and making a literature immensely strong and important for the kids of tomorrow. That is the most essential thing, that the kids are able to read something and say in their blood, "Ah, this is me!"

It is like an epiphany. As a young child, you have a really beautiful experience reading something that you are familiar with, you know. Reading a story about your father and making your father into a figure, a very big figure, as opposed to a sleepy Mexican, the whole thing changes, all the rules change and the authoritarian, colonial way of thinking becomes rubbish, and you become a human being full of pride and integrity.

Visions are very important. I am not talking about visions in a prophetical sense. I am talking about having a beautiful relationship with hummingbirds as a child, you know, and studying them and putting enough faith into that experience to pursue it.

What has been really hard and destructive is that we haven't taken ourselves seriously. We grew up thinking of ourselves as wards. If you are in a mental institution, people put their hands up for pills. You know what I am saying? If you grow up thinking that you are very important, then everything changes.

Crawford: You mentioned the educational system, and one thing I see as a college teacher is that students come into it with a pretty good feeling about themselves, but it is stripped from them in a couple of years unless they are very careful. The institution keeps telling them they are not competent according to its rules. How would you deal with the education of somebody who is in their teens, and not do that to them?

Baca: I think you have to take the person's experience seriously. You have a big responsibility to be open enough to encourage the students first of all—if they are in an English class—to use the language that best describes their experience, and not the experiences of Wordsworth in England; and to have each student reciprocate by giving as much effort as he or she can give to it.

Crawford: Then the problem is going to be that you are going to "marginalize" kids and they are going to stay out of the mainstream culture. It becomes a question of economics, more than anything else.

Baca: It all comes down to the bucks, that's right. I don't give a damn how good you write; if you are starving you are not going to write. So if someone is writing good stuff, the best thing you can do to help them is to find them some money.

Crawford: But if you take them out of the community and stick them in a research place somewhere, you have made them into institutional wards again. You have to enable them to do what they want to do where they are.

Baca: Exactly; you have to "give" them their own environment. But that's a problem not only with Chicanos, but whites and blacks as well. Unfortunately the more you lose yourself, the more accessible you are to the people with the bucks, and the more you are able to compromise, the more they are willing to set you up and give you loads of distinctions. The more you remain who you are, the deeper you stay in your work and your writing, the more they are inclined to ostracize you from their little funds and foundations.

Eysturoy: Has that been a big problem for you? You have a lot of poems about the economics of writing.

Baca: My experience is that the most essential and important thing in my life is writing, but while I am writing I have to work at different jobs, right? And all these other people are writing, not working, but what they write, in my opinion, is not going to stand up to the sun. It is a speck and it glows for a second and goes out, but they are getting all this money, and I wonder how they do it.

A couple of years ago I found this book on funding, and realized that these people had been spending 95 percent of their time sending off for money while I have been working on poems. So it comes down to access to information. A lot of writers spend their time in libraries getting access to information that will enable them to survive, and that hurts their writing.

Eysturoy: Where I come from the fisherman is a poet, or the poet is a fisherman. Don't you think it is a fruitful combination to be a worker and a poet?

Baca: I think that's beautiful and extremely important. A lot of writers today have to ask themselves, "How much time am I going to give to writing and how much to living with people or to the antinuclear movement, for example, and how much am I going to subject myself to what's happening in the world?" You can't have your ivory tower and be a good writer; you have got to have your writing hours and your struggle hours. If you begin to sacrifice one or the other, then you're going to really suffer.

I wouldn't be worth a piss if I let my family starve and they suffered because of my writing too much. I have to write, I have to close the door and go out and work, and then come home and be a father and love them and kiss them. You have got to put all that into one day, which makes it really hard.

Eysturoy: But you also participate in a reality that other people can relate to and are able to put that into your creativity.

Baca: It is very hard, you know. What makes it so difficult is that you go out, like I have done the last couple of days, spend a good many hours planting trees, and then write a tree-planting poem. That's okay, but the experience of actually sweating and straining and having your back hurt and feeling the earth and watering it and looking at the leaves, that's really life, as the Beatles were saying in that song; life is what you live while you are thinking about what life is.

The thing is not *just* to write a poem, you know. I call it commercial thinking; our minds are accustomed to commercials. We see something for seven minutes, then a commercial comes on; we write a poem for seven minutes and then we stop. A lot of poets and novelists and writers are doing it; their thinking is sequenced to commercials. So I have to go in and write the poem down and then I have to give that poem a day or two or a week, to really get the same heavy experience I got out of actually digging the hole and planting the tree. I want the same sort of depth and breadth in that poem as when I planted the tree. That's what is hard, to slow yourself down . . .

When you begin to deal with language you have to be loyal to the language that speaks for the "we" of the people. I say "we," because I don't take all the credit for it; I simply bring in the information; I bring it all together like a big puzzle, and there it is.

Crawford: It has always struck me in your written work and when you talk that for someone who has been through such hardships you are very optimistic. Not that you don't know there are bad things out there, but the way you deal with it is always at the level of opportunity.

Baca: Let me tell you something about that: I once came out of my cell in the dungeon; I was teaching these guys how to write, and they happened to be "soldiers" of this particular gang. The leaders came down and said that they were going to kill me if I didn't stop teaching their people how to read and write, and I said, "Well, what the heck . . ." So I come up from my shower and there are these two guys walking towards me and both of them have knives. Speaking of being opportunistic, having a bright outlook on life? . . . I look at these two guys and I think, "Holy shit, these two guys are going to kill me," right? So what am I going to do? I look around and there is a wash bucket and I pick it up and run at them with a wash bucket, just like the Apaches would do, my ancestors. I went "Wha . . ." and they took off running. It was not that I was courageous or brave, it was just that you cannot just sit there and let it happen. I was lucky in so many instances, but that's the way I approach life, you know; you do what you do and hope for the best.

But I have fallen through some deep holes, and I am not as disciplined as I should be. What you do is that you try to submit yourself, your humanity, to the very, very edge of the cliff where you think you may be able to fly, but you don't actually jump. And you kind of go there and put yourself there; it is that instinct of wanting to do it and not doing it, purposely reversing it—that is where your humanity is able to be creative. You begin to write knowing that you would love to pick up a gun and go down to the police department and blow some of them executioners away, right? And you carry that with you when you write creatively about peace and love and so forth; you have that in you.

Crawford: I see how *Martín* as a poem fills up creative space for you. What about some of the other work you have been doing in the last few years? How does it satisfy you creatively?

Baca: I don't know. I am not being facetious here or humble, but honestly I don't think I will know how to write until I am forty-five. *Immigrants in Our Own Land* was a passionate try to bring life into a really barren, dead place. It was a weapon against sterility, mental and spiritual and emotional sterility. In some of the other things I write, I run the spectrum of the emotions. *Poems Taken From My Yard* was written in a week; I just sat down because I was tired, I sat down in the kitchen and wrote all these poems out. And it was fun, I enjoyed it, and people enjoy them. *Martín* was different. One of the big issues there was that the Chicano experience has been described so much in rural terms. I grew up in a city, a hot, slick kid, and there were millions of people like me who did not have anything to refer to that reflected their experience. So I wanted to write a book that was partly rural, but for the most part incorporated the city experiences, and gave them an element of dignity. You're hanging out by the railroad tracks, but you can have the same dignity as if you were hanging out by the ruins. I wanted to give that dignity back to the people. That is how I approached that.

Eysturoy: You say somewhere that you write to lure yourself to your inner self, "to the very edge of my eye." Is that still so?

Baca: You know what I do as a habit? I go to my office, I turn on the typewriter, and before I start working on this book I am writing, *The Three Sons of Julia*, I will type five or six poems as a warm-up, pretty much like you warm up your engine. I will look out the window and just start. I can see a leaf and start writing about it; then I'll put it away and start writing about my son's expression last night; and I'll put that away and write about fish. And when I think I am sufficiently past the stage of being *crudo* from sleep, I drop all these poems into a big hole in my desk, and then I start on my *Three Sons of Julia*. It would be interesting if I were to show all these warm-up poems to somebody what they would think of them.

Eysturoy: When you started writing, was there more a search for yourself, while now you have moved into a different stage?

Baca: Yes. I have found that I work best in book-length poems, as opposed to a single page poem. I don't think you can imagine Whitman working best in a sonnet. A single poem does not fully describe your poetic temperament as opposed to a book. The book may actually be one poem, but you're like a wild pony and need that much space to say it. And it is those poets out in the wilderness, who have to work and who know a woman's cry of birth and so forth, who know that you have to have a lot of space to write a real poem if you want it to reflect who you are or what you are writing about. So it is really difficult to write those small poems.

It all goes back to what your vision is. If your vision is a very small one of making thirty-five thousand a year, teaching three classes a semester, and having enough time to go to the Caribbean, then your writing is going to reflect that; and if your vision is to reach all these people and have them read your book, crying and weeping, then your vision is going to reflect a much deeper, broader sort of book. So it is who you are. And we are in an age where single poems win ten-thousand-dollar awards.

Eysturoy: Maybe a reflection of the fragmentation of reality that we see in all areas of life?

Baca: I think so . . . I was in Mexico a couple of weeks ago and I was sitting next to this novelist and he tells me, "I have fifty-two books." And I look at him wondering what I should say, and realize that nothing I have been taught or have experienced has enabled me to answer someone who tells me that he has written fifty-two books. Somehow I cannot see how those people can take their lives seriously; there has to be something missing. They fall into a syndrome where they produce a book a year. It is really destructive, too, because your words become ticker tapes and your mind a computer, and all emotions become ideology; you just send it through the computer and it puts it out on the page.

Crawford: You are very prolific, but you are not thinking in terms of product.

Baca: Yes, I am extremely prolific. Everything I do seems like a rockchip in an Indian ruin, with a question of where it belongs. There is a bigger figure to this; something big is looming in the darkness and these are all the clues. So if I can put all these together, I'll find the great God and He'll show me all the secrets.

Eysturoy: In your most recent collection of poems, you end by saying that you use every poem to break the shackles on your legs. What are your shackles now?

Baca: What I meant by shackles are those things that hinder creativity, and there are so many things that hinder my creativity it is incredible. I love drinking whiskey with friends until all hours of the night. I love it, you know, and I should be writing, but I am not. I sometimes find that life is too good to write. I mean, why sit around writing? It is the worst thing anybody could do while you are on earth; there are so many other things to do, you can sing, dance, fight . . .

Eysturoy: But without one you cannot do the other . . .

Baca: That's why writing for me has become a really lonely type of occupation now. It wasn't like that before.

Crawford: When you were in prison, writing would be a way of saving yourself, defining a new identity?

Baca: If I hadn't written in prison, I would still be in prison. . . . I had to go back to my tablet and write in order to find a deeper understanding than the immediate satisfaction or gratification.

Eysturoy: Would you have become a writer if you hadn't gone to prison? Was that experience the catalyst for your creativity?

Baca: Probably.

Crawford: There is also this sense of growth, that this is a new page—I am starting afresh, and I can do what I want.

Baca: You know what I have been experiencing in the last eight, nine years? Learning. I have learned that I didn't know how to be a loving person. I am learning how to get up in the morning and listen to my son. It becomes really sweet when you realize that you have learned what you didn't know. So the process, even as a man, is one of continuous learning.

That's why I have survived, and why the Native Americans and the Chicanos have survived, because we have learned, we haven't stopped learning; even when we don't want to, we learn.

Crawford: You taught yourself a lot about poetry and writing, right?

Baca: Yes, I taught myself everything in writing, and I don't say that arrogantly. Nobody is going to teach you how to write what you see, you know; the only way to learn is to write and write until you are able to come really close to the way you see life.

Crawford: You have a way of saying "seeing" that is unlike ours.

Baca: The way the Indians say "seeing" is how close you can come to the way things really are, the way a deer sees a rock, or the way a frog sees water; we call that "seeing." Every human being has that seeing in them, and someone who gets up and writes every day, all he or she is trying to do is to get close to his or her seeing capabilities; that's where the good poems come, when you are able to see. No class is going to each you that. Lucy Tapahonso is a good example. Her poetry could not have been written by anyone but her. She sees things and she has to use her Navajo culture and this other culture and the English language. She has to put them together in such a way that is Lucy Tapahonso and only her. She can of course read all the books she likes to, but nothing is going to teach her her own voice.

Crawford: I sometimes think that the best a writing teacher can do is to give you some space and encouragement.

Baca: Encouragement is important, but not *that* important. It's a funny thing, and I have to live with it, but I don't encourage anybody. I say that is good, yes, but I'll say that it is good to a lot of people. But if it is someone I think is really born to be a writer, I won't tell that person whether it is good or bad; I won't say anything to that person, because I think the most valuable experience comes from when the person is left in doubt all the time about his or her work and has to struggle that much harder to prove that what he or she is writing says something.

The minute you tell someone that it is good or bad, it is no good. It's like when you go out there and fast for three days, and whatever you find is yours, and that's real. The same rule should be applied to a writer: go out there and find what you are going to find and then develop it.

What it all boils down to is that anybody can write. You can pick up any magazine in the country and find that the writing is very bland. Everything falls into the same pool. It is like the forest rangers who breed fish to stock the streams. The schools do the same thing; they stock the streams of the literary magazines around the country, you know.

As a reader, almost anything I catch is going to be a simple trout. It is not going to be the beautiful experience of seeing the golden carp flash by your eyes. But that's what a poet wants to see. And when you see that in a poem, then you know that all the effort you put into a poem is worth it. As long as from the unconscious will come that beautiful surge of golden liquid that will make a good poem glow, that's what you want.

The grading system fosters the other kind of fish. All those poems about eight inches, right? They all have certain words like *brown;* and you get really tired of catching eight-inch trout. Creative writing programs are fish hatcheries.

Crawford: You have mentioned the Mestizo a couple of times. How would you define Mestizo culture?

Baca: Half of my family are Apaches, on my father's side; and on my mother's side everybody is Hispanic, European. I haven't read much, but I have heard from friends as I was growing up that a large number of the Mexicans that were living here, or Hispanics—whatever you wish to call them—*really* intermingled with the Indians to a great degree. In the dances they played all their music. The Indians would have their corn dances and it would be the Mexicans playing their accordions and their trumpets. That's the way it was. You couldn't have an event without having both people coming together, and that's who I am.

But if you listen to the historians, you get the idea that these two people really never intermingled. I know for a fact that there are pictures of Mexicans carrying La Virgen of Guadalupe through Indian pueblos, and all the Indians are behind her, and they all go around the pueblo blessing the homes. But they are not willing to accept the fact that we came extremely close to being one people. They do studies to set us really far apart, when all I have heard, and my own memory and so forth, tells me that we really were together.

When the Indians ran from another Apache tribe, they would run to a village that was all Mexicanos, and then when those Apaches came, the Mexicanos and the Indians both ran to another village. Everybody was marrying everybody, and the Indians hate the Mexicans more than they do the whites because we were sleeping in their beds, and they were sleeping in our beds; hatred runs highest in the family, you know. So I think that Mestizo means that we are *deeply* mixed bloods.

Eysturoy: And you identify with both groups, not saying that you are Chicano or Indian, but both?

Baca: Yes, I am Mestizo. I go up there to the Black Mesa behind us; the Indians go up there, that's their holy mountain—the Isletas—and I go up there with the Isletas; we sit up there and we talk. They tell me what they think of the yucca blossom—there are a lot of yucca blossoms up there—and I tell them what I think about it, and we find out that we both talk about it in the same way, we both see it in the same way. And it comes from that, you know, that we are really close to each other. That is not to say that we are more spiritual than any other ethnic group; that is just to say that that is the way things are.

Crawford: But a lot of your creative work comes out of the ways those cultures are intermingling.

Baca: Very difficult, John, because I cannot ignore the city experience and I can't ignore my Indian ancestry; somehow I have to pull it all together, the ruins and the holy Red Rock there together with the hamburger stand in the barrio.

The English have a way of saying, "Find your voice," and that represents the egotistical sense of the English people. The Native American way is "to see." It does not entail a voice; someone like Black Elk, his seeing was very strong, nothing could boggle it. But the Anglo people always have this aggressive voice thing—"Your voice is very strong in this piece," right?—while the Indians say, "Your seeing is very strong in this piece."

So, right away, if you send an Indian piece to Harper and Row, they are going to say that his voice is not that good, and that's because it is his seeing that's strong and not his voice. How many times have you heard an Indian scream, except on the warpath? They do a lot of their anger through seeing. They look at you, and you know that you'd better get out of here. It's funny. I think that the seeing is a lot stronger than the voice. I know that when my brother got mad at me, I would look at his eyes, and his voice could have been Mary Poppin's, but those eyes . . .! I'd better get out of that room fast . . .

Eysturoy: So you see your creative process as incorporating all these different aspects of your background, all the ways of seeing that you do—Chicano, Indian, urban—in your search for your own identity.

Baca: Yes. But you know, I think I lost it sometime when I was around eighteen years old. (Laughs) I don't have one personality; I depend so much on writing that whatever I am writing, I go into that personality and I adopt it as my personality. Now I am writing about Julia and I have a lot of feminine thoughts in me now, you know, so that's really who I am.

I know that if I always acted like a father around my kids, my kids would grow up to be monsters. I have to be a kid with them, and sometimes I have to be wrong, and sometimes I have to be stupid. If I was always *the* father, father knows best, I would be crazy and they would be crazy. And my writing is like that. I don't see how I can approach my writing with really hard-core laws; it doesn't work.

Eysturoy: But that also brings a vitality to your writing in that you are searching all the time . . .

Baca: Yes. If there is anything true, Annie, about me, it is that I am always searching, and that is from a really deepseated insecurity. I am always searching.

It was a survival mechanism for years and years, and a very deep one, too. I knew that without my writing I would not survive. I will never forget when I was in prison, there was a workshop conducted by Richard Shelton and Michael Hogan, who was the poet laureate of all prisoners in America, right? I remember the writing that came out of their workshop was really structured. They were pursuing poetical craft while I in my cell was pursuing survival. And I will never forget when they got hold of one of my poems I had sent to my friend within the prison population who went to the workshop. When it got back to me, the criticism was that it was too romantic, too farfetched, too dreamy. And, really, that's the only thing you have to survive with when you are put in the dungeon, to dream. But I stuck with it and said dreams *do* mean something, and to be romantic and think that you can go across the sea on a canoe does mean something. It says something about the human spirit, that without it is devastating.

Eysturoy: What do you think you are searching for in *The Three Sons of Julia?*

Baca: Well, I have an idea that violence and drug addiction is wrong, and I am finding out that these old pieces I wrote fit together really well, but that I need to add a piece about someone who overcomes violence and drug addiction. That is not a search, that's more the *benefit* of searching; you learn how to put things *together* when you are searching for something. I think my searching has taught me to recognize things in their order.

Every barrio, every neighborhood and village has a family of sons. Every neighborhood has a mother without a man who has these three or four sons to nurture, and those sons acquire a reputation of mythological status. "Flaco shot the cops last night," you know, and don't mess with *him*, because Benito below him is another bad dude. It's the Domingo family, or the Redfeather family, or whatever, right? So you have this family, headed by a woman with all these strong kids; and I realize that these pieces that I had written ten years ago, and one that I wrote five years ago, and one I am writing now, all fit together as *The Three Sons of Julia.*

One goes to prison and stays in prison forever; one becomes a drug addict and roams on his motorcycle across the country; and the other one goes to the university, graduates, and becomes a writer. He breaks the violence and the drug addiction, and he does it with integrity and love. And you see, when it is published and goes back to the children and they read it, they don't have to say, "Hey, well, I'm gonna go to prison, you know, like Octavio went to prison," they'll say, "No, Esteban over here, look at what Esteban did, he broke the cycle." So you give them something.

Crawford: This is a book that has had a long gestation, about thirteen years.

Baca: Yes, and I have never been more uncertain about any book in my life than I am about this one. It is very strange after *Martín* going on to get some acclaim, right, that I would try another book and feel so frail in its presence, not knowing what it is. I had thought I would have more confidence . . . but that's how life works.

Crawford: Is there anything else you can think of?

Baca: I'd just say, take the leap into the abyss and uncover some of the mythological artifacts that float around in the mind. The more you fall into that abyss, whether you are a painter or writer or whatever, and the more you are able to come back like a messenger from the land of death, the more you are able to come back with *something,* the more it helps writers like myself to say, "Wow, yeah," and it pushes me forward.

Photo by Cynthia Farah

chapter sixteen
Luci Tapahonso
Interview by John Crawford and Annie O. Eysturoy

Luci Tapahonso was born in 1953 in Shiprock, New Mexico, and grew up on the Navajo Reservation. She received her B.A. degree from the University of New Mexico in 1980 and her M.A. in creative writing from UNM in 1983. After several years as lecturer, she was appointed assistant professor of English, Women Studies, and American Studies at the University of New Mexico in 1987. She has published three volumes of poetry: *One More Shiprock Night* (1981), *Seasonal Woman* (1982), and *A Breeze Swept Through* (1987). Her poems have been frequently anthologized since 1981. She has been an innovator in the intertextual use of Navajo and English in her poems and readings, and in adapting so-called Anglo themes to Indian settings in her poetry (for instance, a poem in praise of Hills Brothers Coffee). This interview—the last one for this volume both in sequence and chronology—was held with Annie Eysturoy and John Crawford in October 1988.

Selected Bibliography:

One More Shiprock Night, poetry (San Antonio: Tejas Art Press, 1981).

Seasonal Woman, poetry (Santa Fe: Tooth of Time Press, 1982).

A Breeze Swept Through, poetry (Albuquerque: West End Press, 1987).

Eysturoy: The question of identity seems to be central to Native American literature in general. Has this been an important question to you as a writer?

Tapahonso: Identity is important, but for me as well as a lot of other Navajo people it's important in terms of what clan we are. My clan is *todikozhi*, because my mother is *todikozhi* and my father is *todich'iin'ii*. *Todikozhi* means "salt water" and *todich'iin'ii* means "bitter water." So when I identify myself that's the way I think of myself, first as my mother and then as my father, and then my last name in Navajo which is Tapahonso, "edge of the big water." And so my identity is in terms of the clan, which places the Navajo person in the world and defines one's relationships to other people and one's responsibility. It places me in certain waters. . . . And so my name is already connected to history, and origin, and my relatives. My identity is established; there's no question in my mind about who I am or from what people.

Eysturoy: Does that make it easier for you, say, to move between the academic world and your Navajo community?

Tapahonso: Anything that I do just adds to my identity, it doesn't detract; I don't waver. In the creation stories, *todich'iin'ii* is one of the four original clans, and Changing Woman created him from her own body, and this happened at a particular place on the reservation. So as far as my ties with location and place are concerned, this is much more important than the fact that I was born in Shiprock and I was raised there. It has to do with the people and the beliefs and the philosophy and spirituality. And so my sense of place and my sense of the Southwest is a link that has a lot of layers, and the land is only a part of that.

I was born in Shiprock in a comparatively large family. While I wasn't raised in a really strict traditional way, it was semitraditional, which was very common in people of my generation. I learned Navajo first, and then I learned English at home as a matter of necessity. I have always connected English with matters outside my home, and I connect Navajo with the language of my home, and food, and sounds, and descriptions, and people telling me about various things, and just everything that was connected with my upbringing, the way that I was taught, the things that were explained to me, the way I was disciplined. English was always on the periphery.

Then when I began writing, I was fascinated with the English language because you could shape something, you could create whole worlds out of words, and people were always doing that; it was fascinating. So I tried to use words in real complex ways. . . .

Eysturoy: Did you try to do this in Navajo as well?

Tapahonso: Not intellectually, the way I did in English. Now I understand that I was fascinated because I already recognized that was possible with any language, whether English or Navajo. But I connected English with the written word, and to this day I can't connect Navajo with the written word. I can't read Navajo well, and I can't write Navajo well. . . . It's agony for me. At one point I could, but now my writing is all in English, and I'm comfortable with that, because of whatever happened with my mental processes as a child. But it's just the writing that is English, and otherwise it's still on the periphery.

So that's how it comes about for me. My reactions and my surprises, everything is always in Navajo first. It takes me a while to cross that space into English, especially if I'm real shocked or something like that. My first reactions are always in Navajo, and when I'm trying to think of how to explain something in English, I have to go real slow because I have to take care of that process first. It's still a matter of finding the exact way to say it that's as close to Navajo as it can be, but it will never be like Navajo, and that's the real challenge. I really like that searching. It's almost painful to do that, but it's really good because when I find it I know that that was it, and that's the closest I can get. . . .

Eysturoy: Do you ever write poems directly in Navajo? I know you have sections of poems written in Navajo.

Tapahonso: I can say poems completely in Navajo, but I can't write them completely in Navajo, because I can't hear all the sounds. When you write in Navajo, you have to hear every sound and I can't. I can't separate the sounds. For instance, if I say *bil dah set'eeh*, which in English means, "They're going so fast, the horse and rider are almost horizontal, and there's dust after them," I can see it in my mind, but if I was to write that in Navajo, I would have a hard time writing that down. It's such a complex thing.

Eysturoy: Is the process of translating the oral tradition into a written language difficult?

Tapahonso: It is difficult, but it's also very good; I mean, how else would I do it? And then I'm fortunate, I really do like language, and my knowledge of English is good.

Eysturoy: In the process of writing, do you ever compose in Navajo and write it down, and then translate it into English later on?

Tapahonso: No, well, I can do a whole poem in Navajo before I write it in English, depending on the context. . . . For instance, the last poem in my book, "There is Nothing Quite Like This," was all in Navajo to begin with, and then I translated it into English. But there are certain words in English that can't be translated, for instance, how do you say Hills Brothers Coffee? How do you say Tony Lama? So it depends on context.

Eysturoy: Have you ever translated poems written in English into Navajo?

Tapahonso: I won't really go any farther in Navajo. There've been poems that I can switch to Navajo from English. But I won't do that much. There's people much more able to do this. They're linguists, and they have a mind with which they can do that. I've accepted pretty much that I can't. But one of my long-term goals is that by the time I'm forty I'll have a working sense of written Navajo.

Crawford: I've heard that Navajo is one of the most descriptive languages in the world, because you can do so much with the endings to locate and modify what is going on. English can paint word pictures, but it can't do what Navajo can with such economy. Does that enter into your poetry?

Tapahonso: The language is very visual, and you're right, you can have an entire picture in three or four words, which is hard to do in English. And you have more of a sense of motion, and of placement in Navajo. One of the examples I have of that is that you can define relationships with certain words, including what stage the people are at. If you describe the action of people sitting together as *bil seka*, that means they're living together, therefore they have a serious relationship and are committed to each other, and there's an indication of the time that they have been together, and all that is implied in *bil seka,* a few syllables.

Crawford: You've tried to work with mixed audiences, in bringing Navajo culture to Anglos while there are Navajos there listening for special things. How does that work for you?

Tapahonso: It works good, because basically you trust that people are intelligent, and the poetry is much more than just words; it encompasses a lot of other things too. A lot of times I'll read the poetry that I have that's in Navajo, but from the context you can tell what it's about and if the people don't understand what it's about they can still respond to it. The language has a lot of expression in it, so if there's an expression of anger they'll pick it up; it's implied in the tone, so it works well.

Sometimes it kind of calms me to read poems that are real funny in Navajo to an audience and I don't translate or say anything about it, I just do it. And I have a real hard time maintaining a straight face because they don't know that it's funny. Or they might have an idea that it's funny but they don't know how to respond. And that's real funny to me because—it's real funny.

So it generally works real well. It gets the people used to hearing another language rather than just English.

Crawford: What do you think of the Anglo writers who for seventy-five years now have gone out to the reservation and tried to interpret what's going on there? I'm thinking of everyone from La Farge to Waters. What problems come out of that kind of excursion?

Tapahonso: Well, I think there's a lot of problems, but to me the most important thing is to point out that anyone's writing is always done out of that person's particular perspective. If you read something and are aware of that, then you're much more careful and more likely not to be wrongly influenced. You know, my writing is certainly filtered through my perspective, so I wouldn't be so bold as to say that I represent the "Navajo Voice" or anything like that, because I know that I don't. . . . So I think the most important thing writers have to realize is that they're writing through their own perceptions, whether that's a white, or Christian, or male perspective.

We certainly see a lot of European influences in La Farge's work, in the portrayal of his characters, because Laughing Boy is really just a noble savage and sort of untouched and unscathed by anything, so certainly he can't die, while on the other hand the female character deserves to die, because she's so evil by European standards. If you can see all those things, it's real important, but a lot of people don't really think about that; they base their perceptions on what other people have written and don't question the way our culture is formed.

Everything that is authoritative and everything that is documented is somehow substantiated, because, yes, "It is true and we have the records to prove it." And that's where the conflict comes in between oral cultures and written cultures. I think that's real important.

Eysturoy: Tony Hillerman has written a lot about the Navajos and uses a great deal of cultural material in his fiction. What is your perception of his work?

Tapahonso: (Laughs) I knew that was coming! (Sighs) Again, it's a matter of perspective. He's so successful, but I think a lot of people don't even stop to realize it is fiction. At some level they might, but when they see Indian people, when they see Navajo people, they think they're knowledgeable because of what they've read. And it's all filtered through Tony Hillerman, bless his heart, his perspective and whatever kinds of intentions that he might have, and whatever sort of confidence he might have in himself as an individual in his knowledge and his ability to write. Now, it would be very unfair, to my mind, for me to pretend or to presume to know so much about white culture or American culture in the Southwest that I would write something akin to "Murder She Wrote" from an Anglo perspective. But that's the difference in the way people are raised, and the way that people believe, and the way that people live. To me, it's a really crucial difference.

Eysturoy: Do you see any cultural transgression in his work? Is he in some cases dealing with cultural material which should not be written about, witchcraft for instance?

Tapahonso: I think that he should be very concerned about the kind of things that he's writing about. He makes them out to be something to be very much afraid of, like you're really treading on thin ice. If he feels that way and he tries to get that feeling across to his group, and if in his research and his talking to people he acquired that knowledge, I would be concerned about the place that I was putting myself in in dealing with things like that if I was him. If indeed there is something to be afraid of . . . but apparently he thinks that's trivial. That's the concern I have about that kind of thing. He talks about things that we don't even talk about among ourselves.

On a personal level you're taught the way that people should be, or an individual should be. Then it's just a matter of adhering to that. It's a matter of standards. And it's not "keeping things secret" or it's not that people shouldn't talk about it, or that it's real sacred or anything like that, it's just a matter of standards. It's sort of like people should wash their face every morning, only it's more serious than that.

Crawford: What I wanted to ask before was, do you think Anglo writers are getting any better at interpreting Navajos than they were in the past?

Tapahonso: I don't know. That's a real general question. I don't know.

Crawford: Let's try this from the other end. The Southwest is becoming more truly multicultural, in that more native people and more Hispanics are writing material that people from all backgrounds are taking seriously. Does that seem to you like a hopeful thing?

Tapahonso: Yes. . . . But we really have to realize that our country is based a lot on the received notion of what it takes to be successful. It takes a long time for minority writers to have a voice. It's hard for people who are not white and male, and so don't fit into the standard category, to be successful writers. But I also think that we've really suffered a setback, and it's directly related to politics, in the last eight years. I hope that with the next administration things'll get a little bit easier. Literature and art are real connected to politics, though they seem like different things.

Eysturoy: Did you find it difficult to break through as a Navajo writer when you started writing?

Tapahonso: No, I think I came up when times were ripe, and I thought it was all going to work out in a matter of time. I was published late by some standards, and then I was published quickly. It wasn't by any means by myself, it was by a lot of fellowship and network connections with other people. Leslie Silko had said "You should probably publish," and I thought "Oh, sure." But she kept telling me that, so I finally did. I finally did it myself, but she basically said, "If you don't, I will. I'll submit it for you." So I did, and I was real surprised that it was published. And things just fell into place after that.

My writing was so private, so personal, and I was really shy, I was really afraid of the way things would fit, but it went very well, and people really liked my work when it came out, so it wasn't really difficult for me as a writer; everything really worked out well for me.

Crawford: I was talking to people recently from the reservation who want to start a little press there, and what I kept hearing from them was awe of the written word. People are really afraid of using that language or seeing it in print, or are worried about how you do something like that. It seems like every step is a struggle.

Tapahonso: If you know the reservation. . . . I know that if I had stayed in Shiprock I would never have been published. So you have to make compromises, and for me, I had to leave. That's the way that it has to be. You can't live in Shiprock and write and be published and teach at the same time . . . you can't have two things at once.

It's real hard because the connections aren't there, and in this kind of thing almost everything depends on networking and connections and word of mouth. Fortunately our writing circle is so small that everybody knows everybody, and people are wonderful; they're real supportive. In just one or two instances are people being competitive, trying to get each other, but that's real rare. In even that case, people are real forgiving; they just let it be, they don't confront it. We're so few that it's futile to be otherwise.

Crawford: You're thinking of Indian writers as a whole?

Tapahonso: No, minority writers.

Eysturoy: Do you find it difficult to cross over from the Navajo world to the Anglo world and back again? Is it difficult to bridge the two worlds?

Tapahonso: No, I don't. I think that's really become a cliché. It's untrue for me, because the way that I was raised, my philosophy, is really in me; the way that I think is very much internal. I could go to India or China and still have a sense of who I am.

It's true that one of the compromises that you make when you leave the reservation is that you can't be there for a lot of things that are really important. You can be there for what you can, you can be there when it is absolutely necessary, but you can't be there for all the day-to-day things. But those are the compromises that one has to make. And I realize that, and feel sad over it, but I also realize there's a balance, in my career and my writing, and I meet a lot of people.

Still, my life *is* poorer in a lot of ways because I left. I realize this when my car breaks down, and I get real upset, I get in a quandary, and I don't know who to call. It would have been easier if I was in Shiprock, where somebody would have seen me along the road . . . you know, they would be there. But I could break down on the bridge, and people would, you know . . . it's a matter of compromises. But I think that you do that anywhere in a modern culture.

Crawford: The idea of "bridging the two worlds" is an Anglo stereotype, isn't it? It's from the Anglo perspective that of course since our culture is dominant, it's going to be hard for you from the "other" culture to do that. But if you don't start out with our sense of cultural superiority, if you carry your world inside you, it looks completely different. Am I right?

Tapahonso: Yes, I think so. But I think a lot of our people do have difficulty.

Eysturoy: You have written mostly poetry, little fiction.

Tapahonso: If I do write fiction, it's short. I don't know how I make that choice. I just get excited about poetry, I just like the challenge of being able to do almost a whole story in a few lines, and thinking about the words I will use, and the words that are most full and vibrant and will encompass what normally ten words can encompass.

Crawford: When you write, have you got an idea about how long it will be?

Tapahonso: No, not really, it's not preconceived, I don't think I will start with so many lines . . . but it kind of works that way. But I think that the most important thing in poetry is that one has trouble writing in as few words as possible. Maybe it's that. You try to think in ways it's never been described before, and throw out all the showy things . . .

Eysturoy: What is your vision as a poet?

Tapahonso: I think it's real complex. It's the ways I think and the ways I react to all the situations that come to the Navajo people—the way that we talk, the way that we laugh, all those things that are part of the Navajo perspective. But I also know how to function in this world, in the professional and business and academic world . . . a whole different way of functioning. I can chair a meeting, I can organize events, I can raise money. So there's that perspective too. It's really interesting to think about. When I'm writing, it's really me, it's my perspective. But in my perspective there's a lot of different things combined. My viewpoint is fairly typical of the Navajo people. It's real complex.

Eysturoy: What projects do you have planned in the future?

Tapahonso: I think having tenure. Here or elsewhere, hopefully here. (Laughs)

Crawford: We'll keep that in, just in case anyone's listening.

Tapahonso: And writing more, and devoting more time to writing than I am now. I think that's real crucial, but that means teaching less. Again there's compromises there, but I'd much rather be writing. And my children. My youngest will be a teenager soon, and Lori will be off on her own pretty much. And that they will do well in whatever they do, but will also contribute meaningfully to their community. And going back and building a home. I can see myself having a home that my children and I can go back to, and I can stay at, and I can go to in the summertime. Unless something miraculous happens, I don't see myself living there year round. But finally, when I retire, and I have no more reason to work for money, I'll go back and live there! (Laughs)

Contributors

CHARLES L. ADAMS currently serves as director of the Frank Waters Society and edits its annual journal, *Studies in Frank Waters*. He has published numerous articles and reviews and edited *Frank Waters: A Retrospective Anthology* for Ohio University Press. With Waters, he coedited W. Y. Evans-Wentz's *Cuchama and Sacred Mountains*. Adams is professor of English at the University of Nevada, Las Vegas, where he has taught for the last thirty years.

WILLIAM BALASSI is a lecturer at the University of New Mexico and has been teaching high school and college English for nearly twenty years. His work has appeared both in scholarly journals, such as *The Hemingway Review* and *Studies in American Fiction*, and in popular magazines including *The Mother Earth News*. His interests include Southwestern literature, American literature, and manuscript study. He is currently writing a book on the day-by-day composition of *The Sun Also Rises*.

SUE BERNELL is the coauthor of a mystery series and has written for commercial and educational publications. She has worked in the media and currently developing a radio talk show featuring many Southwestern writers. One of her first interviews is with Tony Hillerman; she describes it as a continuation of their discussion for this collection. "He is a brilliant storyteller, on paper or in person."

JOHN F. CRAWFORD is assistant professor at the University of New Mexico, Valencia Campus with twenty years' college teaching experience. He is editor and publisher of West End Press and also produces a quarterly newsletter, *Peoples Culture*. He has published articles on multicultural literature, small press publishing, and cultural politics in a variety of books and journals, and he is presently at work on a study of cultural influence in the Southwest, *Here Come the Anglos!* with Patricia Clark Smith.

ANNIE O. EYSTUROY is a Ph.D. candidate in American Studies at the University of New Mexico and now lives in Spain.

NANCY GAGE is a fiction writer and playwright whose work has recently appeared in *Sonora Review* and *New Mexico Plays* (University of New Mexico Press). She also writes for the *Albuquerque Journal*.

KAY JIMERSON is a consultant for the city of Tucson, as well as a writer and teacher. She is working on her first novel. She teaches composition at Pima Community College in Tucson. "Edward Abbey measured and meant every word he uttered during our interview," she says.

DAVID JOHNSON is associate professor of English at the University of New Mexico where he teaches poetry and mythology and serves as editor of *Blue Mesa Review* and *Man, Alive!* newsletter. He is also a contributing editor of *Puerto del Sol*. He says that through his interview with Frances Gillmor he came to know and respect a remarkable writer, scholar, and human being.

MICHAELA JORDAN KARNI, originally from Illinois, considers herself a New Mexican after twenty-eight years residence in Albuquerque. She received her B.A. (summa cum laude in English) from UNM in 1964 and her M.A., also in English, from the same institution. Karni coauthored two romances (Dell) and three murder mysteries (Popular Library), all published in the mid-80s. From June 1987 to December 1989, she was the editor of LINK, a monthly newspaper serving the New Mexican Jewish community. Currently, she is writing another mystery, this time on her own. Karni, who is addicted to community volunteer work, is married to a professor at UNM. They have two children.

LOUIS OWENS is professor of Literature at the University of California, Santa Cruz. He has taught at California State University, Northridge and the University of New Mexico and has published books and articles on American literature, with a special interest in Native American writing. He received a National Endowment for the Humanities award in support of his critical study of Native American novelists in 1988, and a National Endowment for the Arts Creative Writing Fellowship in 1989.

TEY DIANA REBOLLEDO is associate professor of Spanish at the University of New Mexico. Coeditor of *Las Mujeres Hablan: An Anthology of Nuevo Mexicana Writers* (El Norte Publications, 1988), she has also written numerous articles on Chicana writers in the Southwest. She and Pat Mora, she says, have *continuous* conversations.

PATRICIA CLARK SMITH is a poet, critic, and associate professor of English at the University of New Mexico. Most of her scholarly work concerns American Indian women writers.

PHYLLIS HOGE THOMPSON is an accomplished poet, with five published collections and many individual poems in publications such as *Hudson Review, New England Review/Broadleaf Quarterly,* and the *New Yorker*. In addition she wrote a regular column for *The Silver City Enterprise*. She is now at work on a book on Mogollon. Thompson divides her time between Mogollon, Silver City, and Albuquerque.